Coda X 50

D1576689

GOLDEN AGE OF BUSES

Charles F. Klapper

ROUTLEDGE & KEGAN PAUL
London, Henley and Boston

First published in 1978
by Routledge & Kegan Paul
39 Store Street,
London WC1E 7DD,
Broadway House,
Newtown Road,
Henley-on-Thames,
Oxon RG9 1EN and
9 Park Street,
Boston, Mass. 02108, USA
Filmset in 10 on 13 point Monophoto Ionic
and printed in Great Britain by
BAS Printers Limited,
Over Wallop, Hampshire

British Library Cataloguing in Publication Data

Klapper, Charles Frederick

Golden age of buses.
1. Motor bus lines – Great Britain – History
I. Title
388.3'22'.0941   HE5663.A6   78–40635

ISBN 0 7100 8961 9

Contents

Plates

Preface and Acknowledgments

It is a remarkable thing that the British Isles, notwithstanding every kind of discouragement, produced the genius that was crowned with success in two diverse fields of invention more or less simultaneously in the form of the steam railway (which was suddenly developed from comparatively crude mechanisation of railways intended for conveyance of mineral traffic) and in the same part of the late eighteenth and early nineteenth centuries the high-speed Royal Mail coach and mechanised road vehicles. The railway achievements of Stephenson, Hackworth, Trevithick and their contemporaries could have been matched by the road transport achievements of Hancock, W. H. James, Sir Goldsworthy Gurney, Sir Charles Dance and numerous others who are recorded in W. Fletcher's *Steam on Common Roads*. Unfortunately prejudice in favour of the horse and indeed of foxhunting swayed public opinion and was aided by subtle help from the railways, now beginning to feel their power. Until 1865 high tolls were relied upon to keep mechanical traffic at a minimum (horse-hauled stage coach, 4s; steam coach 48s); about this period the unhappy motorist was liable to be prosecuted for damage to the road, undue noise (with nothing in the way of measurement) and all sorts of indefinable dimensional errors. A more virulent attack on self-propelled vehicles on roads was marked by the Red-Flag Act which required three persons in attendance on the vehicle one of whom should walk

xi

60 yards ahead showing a red flag by day or a red lamp by night; speed was limited to 4 m.p.h. in the country and 2 m.p.h. in towns, with further restrictions at the discretion of the Local Government Board. These penal restrictions were lifted in 1878, but it was not until after 1896 that the present state of affairs was assumed; one cannot help wishing that a little more tolerance had accompanied the vital period of changeover.

Like most books, this one owes a tremendous amount to my friends – particularly to my friends in the Omnibus Society who have been so tolerant and have given me so much help.

The Omnibus Society began as a result of a meeting at the Commercial Motor Exhibition of 1929 at Olympia of a group of friends who already knew one another in railway circles. At the end of the afternoon Charles E. Lee and I said to one another simultaneously, 'We have enjoyed ourselves so much, can we not meet again?' A meeting was held the next week at Lee's home and the Society took off with a programme of meetings, a monthly magazine, and meetings and visits in which representatives of the industry have always co-operated, notably A. Douglas Mackenzie of Southdown, Herbert Baker of Brighton, Hove & District, and Donald Sinclair of BMMO.

Those who have helped with this book include Noel Jackson, Dick Riley, John Cummins, R. G. Westgate, R. R. J. Durrant; Eileen, my dear wife to whom I owe so much; Charles E. Lee, who when I was stricken by illness, completed three chapters, on independents in London, coaches and small proprietors in the provinces; to all these I offer heartfelt thanks; I am especially indebted to my old friend Charles E. Lee who taught me the rudiments of weekly technical journalism.

The author and publishers are grateful to the following for permission to print photographs: Chemins de Fer Métropolitains de Paris (RATP), no. 1; Ian Allan Ltd (*Modern Transport*), nos 2, 3, 10; London Transport Executive nos 4, 13, 22, 31, 36, 38; British Leyland UK Ltd (Leyland Truck & Bus division), nos 5, 11, 14, 18, 19, 33, 34, 37; The Western National Omnibus Co. Ltd, no. 7; W. Noel Jackson, nos 20, 39; F. R. Logan Ltd, no. 21; Central Press Photos Ltd, no. 32; Times Newspapers Ltd, no. 40. Every effort has been made to trace the owners of copyright material. Where contact has proved impossible we apologise to those concerned.

1
When was the Golden Age of the Bus?

When was the Golden Age of the Omnibus? This is a question I have often been asked, especially since it became known that I was proposing to produce a companion volume to the *Golden Age of Tramways*. I should first of all emphasise that to say that there has been a golden age does not necessarily imply that the bus is defunct, but is merely an indication that there have been periods that one can consider halcyon and look upon in retrospect with pleasure. In lecturing upon the economics of the bus business in the august theatres of London University I have often had recourse to what one may call the alternating current diagram to show the fluctuating fortunes of the busman's trade—early success, followed by the evils of competition, bankruptcies, amalgamations, consolidation, retrenchment, renewed prosperity, followed by resumption of competition, bankruptcies, fresh consolidation and a return of prosperity. One can trace a variation of this theme with the introduction of mechanical power, a sorry story made sorrier by the innate conservatism of the British people as a result of which British internal-combustion-engined vehicle manufacturers were unable to test and improve their products in the hard school of experience and Continental rivals gained a head start on us.

Competition and mechanical failure having reduced the industry to dire straits, once more consolidation and a setting of the house in order had to be imposed to bring financial stability. Then many rushed to step on the new bandwagon of mechanical satisfaction and prosperity, competition was again rife and the cycle of events was seen again. Not until the London Traffic Act (1924) and the Road Traffic Act (1930), and the creation of the London Passenger Transport Board in 1933, was it understood that satisfactory bus operation requires a monopoly (albeit a controlled monopoly) for the operator. Even then the Conservative party and, indeed, many of the general public, are violently opposed to transport monopolies, and seek to try the effect of competition yet again. Economically the golden age of the bus has thus been ephemeral: the period of maximum prosperity was probably around 1951 when pre-war traffic had grown for several reasons including its stimulation by the restrictions on petrol for private cars. There was an absence of outlets for surplus cash, rationing caused everyone's food bill to be frugal and at the same time prompted travel by housewives to new shopping areas in endeavouring to add variety to the household menu, so that there was little to make families count the cost of travel. The cinema and live theatre still reigned supreme for entertainment and the competition of the television set had not made itself felt, so that evening traffic still filled a valuable role in contributing to the bus operator's revenue.

Previous booms in the bus business had brought expansions of business—in 1911 when the reliability of the B-type bus and its contemporaries was being realised; the post-war boom when the virtue of the services rendered by the bus were realised steadily over the length and breadth of the land and the bus, through ingenuity of design and relaxation of restrictions by that most authoritarian of regulatory bodies, the Public Carriage Department of the Metropolitan Police, was growing in size and becoming a more economic unit, even capable of taking on in combat its firmly entrenched rival the electric tramcar; at the same time in this period anyone who could afford to adapt a Model T Ford could make money by opening up rural routes; then, after 1925, there was a rush to establish express coach services. This led to the growing railway interest in investing in bus services and rivalry led to a Royal Commission, then to regulation, manifested in the Road Traffic Act (1930) and the higher levels of taxation following the Salter Report. At this time too the petrol-engined bus reached a peak of perfection, followed by the diesel engine; designers and manufacturers continued to play their part so that the vehicle was worthy of the 1951 peak of prosperity. In adversity since, the vehicle builder has continued his valiant support of the operator.

From the author's viewpoint, growing up as a boy in London, there were several periods when the bus was at its most fascinating. The developing years and the period of mechanical failure had almost passed when I began to take a keen interest in the vehicles on the streets. I can remember seeing a vehicle, submitted for approval at our local police station where they occasionally carried out public carriage inspections, having ignominiously to be towed away instead of receiving the accolade of approval, and I have a vivid recollection of being on top of a De Dion on Bayswater Road *en route* to one of Imre Karalfi's gorgeous exhibitions at the White City and alongside Kensington Gardens coming to a halt from which there was no restarting. Simultaneously, it came on to rain rather vigorously. After a wondrous time at the White City (petrol trams round the grounds, boats on the lake and the Reynard road train for a further trip round the exhibition, a look from above on the Flip-Flap, and model railways and full-size equipment galore in the palaces devoted to transport) I demonstrated on the way home (at the age of three!) that I could read in a sort of way, sorting out Union Jack buses from Vanguards, and even apparently reciting the details from destination boards.

From 1911, when the Great Eastern of London fleet was renewed by its Straker-Squire fleet, first in bright yellow, then with 'Generalised' route boards and finally in the sombre General red livery, to the war of 1914, was a truly halcyon period. The changeover of the General fleet to the B-type, the all-too-brief period in 1913 when buses at selected garages appeared in a red, white and green livery and the development of vast numbers of new services, operated from new garages, happened almost too swiftly to be taken in, yet with the leisurely time-scale of youth each phase seemed to last weeks and months, so that one was lulled into belief that whatever existed would never change. Only a character of iron resolution, such as Charles E. Lee, could discipline himself into recording everything that happened in the most meticulous detail. Going laboriously back over the searchings of memory and the meagre published records, how one wishes that one had written a record of the date that one first saw a B-type in Associated livery, maroon like contemporary Generals, or still more surprisingly found the service to Hackney Wick operated mostly by green, white and grey B-types in the livery of the Metropolitan Steam Omnibus Co. Ltd, on whose vehicles I had last ridden amid the aroma of paraffin only a few months before between Brixton and Clapham Common on the peculiar cross-country route which served Acre Lane at one end and Walham Green at the other. It was probably the bright appearance of the B-type Metropolitan Steam fleet that turned General board-room thought towards a lighter red, relieved with white for their own vehicles, says Ted Gaffney, an expert on London bus liveries.

Then one splendid May morning in 1913 I was overtaken by an MET

Daimler, resplendent in blue on service 51 from West Kilburn to Ilford and with its sleeve-valve engine even outdoing the silent B-type in its suppression of decibels to a soft hiss from the carburettor intake. Later that year I discovered a Southern bus – a B-type – on service 71 at Petersham and saw numerous examples of the Central Leylands in dark blue (almost black) and primrose yellow with a red surround to the fleet name as at various times they operated on 10, 35 and 40, services which began at the Elephant and Castle, close to their garage off Walworth Road. The combination of associated companies was completed by the Tilling petrol-electric fleet which I first saw in 1911, but thought dull because the livery was hardly distinguishable from the General Gearless, whose small band of Daimlers was at first notable for the pearly grey livery (but later, like the victims of magic, turned blue) and from the beginning of 1914 the white National Steam Car fleet, which had, of course been pursuing its independent way and originally-planned services for five years before that, and continued even after association with the General to retain a distinction of style, including a route board which embodied the extreme destination and only reluctantly the imposition of service numbers on the vehicles.

The colourful phase came to an end with the takeover of the red Premier De Dion and primrose Allen Straker-Squire fleets in 1916; a still more colourful epoch followed the initiation of the Chocolate Express in 1922, with more than 500 buses in violent competition, compared with the 1914 fleet of roundly 2,950 buses at its ephemeral daily maximum, operating as 'LGOC and Associated Companies'. Away from the Metropolis the period after 1919 produced entertaining progress as the bus became familiar on one road of the British Isles after another. Unlike the tram the bus leaves no spoor – nothing is so temporary as a tyremark – and when it has gone and the exhaust is no longer heard it is as if it had never been. But in England and Wales the operators did leave a mark of their services by putting up roadside timetable boards. For some reason Scottish operators (could it be that they were too parsimonious?) disliked this simple means of advertising the existence of a service despite the fact that so much of the time the bus is invisible to the impatient customer.

As with the whole career of the tram, many of the memories of the developing days of the bus are aural – the creaking of valve springs and leaking of compression past ill-fitting gaskets in the early days, the quiet running of the Bs and Daimlers, broken only by the pounding of solid tyres on potholes, a staccato rhythm which for some reason I associate with the kinky route across Stoke Newington through Brownswood Road, Lordship Park, Manor Road and Northwold Road followed by the erstwhile 87 and, after the First World War, by 106. Another noise memory of the B-type was the distinctive big-end knock attained at a certain stage of wear, loud enough to make dramatic suggestions of connecting rods charging through the sides of crankcases.

Another crescendo of sound and thrashing fury was produced by the TTA1 type Tilling-Stevens on attempting a steep hill. Shooters Hill was probably the nearest they were to defeat. Fortunately they were seldom fully loaded at the end of the journey. If they did have thirty-four on board the hills of the Epping Forest area were all they could tackle when they were allocated to turns on 10 (to Woodford Bridge, with its sharp rise to the terminal pub) or 10a, with several hills to surmount on the way to Buckhurst Hill. On easy throttle on such rises as Clapton Common their frittery purring hum was a delight to the ear and I well remember going to Finsbury Park on 42 on summer evenings on several delightful occasions at a time when my father sought exercise by an hour or so's rowing on the park lake. A descent after park closing time through Tollington Park to Stroud Green Road, full of boys on bicycles hooting with a pip-squeak device, which for the time had outclassed the bell as a popular warning of approach, is another recollection. The TTA1s could also be heard working hard on that remarkable cross-country service, for so many years an exclusive Tilling preserve, 75, from Woolwich to Croydon.

The National Steam Car vehicles were comparatively silent, with a hush-hush exhaust as they started off, and I often saw them show a clean pair of heels to a following B-type. When the throttle was wide open the naphtha jets would roar and I recall seeing one coming round The Pavement to Clapham Common Station on a wartime evening with a rosy glow reflecting from the road surface (what an embarrassment they would have been to ARP officers of the Second World War!) and suddenly vanishing in a cloud of black smoke like the genii in a pantomime as a blow-back took place. I was sorry when the National fleet was rusticated to scrapyards in Essex and Bedfordshire.

The development of the provincial bus seemed more spasmodic to a London-based boy; the green Maidstone and Aldershot fleets made occasional impressions and by contrast the East Surrey blue livery impressed itself as being a country upstart which had somehow baulked the General of its threatened progress down the Brighton road. A 1917 holiday at Bexhill revealed the Chapman fleet running so certainly on town gas from balloons that gas standpipes were provided at its stands at Pevensey and elsewhere so that coaches did not have to be dependent on supplies at its Eastbourne garage. Southdown also appeared fleetingly on the excursions of this holiday, but to a large degree while one was a youth one was dependent on hearsay for the news that Tilling had a big fleet in Brighton, and could be seen in such places as Ipswich. Railway strikes provided insight into provincial arrangements, a Mersea Island Straker, looking, livery and all, remarkably like Allen's fleet which had vanished from London in 1916, appeared in Bow Road bound for Essex in the 1919 strike, but the gleaning of information in bulk had to wait until in 1921 my friend Charles E. Lee, then one of the most youthful editors in Fleet Street, produced the *Travel by Road Guide* with a most comprehensive timetabled account of the bus facilities available throughout the country. This attempt at a *Bradshaw* of road services unfortunately did not survive for long commercially – operators made too many service alterations for the printers to keep up with month by month, or at any rate for the publishers to stand up to costwise. Soon after from the height of the Cotswold escarpment I saw a white National (petrol, by this time, of course) making its way from Cheltenham towards Stroud, penetrating territory disputed by blue Bristol I-types of the Bristol Tramways & Carriage Co. Ltd. I was accompanied by another indefatigable bus enthusiast, W. Noel Jackson, whose interest in road transport I happily discovered while we were in the sixth form together. One of the most fascinating aspects of the growth of the 1920s was, indeed, the sweeping across the country, from Essex and Bedfordshire to the South Western Peninsula, of the activities of the National Omnibus & Transport Company, opening garage after garage and occasionally buying businesses. Where so many operators developed round a nucleus town, like Hants & Dorset round Bournemouth or Wilts & Dorset round Salisbury, National's development was linear, like a burst of white or green flame, only parallelled by the sudden expansion of Ribble from its Preston nucleus – but admittedly mainly by purchase – to Carlisle. Other firms stayed mainly based on a centre, even when they grew as big as the mighty Birmingham & Midland; United Automobile developed from several centres where the Hutchinsons, père et fils, had seen opportunity, so that eventually UAS buses could be seen from East Anglia, through Lincolnshire and the North East industrial complex, right up to the Scottish border and Edinburgh, rather like the spread of National, but on a quite different foundation. The huge growth of Crosville, known to so many by the articulate pen of its managing director for many years, W. J. Crosland-Taylor, was a product of the railway investment era by which it overflowed from its home Cheshire, with a little area in Merseyside Lancashire, to all North and Mid Wales.

In the end of the roaring twenties the long-distance coach came into its own. It had been given a boost for holiday purposes by railway inadequacies, when men like Len Turnham flogged coach rides to Brighton to queues waiting at the Brighton Railway's Victoria booking office. Friends made then by the road vehicle stayed with the coach, particularly when the six-cylinder engine and pneumatic tyres added luxury to the enjoyment. In 1925 the first all-the-year-round long-distance service was inaugurated by Greyhound from Bristol to London, and like many other people we as a family began to think in terms of all-coach and bus holidays. This was aided by the organisation of coach services, using stations such as London Coastal Coaches at Victoria, London, or St Margarets, Cheltenham, or the double-deck establishment in the Square at Bournemouth as meeting points of services.

The final period of the golden days of the bus was when it was making big money in the days of post-war euphoria; people wanted transport, but many had despaired of getting delivery of a car of their own. Conscious that my pre-war model (delivered in 1947) had done a huge mileage and was due for replacement, I actually ordered a car early in 1952 and was appalled to have a very friendly letter from the distributor offering delivery in rather over four years. Many must have been in like case and to a very high proportion of the population the bus and coach were the only means of transport. Operators were able to make a success of services to the most remote hamlets; in towns close headway services could survive while duplicating existing facilities and Saturday afternoon was still a busy time; traffic commissioners relaxed their prohibitions on duplications, especially of long-distance coach services, and even encouraged new developments. There were no shortages of staff or spares, so that the first requirement of a bus service, reliability, was easily met.

So the interest of the bus and coach has had fluctuations and the interpretation of its golden age can be a very individual one. To me, since seven of us first gathered together in 1929 at the Commercial Motor Transport Exhibition and decided we must meet again and did so within a few weeks at Charles Lee's home to formulate the constitution of the Omnibus Society, its interest has been unflagging and its golden age continuous. This book owes a good deal to my friends in the Omnibus Society, for information gathered over the years, photographs supplied for this volume and for generous help with specific queries; a special word of thanks is due to Charles E. Lee, who, when I was ill, completed three chapters for me. To all of them, my heartfelt thanks. And a special word of thanks to my wife, of whom a prominent bus company general manager once said, 'she must have walked round more bus garages than any other woman in the country'; to her companionship and interest I owe much.

2
Origins

It would be agreeable to find that the bus was at least as old as some of the vast cities of antiquity, but although we know that some ancient civilisations had merit as town planners and that for both administrative and military purposes road systems were not merely desirable but were so well engineered that they have endured for millennia, there is no evidence of such a development. Indeed, the tough athleticism of the average man and woman and their capacity for tireless walking in those ancient times (and even much less remotely, within living memory) seems to argue against any internal town transport until after the Renaissance.

It was a combination of science and nobility that brought the first collective public vehicle service into being in the Paris of 1662. The scientific side of the partnership was represented by Blaise Pascal, inventive mathematician who also fathered the calculating machine; in the custom of the day he sought the patronage of the nobility, who provided the working capital for the venture. A company was formed by the Duc de Rouanes, Governor of Poitou; others concerned were the Marquis de Sourches and the Marquis de Crenan. A monopoly franchise was secured from Louis XIV, with the Draconian threat that unauthorised rivals would have their vehicles and horses confiscated. On the other hand the lower orders – specifically the rude and savage soldiery and peasants – were excluded from the *Carosses à Cinq Sous* when they began operation, with a great deal of ceremony, on 18 March 1662. The coaches seated eight persons each, the routes were short and evidently did not fulfil any lines of desire, as modern planners term them, and after a short burst of popularity with the nobility and gentry the business came to an untimely end through the lack of a cash flow. By that time Pascal, who even before the invention of the public service vehicle had suffered poor health and claimed in 1659 to be 'in a state of annihilation', had been dead for some months. His admirers, who set up a Pascal museum at St Hymer in Normandy, have not emphasised his ephemeral connection with public transport.

If too limited a market and too small a vehicle killed Pascal's idea, it could not prevent there being a growing demand for personalised transport, as town life become more complex, among the executive classes. This took two forms – the privately owned carriage and various types of vehicle which were available for hire, including hackney coaches in London (despite repressive measures and complete bans, arising in London from royal favour in the seventeenth century being given to providers of sedan chairs) and fiacres in Paris. Although there was a St Fiacre, canonised for converting a large part of France to Christianity, he lived in the seventh century and it seems he was a patron saint of gardeners and not of cab owners. The fiacre took its name from having plied from a house named in honour of the saint.

During the eighteenth century the need for public transport on inter-city routes without the high cost of maintaining a private carriage became manifest all over Europe and in Britain, with the introduction of better foundations for roads and better surfacing through the efforts of engineers such as Macadam and Telford, culminated in a network of mail coach services, with a chain of provision of post horses for the haulage of private carriages as well as relays of coach horses. Some of the coaches in their last days before the coming of the railway were timed at speeds of up to 12 m.p.h. But, in general, each passenger made a personal contract with the operator and individual journeys were recorded; this involved the use of booking offices, usually based on inns in this country. On short routes it involved a considerable loss of time in operation, partly through carriage of parcels, so that a journey from Marylebone (then part of Paddington) to the centre of the City of London at the Bank of England is said to have taken up to three hours at a cost of three shillings (15p) for an inside passenger.

The time was ripe for an improved system of urban travel and after some abortive attempts it came in Paris in 1819 when Jacques Lafitte (later well-known as a political figure) began services across Paris at a fare of 2½d (1p) with vehicles which would pick up and set down passengers at any point of the route. A name had yet to be found for them and this was done by Stanislaus Baudry, a former Army officer, who began a bus service at Nantes to some baths in which he was interested as the 'Voiture des Bains de Richebourg'. He seems to have had keen critical insight which made him realise that a shorter title would be good for business. In the town was a grocer's shop owned by one Omnes and with true supermarket instinct the grocer called it 'Omnes' Omnibus' to show the wide range of commodities stocked. As soon as he saw it Baudry felt that if his vehicle was 'for all' the title 'l'Omnibus' as a fleet name could hardly be bettered. He prospered and with the aid of some partners arranged after negotiation with the Paris authorities to introduce 100 omnibuses to ten routes on the streets of the capital. Among police conditions were that more than one horse should be employed and that the seating capacity should be between 12 and 20. Although Baudry was not in the bus business for long (he failed in 1829 and appears to have followed the last resort of many bankrupt busmen by committing suicide) his inspiration 'omnibus' proved an enduring and popular name for a new type of business which provided a service for all comers without any formalities.

The success of these and other operators who joined in what appeared to be a good thing aroused the interest of George Shillibeer, a native of Tottenham Court Road. Shillibeer was a naval man, rendered redundant after the Napoleonic wars. He learned the art of coachbuilding with Hatchetts of Long Acre and set up in Paris, where his products not only included elegant coaches for the society that was reviving after the shocks of the 1793 revolution and the subsequent wars, but included two luxurious buses that Lafitte was providing for the common man. It occurred to Shillibeer that London would open an opportunity for a similar service of omnibuses and he set about assessing what his chances were likely to be. He quickly discovered the strength of the opposition – the short-stage operators were well-entrenched and the proprietors of hackney coaches were extremely jealous of any idea that would compete with their profitable operations and were protected throughout the paved area of the city from stage-coach competition. The only route in London apparently open to a newcomer, with a vehicle plying for hire along its route, was to avoid 'the stones' or the paved streets of the central area and this was why Shillibeer began to operate from the 'Yorkshire Stingo', not far from St Marylebone Church, to Moorgate and the Bank of England over the unpaved surfaces of what was then still known as the New Road. This eighteenth-century bypass is now better known as the Marylebone, Euston and Pentonville Roads. The 'Yorkshire Stingo', now demolished, was known as Paddington, a name which travelled westward with the coming of

1 (*left*) The very first bus: Pascal's *Carosse à Cinq Sous* in Paris, 1662

2 (*below*) Walter Hancock's steam bus 'Era' which ran between the City and Paddington with 'Autopsy' daily between August and November 1834, carrying nearly 4,000 passengers

the Great Western Railway terminus beyond Paddington Green.

Three-horse buses were Shillibeer's choice; he built two for the start on 4 July 1829. They seated 22, 11 on each side, longitudinally or, as another account categorically states, 'seated from 16 to 18 persons'. The conductor stood at the back and at first he was supplied with a uniform resembling a midshipman's in the Royal Navy. The first men to be engaged spoke French well; some lady passengers were reputed to ride solely to improve their French conversation! The journey time of the buses was much reduced over that of the short-stage coaches which are variously credited with taking 2, 2½ or 3 hours on the journey and charging at least twice Shillibeer's fare of 1s (5p) or 6d (2½p) from either terminus to Islington, roughly half-way. Adherence to a previously announced timetable, avoidance of the delays at the booking offices while the journey of each passenger was entered in a book (hence the term which still applies to modern transport media), and the quick passage of the relatively traffic-free New Road route made a difference. Short-stage coaches running via Oxford Street had the detours of St Giles High Street and the descent into the valley of the Fleet and rise up Snow Hill. Fleet Street in those days suffered the obstruction of Temple Bar and there was no Queen Victoria Street.

Shillibeer had been agitating the London scene from the mid-1820s; he cast his eyes on cabriolet licences and sought Treasury permission for omnibuses, under the name of 'Economist', in 1828. Because of the hackney coach monopoly, permission to ply for hire was not granted. The route he chose for his initial venture, was, however, outside the monopoly area. He advertised trips at 9, 12, 3, 6 and 8 o'clock from Paddington and return journeys an hour later. The short-stage opposition via Oxford Street provided perhaps 150 journeys a day.

Shillibeer, while employing a vehicle of a rather cruder nature than the coach (except that at first he supplied his passengers not only with French conversation, but with newspapers and magazines in the best launderette or hairdresser's style) had thus established two new principles of operation – regular service, no matter what load was presented, and picking up and setting down without formality anywhere en route. In addition speedier service and lower fares made their approach. The established opposition made the most of what objections they could – they annoyed Shillibeer by calling him a Frenchman on the score of his unusual name and of his having lived in France and – quite unnaturally, it seemed to them – being able to speak a little French. As is often the case with innovations, the method of operation was judged illegal. Shopkeepers, anxious for carriage folk to be able to stop outside their premises without let or hindrance, laid informations against the omnibus and its imitators when it stopped for passengers; realising that the omnibus was working in the public interest, the City magistrates dismissed the charges so brought or imposed only nominal fines until the situation was put right by the Stage Carriage Act (1832). As early as 11 July 1829 the first of these prosecutions took place for waiting longer in Bartholomew Lane than the Paddington stages were allowed and the Lord Mayor, who presided, said as he dismissed the charge that the omnibus had advantages of a 'high order'. Many operators hurried to put vehicles on the lines of the omnibus in service, many only 14-seaters like the majority of those in Paris, and requiring only two horses. Shillibeer was subjected to imitation even to the adoption of the name 'Shillibeer' by ruthless rivals, so that he had to repaint his vehicles 'Shillibeer's Original Omnibuses'.

Shillibeer, who had little business acumen, although the reasons for his failure where so many gained prosperity are not easily apparent, was in financial trouble by 1831, the omission to pay the amount of mileage duty on his vehicles as stage coaches attracting bankruptcy proceedings against him; the Board of Stamps and Taxes was the petitioning creditor. The Stage Carriage Act of 5 January 1832 had been delayed in its passing owing to a change of Government and new rates of duty came in during October. One thing which the user inherited from the 1832 Act was the allocation of 1 ft 4 in. (41 cm) of seat width for each passenger.

Although Shillibeer's principles brought success to many entrepreneurs and transport to millions of those not sufficiently affluent to become carriage folk on their own account, he did not prosper greatly himself. He went into partnership with William Morton, a former innkeeper who was an alcoholic, and eventually Shillibeer made over to Morton the original Bank and Paddington route and the partnership was dissolved. The fresh start Shillibeer felt he must make he carried into effect by hiring premises in Old Kent Road in the autumn of 1833 and in May 1834 he put most of his efforts into a service from London to Greenwich and Woolwich. But it was an unfortunate time – fare cutting was in full swing in 1835 on Thames steamboat services causing Shillibeer to bring his Woolwich fare down to 1s, and the London & Greenwich Railway was about to open its first section in 1836. He seems to have had great difficulty in controlling his conductors after the brief experiment with friends' sons in midshipman-like uniforms, and despite investigation of various checking systems he also seems to have been regularly swindled by his employees. In the spring of 1836 he had endeavoured to escape his creditors by fleeing to France. On his return he had a period in the Fleet prison and when he emerged he patented a funeral conveyance and set up in City Road as an undertaker. This conveyance became known as a 'shillibeer', the play upon a 'bier' being too tempting for cockney wit. After that there was no hope of what the Londoner has familiarly called a 'bus', at least as early as 1832, ever being known as a shillibeer. London's pioneer of bus operation died at Chigwell at the age of 69 in 1866. A memorial plaque was placed in Chigwell Parish Church by London busmen to mark the omnibus centenary in 1929.

3
Consolidation

Another activity in which George Shillibeer took part at the start was the formation of associations of bus proprietors. Competition had led to physical violence between drivers and conductors and ruthless and dangerous driving of the buses on the New Road service which by September 1831 was operated by a total of no fewer than 90 vehicles. A meeting at the 'Wheatsheaf', Edgware Road, with Shillibeer in the chair, decided that instead of rivalry, co-operation should prevail. Over one-third of the buses (33) were taken off the service, leaving 57 to work a regular 3-minute headway which was established from 0800 to 2200 hours. Inspectors were appointed to regulate the service on behalf of the committee of proprietors. Three years later, at the complaint of residents of Limehouse and Poplar, a meeting was held by the Blackwall proprietors, although it may not have been effective, as the operators on Commercial Road, which presumably would have included the former, were combining as the Metropolitan Omnibus Proprietors Association in 1836.

So the great associations which controlled the operation of the London bus to the end of the horse era were born. They saw to it that rivals who had not bought their way in were treated as pirates and were harried off the road; they also carried out inspection duties and kept close watch on receipts, so that if they rose too high more buses were put on and if they fell the service would be thinned to suit the circumstances. The 'road director' of the association, corresponding to a modern traffic manager, had great power.

At first the licensing of buses was looked upon mainly as a source of revenue and a matter for the Commissioners of Stamps, who exacted an annual fee related to carrying capacity and a variable duty which was a function of the mileage covered. Under an Act of 10 August 1838 the Home Secretary appointed a Registrar of Metropolitan Public Carriages. With the usual pathetic faith of authority in the efficacy of the written word, the vehicles were required to be inscribed both inside and outside, with the words 'Metropolitan Stage Carriage', and the Stamp Office number as well as the number of passengers they were licensed to carry. Numbered badges were also instituted for drivers and conductors operating within 10 miles of the General Post Office to indicate that they had an official licence. In 1842 the mileage duty was reduced from $3d$ a mile to $1\frac{1}{2}d$. Five years later the Commissioners of Stamps relinquished their duties in respect of stage carriages in favour of the Commissioners of Excise and in the same year (22 July 1847) the Towns Police Clauses Act gave police forces in general the duty of administering hackney carriage operation within five miles of the general post office of any town (or other distance if the local Act named it); the term hackney carriage did not include stage carriages, but in many other clauses stage carriages were included, especially in the event of traffic diversions ordered by the police in case of public processions, rejoicings or during the hours of divine worship on Sunday, Christmas Day, Good Friday or days appointed for public fasts or thanksgivings. Stage carriage operators were relieved of any penalties for deviations from their specified route.

During the 1840s the double-deck bus began to emerge. Stage coaches, of course, had carried outside passengers in the proportion of, say, six inside and eleven out. Force majeure played its part in moulding the double-deck bus, starting with a seat or two either side of the driver or transversely behind him. Small capacity buses rapidly filled in the peak hours or at other rush periods – the railway mania was on – and young bloods decided that to sit on a bus roof was the thing for the athletic male. W. Bridges Adams, well-known for innovation on the railway, in 1847 began to build at Fairfield Works, Bow, buses with clerestory roofs which accomplished three things – more headroom in the centre gangway, better ventilation and a longitudinal roof seat for outside passengers down the centre of the vehicle on which male passengers sat back-to-back. A footrest was provided inside the width of the wheels – an improvement over sitting on rounded roofs precariously with the legs dangling over the sides. Steps or rungs provided access from the street and the similarity to mountaineering in attaining the roof seat easily demonstrates why in early Victorian days it simply was not done for ladies to essay the ascent. The Economic Conveyance Company, with Adams & Co.'s buses, now popularised the top deck by charging much less for seats up aloft.

Although established operators did not approve of the lowered upper-seat prices of the Economic Conveyance Company the great crowds in London for the Great Exhibition of 1851 soon persuaded them that there was money in fastening a board along the centre of the roof for the accommodation of extra passengers and never mind any reduced tariff for the discomfort. So the resemblance of the narrow slip of wood to the household knife-cleaning board that still persisted into the twentieth century before the days of stainless steel cutlery, gave rise to the phrase 'knifeboard' applied to back-to-back seats. Although buses remained small they needed at least two horses. In the Manchester area John Greenwood, whose adoption of Haworth's inventiveness brought him into *The Golden Age of Tramways* for operation of tramrail-guided buses, introduced a three-horse double-deck bus in 1852. Although the conductor was still accommodated on a little step (sometimes called a 'monkey board') at the back, outside the body, there was room for 16 inside and 24 on the roof, making 40. Longitudinal footrests took the feet of those sitting on the knifeboard down each side above the wheels and the passengers' backs were supported by the clerestory ventilating the interior. John Greenwood's great innovation was the driver's brake pedal, which applied brake shoes to the steel tyres of the rear wheels and avoided the driver having to foresee conditions on any gradient and to apply a skid pan after he had stopped at the top of a bank, rather like the old Great Western Railway notice: 'All down goods and mineral trains stop and pin down 10 brakes.' Greenwood's drivers were able to drive with that much more assurance and the steeds were relieved of a great deal of strain, since holding back a heavy bus on a slope was as hard a task for the horse as throwing the animal into the collar to climb a gradient. Conservatism among bus operators was such that two decades elapsed before Greenwood's innovation was generally adopted. Birch Brothers was the first coachbuilder to build buses with brakes. Bell communication between conductor and driver was another innovation pioneered by Greenwood on his services based on Salford and Pendleton and adopted eventually by universal acclaim.

Some of the French origins of the bus continued to create an aura about it. According to Henry Moore, nineteenth-century historian of the omnibus, one of the London proprietors took the fleet name *Les Dames Blanches* from Paris without translation, whereas *Les Favorites* was a title at least mildly anglicised as 'Favorite'. The endeavour was to distinguish services by the catchy names and John Clark, who ran the 'Eagle' line from Pimlico to Blackwall via Hyde Park Corner, having received a gracious bow from Queen Victoria on horseback when he took his bus out of her way, renamed his buses 'Royal Blue', painting them accordingly. Incidentally Royal Blue, then operated by Charles Randell, was the last horse bus service I saw in London, when he revived a connection between Victoria and Kings Cross stations in 1916, a wartime period when horse fodder was easier to come by than petrol. But names of buses in the lush years of competition exhibited a great variety, ranging from 'Emperor', 'Victoria', 'Wellington' or 'Napoleon' to 'Citizen', 'Hope' or 'Paragon'. The largest fleet in the 1830s appears to have been thirty-one, but one to six buses was more usual. The names and liveries of the associations tended to be more prominent later. Apart from 'The Times', 'Wellington', 'Favorite', 'Royal Blue' and 'Atlas', with 'City Atlas', these appear to have favoured territorial forms such as 'Dalston & City', operated by two proprietors who each contributed a bus, and went into the London General Omnibus Company on the first operating day, 7 January 1856. 'New Road' seems to have covered many services, including links between Paddington and the Eastern Counties Railway terminus at Shoreditch as well as connections between the Great Western Railway and the Brighton and South Eastern Railways at London Bridge. The Bayswater Association was also known as 'John Bull'; the greatest of the associations was probably the Atlas & Waterloo Omnibus Association, of which William Samuel Birch was chairman – an honorary office – from 1890 to 1907, which had 46 buses in 1868 and 357 at the end of the century.

The mergers of principal proprietors that were an almost inevitable outcome of unregulated competition and hard times began to come about after the first quarter century of bus operation. With the end of the holiday atmosphere and return of the provincial visitors that had crowded London in 1851 bus traffic began a decline and operation was claimed to be unprofitable from 1852 onwards. Gladstone, the then Chancellor of the Exchequer, was so impressed by what principal London bus proprietors told him in 1854 that in the following July he reduced the mileage duty from $1\frac{1}{2}d$ to $1d$; it was a timely move because bad harvests and the outbreak of the Crimean War had sent the cost of horse fodder soaring. The duty was abolished altogether in 1869, the year of an Act transferring licensing to the Commissioner of Police of the Metropolis. This was carried out in 1870.

In Paris a merger took place from 1 March 1855 following a recommendation by the Prefect of Police and the possibilities of a similar amalgamation in London for producing economies were at once obvious. The Compagnie Générale des Omnibus de Londres was registered under

French law on 4 December 1855. Apart from the source of inspiration there was a good reason for forming a large joint stock company in France. Until earlier in 1855 English law did not recognise the limited liability company unless formed by Act of Parliament. This was all very well for railway undertakings but seemed somewhat cumbrous procedure for a merger of bus businesses with no need of statutory powers for other purposes. The advantages of the ability to form limited liability companies in England took some time to percolate the business community. Early intentions had been to name the new amalgamation of interests 'The London Omnibus Company' but a company of this name had been already registered and as a result the anglicisation of the French name was rendered as 'The London General Omnibus Company' in the first prospectus of the company. In this the *gérants*, or managing directors, were set out as MacNamara, Carteret, Willing & Co., (MacNamara and Willing were both substantial London bus proprietors who in 1856 sold 27 and 9 buses respectively to the LGOC, including some mail coaches in the case of MacNamara) and the capital was announced as 25 million francs or £1 million, of which it was proposed to issue £800,000.

The merger in London lacked the official backing given to the Paris amalgamation and so it did not become so complete. The BTC records, quoted by T. C. Barker and Michael Robbins in an appendix to Volume I of *A History of London Transport* (Allen & Unwin, 1963) show 586 buses delivered to the London General Omnibus Company by Messrs Orsi and Foucaud between 7 January 1856 and 9 December of that year; the purchase price was £510 per bus but there were additional payments for premises and Wilson of the Favorite line, with 48 buses, received £44,000 in all. The willingness of this largest of the London proprietors (and a much-respected man) to sell his business to the new company played a great part in persuading smaller fry that to throw in their lot with the combine was sensible. But feeling against 'the Frenchies' was aroused and in the upshot some 200 buses in London did not become London General property. So working by the associations continued throughout the horse operating era and the London General company found it expedient to continue to belong to and support the associations in their control of routes.

By February 1856 the new company had organised a competition for an improved design of vehicle; the £100 prize was awarded to R. F. Miller of Hammersmith, but in fact improvements were incorporated from others of the 74 designs submitted and a programme of improving the fleet by rebuilding existing buses and building new ones to the new standards was begun. Besides a better fleet the nascent LGOC had other ideas for popularising their services, such as packets of tickets at 10 per cent discount for a supply worth £1 and correspondence tickets by which for a 6*d* fare a journey could be accomplished anywhere in the central area with one change of vehicle, to the next following bus at nominated points, on Mondays to Saturdays. To take advantage of the offer of two 4*d* rides for 6*d* the passenger had to have his correspondence ticket stamped in one of the offices provided. From April 1856 the passenger on the Barnet mail (fare 1*s* 6*d* in, 1*s* 0*d* outside) was allowed to change for other destinations at Highbury or The Angel; offices for transfers were then opened at 109 Bishopsgate Street, Brompton ('Gunter Arms'), Regent Circus (now Oxford Circus), and Whitechapel (56 High Street), and during 1857 at Edgware Road and Notting Hill Gate. Moore also mentions a Cheapside office, but no matter how successful the system proved in Paris for a 3*d* fare, the 6*d* transfer in London was not popular and use of the tickets fell considerably in 1858, and at the end of that year the facility was withdrawn altogether, the basic fare on some routes being reduced to 3*d* in compensation. The company saved something like £1,500 a year on rent of the correspondence offices. The contract ticket arrangement was withdrawn in 1859 as it proved open to abuse.

In Paris Alphonse Loubat, experienced in tramway construction in New York, got tramways going in 1853 and also saw a wheel-changing device accepted so that at the end of the tram lines flat tyres could be adopted and the vehicle could run as a bus over streets without tramtrack – an idea which the English inventor W. J. Curtis (pioneer of cable traction) had also demonstrated. Loubat sold his enterprise to the Compagnie Générale des Omnibus de Paris in 1855 and the Paris board of the London company became interested in tramways to the extent that the Compagnie Générale des Omnibus de Londres appointed James Samuel as engineer with tramway construction in mind and on 13 October 1857 the London Omnibus Tramway Co. Limited was incorporated to apply for powers to build tramways on the streets of London within a 20-mile radius of the General Post Office. In 1858, when the London Omnibus Tramways Company's Bill for its route from Bank to Notting Hill Gate via City Road, Euston Road and Sussex Gardens, with a branch from Kings Cross to Ludgate Circus via Farringdon Road, was before Parliament, the First Commissioner of Works in Palmerston's Government was Sir Benjamin Hall, Bart (afterwards Lord Llanover) whose fame is perpetuated by the great clock of the Parliament building, Big Ben. He was an implacable enemy of tramways, his carriage having twice been overturned on crossing of South Wales plateways, although they were quite a different animal from the grooved-rail street tramway. Because of this prejudice the LOTC Bill was thrown out and the episode proved just another example of that amateurism in British

3 (*above*) An artist's impression
of an angry encounter between
Hancock's steam 'Enterprise'
and a four-horse coach

4 (*left*) A garden-seat horse bus
of the LGOC; it seated twenty-
six; 'Favorite' was a name
associated with the time
worked

government which seems to have affected all its dealings with transport over the past two centuries or more. The LGOC accepted this verdict on street tramways as more or less final, although it registered the title 'London Omnibus Tramway' again in 1860 and kept a nominal company in existence until 1882, by when its interest in providing tramway tracks had evaporated, although it contracted to provide horses for other tramway companies, which obtained powers from 1869 onwards in the Metropolis and were covered by the general legislation of the 1870 Tramways Act, which did not make long-term investment any more inviting to entrepreneurs such as the LGOC.

More important than its abortive tramway venture was the incorporation of the English London General Omnibus Co. Ltd as a limited liability company on 16 November 1858 with a capital of £700,000, and an exchange of shares effected the changeover as from 1 January 1859. Production of an annual report and accounts in French continued at least until 1911 when the English company gained new vigour from the success of the B-type motor bus. By then French shareholders were in the minority. It is of particular interest that the formation of large bus undertakings in the great provincial cities seems to have been largely as a result of the introduction of large-scale capital provision by tramway companies. With some notable exceptions, such as Greenwood and his associates in the environs of Manchester, who, as we have seen, had a leaning towards the fixed track undertaking – bus operators showed a sturdy independence of big business and outside finance in the nineteenth century which is in curious contrast to the joint stock provision of capital and the ramifications of the money market in which railway promoters showed such acumen and which occasionally led into financial disaster, issue of debenture stocks at high rates of interest, or long periods of unremunerative existence in receivership.

In Liverpool the Liverpool Tramways Company of 1865 merged with the Liverpool Road & Railway Omnibus Co. Ltd on 1 January 1876, the combined concern being styled the Liverpool United Tramway & Omnibus Co. Ltd. In 1880 the Manchester Carriage & Tramways Company emerged, but the Glasgow Tramways & Omnibus Company leased tracks from Glasgow Corporation much earlier, in 1871. The attractions of real estate and the complications of the Tramways Act no doubt persuaded big business to invest in tramway companies and thereafter to consolidate with the local bus interests. A different amalgam of local transport interests was manifested in Bristol, where the tramway company formed an alliance with cab proprietors. The Bristol Tramways Co. Ltd was formed in 1872 to lease and operate tramways laid by Bristol Corporation and the amalgamation with the Bristol Cab Co. Ltd as the Bristol Tramways & Carriage Co. Ltd took place in 1887. The Brighton and Hove conurbation was the scene on one of the all-bus amalgamations, the majority of the horse bus proprietors coming together in 1884 as the Brighton, Hove & Preston United Omnibus Co. Ltd. But in general it remained true that bus businesses were on a local scale and there was a strong tramway element in the development of motor bus undertakings.

In the meantime, developments in horse bus design and operation were numerous and must be recorded. Operational difficulties were very much as those of today – with a driver and conductor as crew a 14-seat bus was highly labour-intensive and inspired endeavours to increase seating capacity. The London verdict on Greenwood's and other three-horse buses in provincial cities was that vehicles seating over 40 were all very well for flat routes, but were not suitable for traversing Pentonville Hill, the steady ascent of Camden Road and other notorious hills, including Ludgate Hill. As a result of an expedition by MacNamara to Glasgow and Manchester some of these three-horse buses were built for such routes as London Bridge Station to Tollington Park, but in general they were felt to be monstrosities on the streets of London. A fleet of 20 which had been brought to London by Greenwood & Turner of Manchester for the 1882 Great Exhibition was purchased at the end of that summer.

In Le Havre the Entreprise Générale des Omnibus experimented with a coachbuilt three-horse 24-seat bus which had a curved outside staircase and a top cover remarkably similar to the London NS bus of 1925, but in 1858 it proved too heavy even for three horses. The nearest London attained to a top-covered horse-bus was a light wagon tilt in the last years of the nineteenth century, but a similar vehicle with a light canopy, used for transport of Paris postmen in 1860 like the 'accelerators' of London introduced by our Post Office in 1830, has been commemorated on a French 30-centime (plus 10 centimes for charity) postage stamp.

In London some single-deck vehicles with 12 or 14 seats remained, on light traffic routes, in the outer suburbs or on such routes as Middledich's from West India Docks Station to Millwall Dock Entrance on the Isle of Dogs. One horse sufficed for their haulage and costs were saved further by eliminating a conductor; passengers passed their pennies to the driver through a hole in the roof. The knifeboard double-decker settled down to be a two-horse 26-seater; then, after some division of opinion in the late 1870s a Scottish group investigated the latest in buses of Paris and elsewhere in Europe and formed in 1880 the London & District Omnibus Co. Ltd. On 7 April 1881 the company was renamed London Road Car Co. Ltd and a few days later put to work their unconventional buses with very small front wheels and a front entrance. The driver sat aloft above the front wheels with practically no back support; behind him were two straight staircases coming up from either side to feed a central steep flight of steps to the knifeboard top deck. These were rapidly superseded by more conventional vehicles on which passengers were less accident prone and the London Road Car Company, which displayed the Union flag to emphasise that it had no French connection, began to build buses with garden seats on the top deck, in which they were soon imitated by the General. As the Road Car fleet increased above 400 they gradually assumed the popular title of 'Union Jack'. This innovation enabled ladies to ride on the top deck of a bus without offending Victorian decorum, provided, of course, that 'decency screens' were fitted. Why the garden seat bus did not appear earlier in London is a mystery. Garden seats had been on Continental double-deckers much earlier although the horse tram designers were seemingly even more conservative than the bus men in clinging to the knifeboard pattern. These provided a good anchor for advertisements either on enamel plates or printed on paper. Charles E. Lee has done splendid work on the dating of lithographs because of his comprehensive knowledge of the dates of presentation of plays, since nearly every street scene includes at least one bus with an advertisement of a stage production.

The introduction of new competition, such as was provided by the Road Car fleet and the Railways & Metropolitan Omnibus Company, formed by Sun Insurance executives and other users of the Waterloo–Waterloo Junction interchange who provided a service from the City to Waterloo to rival the South Eastern railway service kept the proportion of General vehicles down to about 70 per cent of the total in London throughout the horse bus era, despite purchase of such sizeable firms as the Richmond Conveyance Company in 1865. Some of the new competition produced original routes; the London Road Car Company began with Victoria to Liverpool Street, which, strangely, was not catered for by bus even before the completion of the Inner Circle underground service in 1884. The journey involved using a Camden Town Omnibus Association vehicle to Charing Cross and using a London General from there; but rather than make a joint through route with the Camden Town Association and so let the Camden Town proprietors into a partial share of a General service, the LGOC let the Road Car wax fat on its innovation which gave the newcomer a better start than it could have anticipated. Andrew's Star Omnibus Company began several new routes on the south side, including Camberwell Green to the Strand, Camberwell to Tulse Hill, Camberwell, Loughborough Junction, Brixton and Clapham, The Plough. A route from Elephant and Castle to Earls Court via Kennington Lane, Victoria, Sloane Square, Sloane Street,

Brompton Road and Cromwell Road, despite its dog-leg course, was also a success and eventually incorporated in the Atlas & Waterloo network.

In the associations of which it was a member it was standard practice for the LGOC to buy the times of retiring or deceased members and to take over rolling stock, horses and premises at an approved valuation. Times often changed hands at round about £250 and anyone who sought to operate outside the associations was dubbed a 'pirate'. Of course, some proprietors were determined to remain independent; Thomas Tilling was a leading example. As well as a bus fleet so formidable that the LGOC looked upon him rather as if he were their south-eastern division, he was a jobmaster with several thousand horses, but other dyed-in-the-wool independent operators included Tibbs, who later formed the Associated Omnibus Co. Ltd, Birch Brothers, at one time presided over by the redoubtable Widow Birch, Balls Brothers of Brixton and Andrews Star Omnibus Company, an interloper based in Cardiff. Myll Newstead was another provider of horse buses on an original route, between Oxford Street and People's Palace, travelling via Hart Street, Clerkenwell Road and Commercial Street to Whitechapel Road and standing in a place where only horse buses could have turned, in Harford Street, opposite what is now Queen Mary College, off Mile End Road.

Towards the end of the nineteenth century the standard London horse bus was a splendid example of coachbuilding skill, with garden seats on the top deck for 14 passengers and longitudinal seats inside for 6 passengers on each side, a total of 26, a good load for two horses. A bus at the turn of the century cost about £150; the LGOC built for its own use about 30 new ones in its North Road, Holloway, coach shop each year. The usual daily quota of mileage for a bus was about 60 and there were ten horses for each bus, with extras where the routes were hilly. Each pair of horses worked about $4\frac{1}{2}$ hours in the day and their working life as a bus horse was about five years.

Another development which was adopted first by the tramway companies was a ticket system. Over the early days of the bus the financial arrangements were haphazard and the takings were divided roughly in four; driver, conductor, ostler and proprietor. The suspicions that Shillibeer had of his men were possibly justified but in the absence of any system that could be audited there was no proof and if the returns fell short on any route in the light of previous experience it might have been due to extraneous causes.

The trams imported the ticket check and the London Road Car Company adopted it on their buses. When the LGOC endeavoured to adopt it also a decade later it was met in the first week of May 1891 by a strike. Tickets were, however, accepted after a very short interruption and the bell punch became the most usual system; tickets were distinctively coloured according to price and were punched to indicate the passengers' destination as a curb on over-riding. 'Shorts' or 'overs' could be checked by a count of the clippings of each colour. Old-time inspectors (or 'jumpers' as they were commonly known) pursued perpetrators of fraud with relish. I remember one telling me that when newly-promoted from conductor to inspector he took his lunch in an old-fashioned dining-room frequented by bus crews and overheard from the little boxed-off seat where he was ruminating after his meal, 'What do you think of old George being an inspector? He'll never catch me, I can tell you!' He finished the tale by saying, 'Catch him? Why, I caught him before he got to the end of the road.'

Just after the middle of the nineteenth century authority began to interfere with London bus operations, beginning in 1863 with the City of London Traffic Regulation Act. The Metropolitan Street Act (1867) gave more complete control, including, specifically, that buses should stop on the left-hand side of the carriageway, instead of whichever side a passenger demanded. At first this applied to a 4-mile radius of Charing Cross, extended to 6 miles from 1885 onwards. Certain traffic innovations followed, including the one-way operation to and from Liverpool Street Station terminus.

The last LGOC knifeboard bus came out of service in 1907 and the last LGOC garden-seat horse bus units were withdrawn from the Moorgate–London Bridge service on 25 October 1911, but other operators continued to have horse buses in service and some acted as contractors to the LGOC. Three years later the principal routes operated were across Blackfriars Bridge and from Somerset House to Waterloo Station across Waterloo Bridge, both at $\frac{1}{2}d$, and provided by Fred Newman. The last regular London horse bus service was suspended on 4 August 1914, when the horses of Thos. Tilling Ltd on the Honor Oak–Peckham Rye service were requisitioned by the Army. The maximum size of the LGOC horse bus fleet was probably attained in 1905 when the LGOC possessed just over 1,400 vehicles, worked by 17,000 horses. The very last horse bus of all was operated on 13 June 1931 by the Gateshead firm of T. Howe across the High Level bridge across the Tyne. The toll on this bridge was then $\frac{1}{2}d$ for pedestrians, so that the toll on the bus of $2d - \frac{1}{2}d$ a wheel – enabled a $\frac{1}{2}d$ fare to be profitable to the proprietor and attractive to the rider.

4
Mechanisation

England gave the world the railway system as a complete innovation about 150 years ago; it is sad that we did not have success in introducing mechanical road transport to the world. A number of Englishmen and Scotsmen were interested in the necessary technical developments but they were defeated by prejudice, vested interest and the conservatism that seems to afflict the British in their relations with the horse and the official disinterest and apathy that envelope all questions of mechanical transport. The road authorities led the campaign against the mechanisation of road vehicles, fearing that the motorised vehicle would increase damage to highway surfaces. Support was lent to the campaign by lovers of the horse, and public house landlords and brewery interests who saw the horse as a support of their trade; they were backed by all those who made their living out of the horse-hauled stage coach. Curiously they obtained further ammunition from surprising quarters: George Stephenson once delivered the dictum that 'steam carriages on ordinary roads would never be effective, or at least sufficiently serviceable, to supersede horse carriages'. James Watt was even more emphatic in his campaign against steam traction on common roads and had a somewhat stupid covenant put into the lease of his house, Heathfield Hall, to the effect that no steam carriage should on any pretence be allowed to approach the house.

MECHANISATION

The origins of steam locomotion on rail and road were parallel. Nicholas Joseph Cugnot made a steam tractor for gun carriages back in 1769, but it came to grief when it turned over; the boiler and a direct-acting pair of cylinders were carried ahead of a single front wheel and the load was to be carried on a pair of trailing wheels. Like all three-wheelers it tended to overbalance and it managed to do this in central Paris while running at three miles an hour. The immediate result was imprisonment for Cugnot. William Murdock made a miniature high-pressure steam road locomotive, also a three-wheeler, in 1781, to Watt's great displeasure. Watt was afraid Murdock's inventive and mechanical genius would be diverted away from the interests of Boulton & Watt, in whose employ he then was, at the princely starting wage of 15 shillings a week. When this tiny forerunner of steam vehicles was over 100 years old it was still capable of running at 8 m.p.h. Despite his prejudice against steam power on roads, James Watt seems to have made drawings of a change-speed gearbox. Geared drive was not usually thought necessary by the early workers on steam road vehicles. William Symington also made a model road carriage which performed in a highly satisfactory manner about 1786, but then turned his attention to ship propulsion.

Richard Trevithick, 1771–1833, was a real pioneer in the use of high-pressure steam for motive power of both road and rail machines; he made many models of steam locomotives from 1796 onwards, although the statement by Dr Samuel Smiles that he was a pupil of Murdock's is incorrect. In the last weeks of 1800 he began to build a road locomotive in John Tyadis's shops at Weith, Camborne, Cornwall, at a time when he had a team of men under him to repair mining plant and pumping machinery, and the task was evidently a part-time one as, according to one of Trevithick's contemporaries, it was Christmas Eve 1801 before the engine was ready for trial. It was a single-cylinder machine, intended to run at a pressure of 60 lb; the cylinder was immersed in the boiler, the drive by crank, with no intermediate gearing and the exhaust steam was turned into the chimney to create a blast on the fire. Captain Andrew Vivian had some part in the building of this engine and by the end of 1801 he was in partnership with Trevithick. In 1803 a four-wheeled carriage was built and this was assembled at Felton's coachbuilding shops in Leather Lane, London; closed passenger accommodation of carriage type was provided. The cylinder was immersed in the boiler and had a long stroke towards the front wheels; the drive was by crank to a train of gear wheels and the final drive to large back wheels which surrounded the passenger accommodation. Vivian and Trevithick exhausted their finances on steam coach operating experiments; unfortunately they did not secure any person of substance to back them financially. Trevithick's forte was experimentation rather than exploitation and in 1804 he was immersed in the problems of making a locomotive for the Penydarren plateway. This machine had flangeless wheels because the guidance was performed by the flange of the tram plates, but as the Penydarren locomotive weighed roundly 5 tons, it managed to break a number of the cast-iron plates on the 9-mile passage from the Dowlais steel works to the canal. Trevithick established the fact that smooth wheels were sufficient for traction, and that the exhaust from the cylinders could be used to draw up the fire and maintain steam pressure during a fairly long run, two facts which, in the absence of a technical press to disseminate news, were overlooked a few years later. The cylinder layout and long stroke of the road carriage were repeated in the Penydarren locomotive and the one depicted in a drawing preserved at Gateshead; an 8-inch cylinder was accompanied by a 54-inch stroke in the Penydarren tram locomotive, which won a wager of £500 on its only journey.

Others carried on experiments in railway traction, with the result that George Stephenson's *Locomotion No. 1* took part in the opening of the Stockton & Darlington Railway on 27 September 1825 and that after the Rainhill trials four years later the steam railway became accepted as a commercial proposition. These developments stimulated fresh interest in the problems of powered traction on roads, complicated as they were by the problems of compact disposition of the plant and severe weight limits. It must be remembered that so acute were these that it was not until 1863 that steam traction was possible on the 1 ft 11½ in. gauge Festiniog Railway owing to the difficulties of design imposed by the narrow gauge.

In the early part of the nineteenth century numerous experiments were made in the course of which attention was devoted to flash production of steam as required, four-wheel drive (Birstall & Hill) and the need for a differential gear rear wheel). Sir Goldsworthy Gurney built several steam 'drags' which had relative success although in 1825 he was still under the impression that smooth wheels would slip on hills and patented a design of steam-operated legs to assist in such places. Sir Charles Dance operated Gurney carriages between Cheltenham and Gloucester four times a day for four months in 1831, carrying 3,000 passengers over the 9 miles in an average time of 55 minutes (best time, 45 minutes). On 22 June 1831 the service was brought to an abrupt end by a heap of stones strewn across the road 1 ft 6 in. deep, which broke an axle of the carriage. The turnpike toll for mechanical vehicles was then raised to a prohibitive figure, such as £2, where a horse carriage would pay 1s 6d.

The most notable continuous applications of steam to vehicle propulsion were by Walter Hancock and John Scott Russell in London and Glasgow respectively. Walter Hancock was born at Marlborough in 1799. He served his apprenticeship to a watch-maker and in 1824 designed a lightweight and simple steam power plant, which, however, proved of no use for steam carriage propulsion. He took out a patent for a compartmented boiler in 1827 and soon afterwards began to build steam carriages in a works at Stratford. In the meantime his brother Thomas invented the process of vulcanising rubber in 1820 and in 1821 was established in a factory off Goswell Road, London. James Lyne Hancock Ltd is still in business as a rubber manufacturer with headquarters in Westminster, but in 1933, at the time when the Omnibus Society marked the centenary of the motor bus in London, their premises were just off City Road. In 1830 Walter Hancock produced a 10-seat vehicle which he named *The Infant*; he operated it regularly from February 1831 in public service between Stratford and London. He claimed this was not with a view to obtaining a profit, 'but as a means of dissipating any remaining prejudices and establishing a favourable judgment in the public mind as to the practicability of steam travelling on common roads'.

On one of its demonstration runs *The Infant* was made to climb the 1 in 18 of Pentonville Hill after a frost and a shower of sleet had glazed it over, and despite some misgivings Hancock had the satisfaction of *The Infant* breasting the summit while horses which set out at the same time were 'yet but a little way from the bottom of the hill'.

Hancock was a victim of company promoters. *The Era* was built for a group which alleged it was endeavouring to form a company to operate steam coaches between London and Greenwich. As a result this 18-seat vehicle made only various trial trips, one of which was to Windsor. Next he was helping the London & Paddington Steam-Carriage Company which had its offices at 68 Charles Street (since 1885 renamed Moreland Street), City Road. Next door, in 1933, James Lyne Hancock Ltd had their premises and so the party of members of the Omnibus Society were able to speculate on whether they were looking at the site of London's first motor bus garage. The vehicle built by Walter Hancock to the order of the L&PSC Company was completed on 26 January 1833 and delivered to the company at 68 Charles Street for painting. On 22 April it began operation between Moorgate and Paddington, the first power-driven vehicle specifically built for bus service. Hancock's records show that this vehicle, *The Enterprise*, made trips from Cottage Lane, City Road, to Paddington and back, with occasional trips down to Moorgate, on 16 days only, when disagreement between Hancock and the company brought operations to an end. First a clash marked the beginning of May 1833; the *Morning Advertiser* of 4 May recorded that 'the driver of the Paddington bus no. 3926, was fined for driving against and wantonly damaging the steam omnibus recently started upon the Paddington road'. This indicated the vicious resentment of the horse drivers towards the proponents of mechanical power. Hancock had, in fact, discovered that D. Redmund, 'projector and engineer' of the London & Paddington company, was busily engaged in taking his vehicle to pieces in order to build an imitation without paying Hancock any royalties on his patents. The L&PS-C Company never did implement its promised order for two more buses.

At this point Hancock decided to operate his own vehicle and from October 1833 he put his newest, *Autopsy*, on the Finsbury Square–Pentonville service. He fitted up premises in Windsor Place, City Road, as a garage, with coke bunker and water supply and also ensured that water was available at the Paddington terminus. With another new vehicle, *Era*, also a 14-seater, a service was run between Moorgate and Paddington from 18 August 1834 to the end of November when *Era*, renamed *Erin*, was taken to Dublin for eight days of demonstration work, including a run on the Howth road. The year 1835 was passed in demonstration runs in England, including runs to Marlborough and Birmingham, and overhauling the fleet. The bus service in London was resumed on 11 May 1836 and *Autopsy* and *Erin* were joined in July by *Automaton*, a 22-seat vehicle. To September 1836, with 20 weeks of operation, mainly between Moorgate and Paddington but with some runs to Stratford during which *Automaton*, with 20 passengers, in the course of a trip to Romford, covered a mile of Bow Road at 21 m.p.h., Hancock compiled some statistics of his operations. In 4,200 miles of running he had carried 12,761 passengers. The round trips from City to Paddington and back totalled 143, with 525 short journeys from the City to Islington and 44 to Stratford. With coke at 12*s* (60p) a chaldron, 55 chaldrons of coke were used or 76 miles per chaldron; the cost per mile of fuel was thus about 0.8 pence or rather less than 2 pence a mile in old currency. Others of Hancock's statistics included the hours in service each day, averaging 5 hours 17 minutes per vehicle; the average time for the 9 miles, Moorgate to Paddington and back, 1 hour 10 minutes, and the speed up Pentonville Hill, about 7 m.p.h. The cost of the *Automaton* was about £1,500. Hancock ceased operations during 1840, when the enforcement of the Turnpike Acts and higher tolls on mechanically-propelled vehicles, made operation unremunerative.

John Scott Russell, a Scot born in 1808, who later designed the SS *Great Eastern*, had an even shabbier deal in Scotland. From April to August 1834 he operated steam coaches over the 7½ miles between Glasgow to Paisley, run in 40 to 45 minutes at up to 17 m.p.h. The wheel of one of the coaches broke, the machine overturned, the boiler burst and five persons were killed. The Court of Session immediately interdicted the operation of the coaches and the service had to be abandoned – as some contemporary wrote, 'a fine specimen of Caledonian wisdom', especially in view of the fact that it was the result of the turnpike authority having strewn the road with stones. The next heard of the vehicles was their sale by auction in London on 27 February 1835. There is no trace, despite extensive research by Charles E. Lee, of their fate after the sale.

When there were signs of a revival of interest in the steam road vehicle after 20 lost years the railway interests were very strong and their lobby resulted in the Locomotive Acts of 1861 and 1865. The first imposed limits of 5 m.p.h. in towns and 10 m.p.h. in the country and in the second, the infamous 'Red Flag' Act, these speed limits were reduced to 2 and 4 m.p.h. respectively and the requirement was imposed for a man carrying a flag to walk ahead of the vehicle. How justified the enemies of road transport were may be judged from the introduction of a number of steam-hauled vehicles in the 1860s and 1870s, intended for service in Edinburgh, between London and Edinburgh, and in India, as well as R. W. Thompson's invention in 1867 of an improved rubber tyre. Most of the ingredients of motor vehicle design were now being explored in practice. The Ackermann steering was designed in 1818, and based on the ideas of Lenkensperger, and Roberts designed a workable differential (then called 'compensating gear') to enable the driving wheels to rotate at different speeds on curves, in a carriage of 1833, but it fell to French designers later in the nineteenth century to realise the benefits conferred by Ackermann's arrangement of separately pivoted front wheels. Pilot wheels or three-wheeled arrangements were expedients to overcome the difficulties which Ackermann and Roberts had already eliminated; all sorts of rack and pinion arrangements were made to improve the cart steering, but right at the end of the nineteenth century and well into the twentieth William Foden was using cart steering with screw and chain control on steam wagons.

The locomotives on highways legislation continued to be a powerful deterrent to British road transport enterprise, although under Col. R. E. B. Crompton we had some success in demonstrating large Ransomes tractors for long-distance passenger haulage in India. But users of traction engines on roads were harried by prosecutions for blowing off steam, obstruction and damage to roads. If a 15-ton boiler hauled by 15 horses broke down a weak bridge there was no liability on the haulier; if a traction engine was hauling it at the time, replacement of the bridge was enforced on the unlucky haulier, and it was alleged that some highway authorities deliberately neglected bridges in the hope that they would get a new bridge for nothing when a traction engine and a heavy load fell through it. Well

5 (*left*) The Fischer petrol-electric bus of 1903. Apart from its great weight the Metropolitan Police rejected it because it was slightly overwidth

6 (*below*) This Milnes-Daimler was the first motor bus to be owned by a main-line railway, and began work for the Great Western on 17 August 1903. Previously it had worked for a short time for the Lynton & Barnstaple Railway but was withdrawn because of the opposition of horse coach owners and harrying by police

into the motor age diamond-shaped admonitory notices with white lettering on a red ground were to be seen either side of flimsy rail and canal overbridges warning road users of the dire results of exceeding the weight of the 'ordinary traffic of the district'. Curiously a Pickfords tractor fell at Boroughbridge through the Ouse bridge after the Second World War and is the only instance I know.

All this put Britain far behind in the internal-combustion-engined vehicle stakes. R. Street in 1794 had devised a turpentine engine and Sir George Cayley had built an aero engine which relied on gunpowder as propellant in 1808, with hot-tube ignition, and then came a suggestion that inflammable gas could be used to power an engine. Vaporised alcohol was used by Cartwright as early as 1797 and J. J. E. Lenoir designed an engine to operate on coal gas or producer gas in 1860. In this the gas was conducted into the cylinder and fired by an electric spark. The four-stroke cycle was evolved in the next few years and Dr N. A. Otto's name is associated with this most commonly used arrangement – suction, compression, explosion, exhaust or, as the cynic who clearly demonstrated the weak point of the internal combustion engine put it – bang, nothing, nothing, nothing. This is a succinct explanation of the the merits and shortcomings of the four-cylinder internal combustion engine. In the Vienna Technical Museum one can see the world's first motor car, S. Markus's two-seater, which was exhibited at the 1873 Vienna Exhibition. Butler in 1885 was a British inventor who introduced water cooling, but to avoid using Otto's patents adopted the use of uncompressed gas. But whereas Butler produced a motor-tricycle and thereafter faded into obscurity, in 1885 the Germans Benz and Daimler, unknown to one another despite living within a comparatively few kilometres, had each devised petrol-driven cycles and later developed powered carriages, and in the twentieth century the Daimler-Benz interests were merged. In the early 1890s the French had the foundations of the Peugeot, Renault and Michelin firms, as well as Panhard & Levassor (who said of their gearbox transmission, 'c'est brusque et brutal, mais ça va') and with steam vehicles, Bollée, De Dion-Bouton and Léon Serpollet.

It was in 1878 that the notorious 'Red Flag' Act was repealed, but this was no relief to the cause of the British motor industry as the repressive speed limits and other means of harrying the mechanical transport user remained. Emancipation did not come until 14 November 1896, with the alleviation of the speed limit to 14 m.p.h., but there was a saving clause for the Local Government Board to fix lower limits and so the LGB set the figure at 12 m.p.h. The real start of the motor age was with the 1903 Act which sanctioned the speed of 20 m.p.h. for light motor cars. The limit of

34

12 m.p.h. continued to apply to rubber-tyred motor buses and heavier vehicles continued to have still more restrictive speeds. Not surprisingly, British manufacturers of internal-combustion-engined vehicles were practically non-existent in 1896, although Thornycroft, with boat building and steam launch experience, and Sumner and Spurrier, partners in forming the Lancashire Steam Cart Co. Ltd at Leyland, who had made steam lawn-mowers for some years, were quickly off the mark with steam vans in 1896, at Chiswick (in John I. Thornycroft, the sculptor's, shed) and in Leyland respectively. These firms won prizes in 1897 and 1898 for the excellence of their products, but despite the support of the wealthy pioneers of motoring whose activities had paved the way for the repeal of the penal clauses of the locomotives on highways legislation, the fact remained that our motor industry was very weak financially and had little operating experience. It was then bedevilled by financiers who sought to get monopoly rights and a stranglehold on the new industry. Frederick R. Simms, who was in business in London from 1891 as a consulting engineer with the special object of developing the use of Daimler patents in Britain and most of the British colonial territories, two years later formed the Daimler Motor Syndicate, Limited, which attracted the attention of H. J. Lawson, who was earlier the sponsor of the 'safety' bicycle. Whatever may be said of Lawson's methods, it is certain that he envisaged the future role of the motor vehicle more clearly than most nineteenth-century financiers. He offered what seemed a huge sum (£40,000) to take over the Daimler Motor Syndicate and its patent rights; most of the early patents, including the spray carburettor of Maybach, Daimler's partner, were unenforceable in practice. 'Lawson', says Anthony Bird, in his excellent book, *The Motor Car, 1765–1914* (Batsford, 1960), 'was of that class of businessman who continues to amass a fortune by buying, to sell at a profit, that which doesn't exist, from someone who doesn't possess it, with money which he hasn't got.'

The Daimler Motor Company bought the Daimler patent rights from the British Motor Syndicate, which had obtained them from the Daimler Motor Syndicate, and in May 1896 the Great Horseless Carriage Company was floated with a nominal capital of £750,000. Leaving aside the question of finance the Daimler 4-h.p. parcel van of 1897 was probably the first petrol-engined commercial vehicle to be on sale in Britain and had a manufacturing plant (bizarrely named 'Motor Mills') at Coventry where French know-how in constructing Daimlers was employed. Simms left a legacy of soundly-based component manufacture and also originated the term motor car in lieu of the French *automobile* which came into American usage.

Nevertheless it was electric propulsion which very nearly produced the first powered motor buses in England, due to the enthusiasm of Radcliffe-Ward. He ran several electric battery buses and although little is known about them, except that they were not licensed by the police, they appear to have made a very favourable impression. A battery-electric version of a horse bus intended for service in Liverpool also made a fleeting appearance. Registration of the Ward Electrical Car Co. Ltd in 1887 brought a warning salvo from the Metropolitan Police to say that thoughts were turning to power operation of omnibuses. When a Radcliffe-Ward vehicle in 1889 appeared on the streets in trial running it earned some marks for silence and lack of odours associated with hot oil or steam and the later familiar stench of incomplete combustion of vapourised petroleum spirit, but none for speed since it appeared to be capable of only 7 m.p.h. We do not know precisely what the Radcliffe-Ward buses appeared like, and despite the confidence of a daily paper journalist that he had a drawing of it, when challenged he was unable to produce the document. The converted horse bus of Liverpool, dated 1894, is illustrated by Charles E. Lee in *The Early Motor Bus* (British Transport Commission, 1974) and resembles an orthodox 26-seat horse bus, with garden seats on the top deck and the driver perched in the air and bereft of his horses. In lieu he has a steering wheel with a rather unconvincing linkage to cart-type steering and some means of controlling the current. The brake still applies with the driver's own muscle-power by pedal to a brake shoe on the rear wheels. The battery box of this Electric Motive Power Co. Ltd vehicle is stowed between the wheels and, like the attorney from Devon that W. S. Gilbert dreamed up for the Lord Chancellor, looks somewhat undersized.

The London Electric Omnibus Co. Ltd was again inspired by Radcliffe-Ward to forecast the introduction of an electric bus service at the end of 1896; the first vehicle, a 10-seater, at last made its appearance on the streets in the last days of 1897, but it failed to carry a single fare-paying passenger.

Between 1897 and 1903 was the wagonette stage, in which numerous vehicles of about 10-seat capacity, with 10-h.p. petrol engines, endeavoured to prove their worth in several places up and down the country. Norman D. Macdonald, whom I met many years later when he was taking vivacious interest in the London & North Eastern Railway endeavour to beat the four-hour time each way between Kings Cross and Newcastle upon Tyne on 5 March 1935, in the course of which 108 m.p.h. was reached on rail for the first time in this country, managed one of these ventures, with MMC and Daimler machines. This was the Edinburgh Autocar Company, which began operation on 19 May 1898 and had to give up in just over three years. The high cost of the solid rubber tyres and of repairs in general crippled the venture.

MECHANISATION

During this period the only safe bet for someone hoping to operate motor buses as large as the contemporary horse bus appeared to be the use of steam propulsion. A great deal of attention has been paid by historians to the steam bus with prominent boiler and chimney carried on steel-tyred wheels and with a modified horse-bus body surmounted by a light canopy, built by E. Gillett & Co. of Hounslow for the Motor Omnibus Syndicate Ltd; this clumsy machine was granted a licence by the Metropolitan Police on 21 January 1899 and seated 10 inside and 14 out. There are numerous reports of its appearance at various places around Hounslow, but it did not engage in regular service. One of Lawson's projects, the London Steam Omnibus Co. Ltd, is not next chronologically as it was incorporated on 30 June 1898; it issued a prospectus of a most exuberant character during the next few days, but its enthusiasm for the steam bus took over a year to cool, until it finally made up its collective mind that no suitable steam bus was forthcoming. It had hoped for a De Dion fleet on favourable terms. On 6 September 1899 it changed its name to the Motor Traction Co. Ltd. A prototype Daimler petrol bus assembled in Bristol by Brazil, Holborough & Straker, with two riders alongside the driver, four on a pulpit above the roof and eight or ten on a typical German single-deck bus layout, ran in London in 1898 and when the company at last launched its venture the chassis was similar, but the bodywork was of 26-seat horse-bus type, painted white, with the owning company's name along the rocker panel. Steel-tyred wheels of wooden cart type were still favoured and service began with two of these vehicles, reputedly designed by Sidney Straker, on 9 October 1899 between Kennington Gate, Westminster Bridge and Victoria Station, the length of two of G. F. Train's abortive tramways of nearly forty years before. After a few months the route was changed to run from Kennington to Oxford Circus and in December 1900 the vehicles were withdrawn as there was no hope of making a paying proposition of them. London saw the twentieth century dawn without a single motor bus at work on its streets, but during the years 1899–1903 some 61 vehicles were submitted to the Metropolitan Police public carriage department and accepted.

This was the beginning of a period of exploitation of the British market by a swarm of Continental manufacturers and their agents and, in fact, very few of the vehicles were trouble-free; if there were few mechanical troubles, the quality of tyres left much to be desired and I remember seeing a spectacular parting of a tyre from a wheel of a Great Eastern bus as late as 1911, but earlier it was a frequent occurrence. It is not surprising that some of the early motor buses were carried on steel tyres. Thornycroft, among the English pioneers, produced some massive steam wagons, including what was probably the first municipal tipping lorry – for Chiswick, at that time the firm's home local authority – and an adaptation of this cumbrous machine entered the service of the London Road Car Co. Ltd on 17 March 1902. It had an enlarged 26-seat horse-bus body with a modified, rather straightened, staircase and the top deck extended to carry 10 more seats, totalling 36. A light canopy, pierced by the chimney, protected upper deck customers from smuts and cinders. John Thornycroft evidently thought that steel tyres might slip on granite setts and provided a massive sandbox on each side. The vehicle operated from Oxford Circus to Hammersmith Broadway via Shepherds Bush and was painted on the side with large letters to say 'Hammersmith'. A subsidiary board announced 'Electric Railway Terminus' to denote that it passed the Shepherds Bush terminus of the Central London Railway. Whether it was the lordly General or not that put them up to the idea, errand boys were soon calling it 'the tuppenny lodging house'. In any event, it was so unwise, while in the care of Driver H. Lock, who drove a Lifu in 1897, as to make unexpected contact with a London United electric tramcar and its owners were persuaded to rusticate it to South Africa. Thornycroft, about four years later, entered the petrol field in London, but only produced a few vehicles for the Metropolitan market at that time.

Soon H. J. Lawson was back in the bus field, designing a 27-seat (12 down and 15 up) double-decker on a Canstatt-Daimler chassis, carried on solid rubber tyres. It was operated by C. C. Dennis on a suburban route, from Lewisham to Lee Green and Eltham. Licensed on 3 October 1902, it ran fairly consistently for over a year until the early part of 1904. During 1903 the London General Omnibus Co. Ltd summoned up its courage to order some Fischer petrol-electric vehicles from the USA, but when one arrived it was over-width and special permission had to be obtained from the police for operation. Only the one was delivered and before the year was out the LGOC demanded back the £450 they had paid for it. This era ended with the London General and the London Road Car companies both turning to Thomas Clarkson, who had been interested in the Capel steam car and was now producing 'Chelmsford' steam chassis at such a rate that he delivered two 14-seaters to the Road Car fleet in London on 8 October 1904 and one to the General on 10 October. Both were two-cylinder single-deck steamers and neither lasted very long in service – the LGOC vehicle was withdrawn in the high summer of 1905. Clarkson had already seen that the boiler needed to be bigger and he had provided his later vehicles with this elementary capacity to make steam. The driver could then not see over it adequately from the normal control position, so he yielded to the temptation to put him above the boiler, rather in the position of a horse bus driver. This particular vehicle was being prepared for the Olympia show of commercial vehicles and the job was rather hastily modified to transfer the controls to the new position. W. J. Morison, Clarkson's assistant, had to drive the vehicle from Chelmsford to London. He raised steam, drove down the shop and turned the steering wheel sharp left to go out through the door. Amid imprecations from Clarkson he found the vehicle up against the right-hand blank wall. The steering links had been transferred from one side of the front axle to the other so that left-about turning of the steering wheel turned the front wheels to the right and vice versa. Morison told me many years later that he got through the ghastly journey to London safely except at the top of Sloane Street, where instinctive pulling away from the kerb took him round a left turn and he wrapped the chassis round a lamp post, which a sarcastic policeman offered to move! The first of this type of Clarkson steamer went to work in the Metropolis for the London Road Car Co. Ltd in the autumn of 1905.

Long before Clarkson's buses had got on the road in London, the Daimler Motoren Gesellschaft had made an agreement on 27 November 1902 with G. F. Milnes & Co. Ltd, well-established as tramcar builders, to use the patents of Gottlieb Daimler for Milnes-Daimler Ltd which was set up to manufacture motor buses. This combination eventually lifted us out of the 'wagonette' stage of motorisation, producing large single-deck and 34-seat double-deck buses in, for the times, considerable numbers. With these, fleets were started in various parts of the country, some on an ambitious scale. One fleet was Eastbourne Corporation where the town fathers were determined not to have a tramway system, and another was at Hastings, where the Hastings & St Leonards Omnibus Co. Ltd thought it could show the superiority of the motor bus over the tramcar. Here the horse-bus company dipped a toe in the water with two single-deck Milnes-Daimlers and then, straight from the show at the Crystal Palace, bought a double-decker. This was put to work on a route between Bo-Peep and Alexander Park, about four miles. Nevertheless, soon the motor bus had to give way to the better money-making prospects of the tram, despite the penalties inflicted on the tram by the Doulter surface-contact system along the sea front, because the local authority was half-convinced that tramway wires were bad for the scenery; later this was substituted by the equally erratic and under-powered petrol-electric tram equipment.

The closing down of the Hastings motor bus system gave a demonstration of the power of the twentieth-century machine to survive in different soil. An offer was made in London for some of the Hastings vehicles and two drivers were entrusted with a pair of them to drive to London. At Godstone one of the two broke down. Some cannibalisation was done and for the best part of a week the drivers, having nothing to lose, their employ having been terminated, plied up and down between Caterham Station and Godstone, one driving and the other taking the money. But when all was straightened out, not only buses had transferred from Hastings to London, but also Clarence Freeland, of the Hastings & St Leonards Omnibus Co. Ltd. He joined the new motor bus boom in London which more or less coincided with my own arrival on the scene. One of the reviews announced on 5 April 1905 that the Vanguard line had just been started by the London Motor Omnibus Co. Ltd, that six buses were operating between Brondesbury Station and Charing Cross via Edgware Road, Baker Street and Oxford Street, and that five Milnes-Daimlers a fortnight would be added to the fleet until the total of 100 was reached. Plate 8 shows a Milnes-Daimler, apparently in blue livery, with the fleet name in gold seriffed capitals on a banner on the side panel where horse-bus owners painted some of the route information. The rear wheels are solid, having a toothed drive which gave the Milnes-Daimler what H. G. Wells would probably have described as its mournful ululation, and as Daimler had no faith in Hotchkiss drive through the springs a massive torque rod is incorporated. Motorenbau Daimler even had ideas about applying brakes to the outer surfaces of solid rubber tyres – an idea that might have stood them in good stead in 1906.

5
The Railway Interest

From the earliest days there were associations between railway undertakings and road passenger transport operators for about a century until the connection was gradually all but eliminated under the Transport Act (1947) and subsequent reorganisations. The Great Western Railway, which originally intended to occupy Euston jointly with the London & Birmingham Railway, was compelled, as a result of Brunel's adoption of the 7 ft gauge, to provide itself with a separate terminus on the west side of London and chose a site at Paddington. This was far out in the fields and although a certain amount of growth had taken place through the presence of the terminus of the Regents Canal and the interchange with the Grand Junction Canal, Paddington was still too remote for bus operators to find operation so far out remunerative. A subsidy was therefore offered to bus proprietors for operating to Paddington from the GWR Princes Street office in the City – Chaplin, Gilbert, Horne, and Sherman – who in May 1839, eleven months after the opening of Paddington, asked for and received a contribution by the GWR of 3*d* towards the fare then being charged of 6*d*. Previously, the Liverpool & Manchester Railway had provided free buses from Dale Street to Crown Street Station in Liverpool and for first-class passengers from the Market Street coach office to Liverpool Road Station, Manchester.

A very usual use by railways of road services was the closing of gaps in the railway route. As an example, the Denbigh Hall–Rugby gap on the London & Birmingham route was so covered; for thirteen months in 1839–40 the Basingstoke–Winchester gap in the London & South Western (then London & Southampton) main line was bridged by coach and the London, Chatham & Dover Railway made frequent use of road coaches to provide service where the railway awaited completion.

In the twentieth century a small railway sought the aid of the motor vehicle when slips in the standard-gauge cuttings linking the 2 ft 6 in. Leek & Manifold Light Railway to the main line threatened to delay the opening and two steam buses (on steel tyres) were hired to maintain the connection. These appear to have been the same Straker single-deckers that the Potteries Electric Tramways had endeavoured to use a little earlier and they displayed the same nasty traits, one of them failing at the opening ceremony on 27 June 1904. The bus service, despite its faults, maintained the link until the railway was completed on 1 July 1905.

An early example of through booking was by the London & Croydon Railway from Croydon and other stations to the Bank of England, changing from train to bus at New Cross. This had the advantage to the L & CR that the *per capita* fee for each passenger between New Cross and London Bridge did not have to be paid to the London & Greenwich Railway, owners of the line from Corbetts Lane Junction to the terminus. A confectioner's shop in Lombard Street was named as the rendezvous for outward passengers by bus and the through fare to Croydon was 1s 6d first and 1s 3d second class.

The Great Western Railway, with the largest railway-owned fleet, did not obtain specific powers until the Railway (Road Transport) Acts of 1928. In 1925 the London & Provincial Omnibus Owners' Association wrote to the GWR calling attention to the fact that their operation of buses was *ultra vires*, but stating that it did not wish to initiate legal proceedings. A meeting was suggested with the railway company's representatives and the outcome was a move towards co-operation rather than competition. In particular Crosville agreed to seek GWR consent before opening new routes which would compete with the railway or before making fare reductions on existing routes. Of the constituent companies of the Great Western Railway at grouping in 1923, the Alexandra (Newport & South Wales) Docks & Railway and the Cambrian Railways had motor bus powers; only the Cambrian had operated buses. The Cambrian fleet comprised two undersized Orion double-deckers which worked from 1906 in the Lleyn peninsula. In 1913 they were transferred to a company based on Nevin. The Great Western took up the bus business as a result of being offered two Milnes-Daimler 16 h.p. single-deckers on which 22-seat wagonette bodies with large luggage accommodation were mounted. These had been purchased by the enterprising Sir George Newnes, who had formed a company to operate them between Blackmoor Station on the Lynton & Barnstaple Railway and Ilfracombe. The local horse-coach fraternity was strongly entrenched and followed a course of action familiar seventy years before. There were obstructions on the roads and information about exceeding the speed limit were laid with the county police. Sir George announced his intention of inaugurating the service of the 'Ilfracombe Motor Company' in April 1903; by May he had incurred a swingeing fine for running at 8 m.p.h. and given up. The Great Western Railway had purchased the two Milnes-Daimler vehicles and on 17 August 1903 the GWR bus service had begun from Helston to The Lizard, where the GWR had been in some danger of having to build a costly light railway. The speed limit for the 3½-ton Milnes-Daimlers, which had caused trouble for the Ilfracombe Motor Company in Devon was avoided by removing enough equipment to bring the weight down to 2 tons 19 cwt in Cornwall. Beckoned on by the driver of a donkey cart, suspended through the state of the roads for a short period in 1904, the Helston to The Lizard bus service survived to be handed to the Western National Omnibus Co. Ltd in 1929 and its fiftieth anniversary was commemorated by the unveiling of a plaque at Helston Station on 17 August 1953 by A. E. C. Dent, who was at that time executive officer for road motor engineering of the Western Region of British Railways. I went down by sleeping car train to have breakfast at Penzance and so be in position to participate in the ceremony.

At the end of 1904 the GWR bus fleet totalled 34 and at the end of the following year 72. Early in 1908 the railway bought 14 Milnes-Daimler double-deck buses from the Associated Bus Company and except for the First World War period the advance was continuous, the bus fleet numbering 300 by 1928 and the number of services 168. Although expenses tended to exceed revenue the railway thought this well worth while if it saved capital expenditure on rural railway extensions. In a few cases, however, such as Lampeter to Aberayron, the bus service preceded construction of a light railway. The services were maintained much as any other responsible operator would have done; single-deckers were equipped with coal-gas balloons in the petrol shortage of 1917. No fewer than 80 handy fast Burford buses were added to the fleet for competitive purposes in 1925; joint schedules and inter-available return tickets were established with James & Sons Ltd of Ammanford in 1927 and in the following year a number of acquisitions were made, including the Dare Valley Motor Co. Ltd of Aberdare and F. Rosser of Llanover. The longest GWR bus routes were over the 21 miles from Corwen to Betws-y-Coed and nearly as far from

Brecon to Abergavenny. The most extraordinary GWR bus service was from Aberystwyth to the summit of Plynlimmon, for the most part over the turf of the mountainside, operated with a Morris Commercial coach fitted with chain track on the two rear axles.

The London & North Western Railway fostered a number of horse-bus services in the nineteenth century and bought its first motor bus at the end of 1905. This was a double-deck Milnes-Daimler 34-seater which went to work on 23 April 1906 between Watford Junction Station and Croxley Green in replacement of the town horse bus. The LNWR double-deck buses had 'LNWR' in brown as a fleet name on the white top hamper and the company's coat of arms on the dark brown side panel. From 1907 the LNWR buses in the London area were licensed by the Metropolitan Police. Besides the Watford and Harrow group of routes, there were services based on Boxmoor, Tring and Brownhills, and at Mold, Llandudno Junction and Holywell in North Wales. A Midland Railway service between Desborough and Rothwell ran between 1908 and 1911. Later the connection was turned round to be from Kettering Station.

Three of the railways which formed the London & North Eastern Railway in 1923 had motor bus departments. The North Eastern Railway was the pioneer, with a service from Beverley to Brandesburton on 7 September 1903. The North Eastern management has been criticised for its choice of foreign vehicles, but it might well be asked what different choice could have been made in 1903 in view of the repressed state in which our commercial vehicle industry had existed before 1896 and, in fairness, until the 1903 Act? The North Eastern company began a number of services in County Durham and also linked Ripon Town and Station.

The Great Eastern Railway was another which obtained motor bus powers early in the twentieth century and it began operations between Lowestoft and Southwold as soon as they were obtained, on 24 June 1904. The difference from other railways was that the Great Eastern Railway built 12 of its own excessively clumsy vehicles, with 38 h.p. engines, at its Stratford locomotive and carriage works. But its services were comparatively prolific – Ipswich to Shotley, where motor boats connected with Harwich, Norwich to Loddon, Harwich to Dovercourt and, beginning on 9 September 1905, a series of services radiating from Chelmsford. The latter sounded most sonorous if the timetables were recited as poetry: *Chelmsford, Galleywood and Stock, Chelmsford, Great Baddow and Danbury*, and stops on another service: *Fountain, Good Easter* and *King William IV, Leaden Roding*. The Great Eastern Railway decided in 1913 that it would hand over its bus services to specialist bus operators. In January 1913 the Lowestoft–Southwold service was taken over by United Automobile

Services Ltd, and the following July saw the National Steam Car Co. Ltd take over the Chelmsford group of routes which made the nucleus of the Eastern National Omnibus Co. Ltd. The Harwich service was operated by part of a batch of six 1919-type Thornycroft buses in the plum livery favoured for GER coaches at the time and remained in GE hands for a short period. The Norwich and Loddon service was suspended during the First World War but was reinstated on 15 December 1919, on which date the Beccles and Loddon service of 1905–9 was also resumed. The Eastern Counties Road Car Co. Ltd bought the Ipswich–Shotley service in 1922.

The Great North of Scotland Railway began bus operations on 2 May 1904 over the 17 miles between Ballater and Braemar. Despite difficulties with road surfaces – met by local petitions that the road should be strengthened rather than the buses withdrawn – services flourished and at the time of grouping the GN of S bus fleet totalled 33. A variety of chassis was purchased, but Caledon figured patriotically high in the list. The bodywork of most was built in the company's own Inverurie carriage-building shops. Of the stock, 26 buses were designed for 18 passengers each, but two of these seated 10 extra riders on the roof and some had additional accommodation for mail or goods. There were seven regular services, mainly in Aberdeen-shire, and summer extras, one of which was over the 32 miles between Ballater and Corgarff. The road between Corgarff and Tomintoul, over the 2,000 ft contour, was treated with some suspicion by the GNSR and figured as a 'mountain road' on tourist guides before 1914. In 1929 the LNER introduced an Aberdeen–Ballater through bus, with interavailable return tickets, thereby paving the way, despite battery-electric railcars, for eventual suppression of the Deeside railway service.

The constituents of the Southern Railway were somewhat sparsely provided with powers to operate motor buses; the LBSCR had such powers, obtained in 1906, provided some part of the passengers' journey was made by rail. But the LBSCR did not operate any buses. The LSWR, however, was early in the field as an operator, obtaining two Clarkson single-deckers and putting them on the 19-mile Exeter–Chagford service on 1 June 1904. Some services were also based on Brockenhurst station and that steam-age raconteur, W. J. Morison, once told me that when assistant to Thomas Clarkson he was sent down there to overhaul one of the machines; he pushed it under the goods yard crane, unbolted the cab and lifted it up, effected the necessary maintenance and raised steam. When he started off there was a frightful rending noise and the world rocked about him. He had omitted to detach the cab from the crane hook.

The London & South Western Railway used Thornycroft petrol vehicles on the Farnham to Haslemere route. For the first year the vehicles were

7 (*above*) Clarkson steam buses of the London & South Western Railway at Chagford

8 (*below*) A Vanguard in blue livery exhibited just before the start of service in March 1905

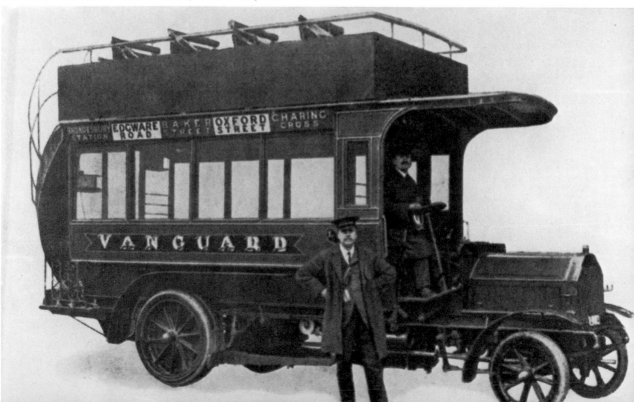

9 (*above*) Milnes-Daimler 34-
seat bus supplied to the London
& North Western Railway, in
service between Watford and
Harrow and Wealdstone station
from 1906

10 (*right*) A Commer of 1908 with
Lindley pre-selective gearbox.
It is accommodating a private
party without the use of
coachwork

maintained by John I. Thornycroft & Co. Ltd, the railway collecting the receipts and guaranteeing 10*d* (4p) a vehicle mile to Thornycrofts. The service began in February 1905 and after a year showed a surplus of £115, so that the LSWR bought the bus. But in the summer of 1913 the vehicles were handed over to the Aldershot & District Traction Co. Ltd. Under LSWR management the service ran three times every weekday in each direction, connecting with trains at Haslemere station and Farnham station and running on at the Farnham end to the Bush Hotel. The professional bus operators increased the service and introduced a Sunday timetable. The railway was surprised and delighted that one of the Thornycrofts had covered 40,000 miles in five years.

The South Eastern & Chatham Railway inaugurated a wagonette service with 12 h.p. 10-seater Panhard vehicles in February 1905 between Canterbury and Herne Bay and another abortive experiment was between Hythe and Dymchurch in 1914. Several of the railway ventures into bus operation were made without very much thought or preparation; they have the stamp of amateurism. The Great Central Railway acquired an 18-seat Milnes-Daimler single-decker and put it to work from Mottram Station to Tintwistle via Hollingworth on 30 June 1905. There is a picture extant showing very considerable wear on the rear tyres. The Lancashire & Yorkshire Railway tried the motor bus in several locations; a pair of Milnes-Daimler London-type double-deckers were seen on a route from Blundellsands Station to Crosby and Thornton in 1907 and later they worked from Chorley Station.

The Mersey Railway began a service of buses to feed its trains at Birkenhead Central Station on 29 January 1906, before the obtaining of Parliamentary powers to operate motor buses, and as the Mersey Railway buses were in competition with the Birkenhead Corporation tramways the Corporation obtained an injunction against the railway company. The Mersey Railway then appealed and upon agreeing to carry passengers from the Birkenhead suburbs only to Mersey Railway stations the injunction was dissolved. But the value of the service to the railway was so diminished that it was withdrawn.

Although, from their attitude to railway charges, the framers of the Railways Act (1921) did not realise the powerful road transport competition to which the railways were to be subjected in the next few years, the about to be newly-formed companies wanted to take some precautions. Accordingly, the Midland and London & North Western Railways applied to Parliament for uninhibited road transport powers in 1922, but were rebuffed. This refusal made the four grouped railways hold back from pressing the matter for some years, but at last the GWR, LMSR, LNER and

SR all obtained the coveted powers in 1928. The Metropolitan, which classed itself along with the main lines, was refused and, as it was running buses at Watford, started in 1927 to connect the Metropolitan & LNER station on the fringes of Cassiobury Park with the station building it had somewhat recklessly built (without rail access) in the High Street, it had to transfer the four vehicles to the associated North West Land & Transport Co. Ltd and later to the Lewis Omnibus Co. Ltd of which John Wardle, commercial manager of the Metropolitan Railway, was chairman. The Metropolitan operated horse buses in the nineteenth century, distinguished by a red umbrella, feeling that by this means it could almost claim to serve such places as Piccadilly Circus; the District used contractors for the same purpose. The Metropolitan's plunge into the horse-bus business is one of the peculiar deeds of that company in the light of the fact that it had secured LGOC assent to a non-competitive pact. In fact except for short periods in 1914 to 1916, when LGOC bus 44 ran from London Bridge to Shepherds Bush largely along the Metropolitan and Hammersmith & City Railways this was observed by the General.

Upon the four amalgamated railway companies being granted road powers it at first seemed likely that sharp competition would develop with existing operators. Very little pattern in their initial actions can be discerned – the LMSR took over a service from Rochdale Corporation and began some services in Scotland and in August 1929 purchased the entire undertaking of Crosville Motor Services Ltd. The LNER similarly purchased an interest, sometimes through the former Great Central cartage subsidiary Thompson McKay & Co. Ltd in a number of small operators, including Robert Emmerson & Co. Ltd of Newcastle upon Tyne, Redwing Safety Motor Services of Redcar, Eastern Express Motors of West Hartlepool, Reliance Express Motors of Darlington and Blumers Motor Services, early in 1929 and indicated its interest by painting one side of the vehicles in LNER livery while the other side continued in the original colours, giving a bizarre effect.

When things settled down it became apparent that the grouped railways were of the same opinion as the pre-grouping railways and felt that bus operation was a matter for specialists, so that there was very little extension of outright purchase of existing bus undertakings. The second method, amalgamation with existing companies, was in practice confined to the Great Western Railway, because only the GWR could contribute a fleet of buses of any importance. Third, joint committees were set up between the railways and municipal transport committees; in these local traffic within the municipal boundaries was allotted to the municipal undertaking, services to places a short distance outside the boundary were shared and the long-distance services were exclusively railway owned. Arrangements were made with Halifax Corporation in March 1929 by the LMS and LNER jointly, with Huddersfield Corporation beyond the town boundaries later in 1929 by the LMSR, with Todmorden from 1 January 1931 by the LMSR, and from 1 January 1929 with Sheffield Corporation and the LMSR and LNER. Much-publicised arrangements with both the LMS and LNER and Leeds Corporation in the summer of 1929 were not consummated and the negotiations that were reported at the same period between the Great Western Railway and Caerphilly UDC did not materialise in an arrangement of this sort. The fourth, and most common, means of the railways taking an interest in a bus concern was the purchase of not more than 49 per cent of the ordinary share capital and the railways were surprised to find what a cheap expedient this was.

The Great Western Railway merged an appropriate part of its fleet with that of the National Omnibus & Transport Co. Ltd to form the Western National Omnibus Co. Ltd as from 1 January 1929, the operating area being Devon and Cornwall south of a line through Newquay and Okehampton. The vehicles were contributed by NO & T 225, and GWR 115; the shares being £360,000 and £180,000 respectively.

The Western Welsh Omnibus Co. Ltd was a renaming in June 1929 of South Wales Commercial Motors, a National Electric Construction Company undertaking in which the GWR took an interest. The large independent undertaking of the Bristol Tramways & Carriage Co. Ltd was another Great Western Railway investment of January 1930. In December 1931 this controlling financial interest was transferred to the Western National Omnibus Co. Ltd. Another Welsh investment by the GWR was the Wrexham & District Transport Co. Ltd, a British Automobile Traction subsidiary in which an interest was purchased in November 1939; the name was changed a year later to Western Transport Co. Ltd and it took over GWR bus interests north of a line from Aberayron to Hereford, those south of this line going to Western Welsh. It also took in seven Corris Railway bus services based on Machynlleth, these having been transferred to the GWR through the purchase of the Bristol Tramways & Carriage interests reinforced by Act of 4 August 1930. Both were investments of Imperial Tramways Co. Ltd, formerly owners of the Middlesbrough tramways and the London United Tramways.

The LMSR and the LNER and later the Southern Railway were much assisted in obtaining their bus company interests by the Tilling & British Automobile Traction Co. Ltd and, in the case of the northern railways, the British Electric Traction Co. Ltd. It was agreed that the appropriate railway company should offer a price sufficiently attractive to the ordinary shareholders in the operating bus companies. Tilling & British or the BET would then sell a portion of their own holding to the railway to make the railway holding equal their own; it was part of the bargain that the railway should offer to buy from all the shareholders so that the holding company should not be forced to provide more than the same proportion as the private shareholders. The same interests were afterwards introduced as partners in businesses which the railways purchased outright. There seems to have been only one instance of competitive bidding by the railways and a holding company and this took place between Tilling & British, who offered 27s 6d (£1 37½p) for United Automobile Services Ltd, when the LNER offered 30s (£1 50p); eventually the offer was a joint one, after some negotiation between J. F. Heaton for Tilling & British and Sir Ralph Wedgwood for the LNER. It is typical of prices paid for bus company shares that the Southern Railway paid between 26s 6d (£1 32½p) for shares in Aldershot & District and 65s (£3 25p) for Southdown shares. Where territory of more than one railway was concerned, the railways concerned each purchased a proportion of the bus company's shares – thus half of the Birmingham & Midland Motor Omnibus Co. Ltd shares were obtained as to £160,000 by the GWR and £240,000 by the LMSR, and of the £672,069 ordinary shares of the newly-formed Eastern Counties Omnibus Co. Ltd £163,243 went to the LNER and £22,419 to the LMSR. The investments of the Southern Railway were not charged to capital account, but to revenue, but the usual holding of the Southern Railway was 30 per cent of the issued capital, owing to the high proportion of independent shareholdings in the principal companies in which the Southern invested; in the Southern National and Southern Vectis companies the railway holding was 50 per cent with Tilling (originally National) and Tilling & British Automobile Traction respectively. In the case of Devon General Omnibus & Touring and the Thames Valley companies the GWR holding was roundly 30 per cent and the Southern 20 per cent.

A certain amount of rationalisation of bus company operating areas took place after the railway investment in the bus business, no doubt as the result of a less parochial view. Thus the Eastern Counties Omnibus Co. Ltd just mentioned combined the East Anglian section of United Automobile Services Ltd, based on Norwich, which had become a Tilling & British company at the time of the railway investment, with the Eastern Counties Road Car Co. Ltd, a Tilling and British (although Tilling managed) subsidiary dating from 1919 and based on Ipswich, the Tilling & British associate Ortona Motor Co. Ltd of Cambridge, and another Tilling & British associate, the Peterborough Electric Traction Co. Ltd, until 1928 a British Electric Traction tramway undertaking. This had the effect of concentrating United Automobile activities on Northumberland, Durham and North Yorkshire and the headquarters was moved from the offices at York, midway between the North East England and East Anglian operating areas, to Darlington. On 1 January 1931 adjustments were made between the territory in Lincolnshire of United Automobile Services Ltd in anticipation of the establishment of the new Eastern Counties company on 14 July 1931.

In Cheshire and North Wales a merger of interests was based on the Crosville undertaking which was suitably enlarged. In August 1929 an announcement was made of the imminent purchase of the Crosville company by the Great Western and London Midland & Scottish Railways jointly, but in October the LMS carried out the purchase alone and for a time the Crosville vehicles appeared in maroon livery with Crosville–LMS as a fleet name. Equal participation in Crosville by Tilling & British Automobile Traction took place in December 1929 and to assist this arrangement the LMSR made offers to shareholders in the Tilling & British Llandudno Coaching & Carriage Co. Ltd (Royal Blue) and subsequently the LMS also purchased Holyhead Motor Services (Mona Maroons), UNU Motor Services, and Brookes Brothers (White Rose of Rhyl) and a new Crosville Motor Services Ltd with equal shares by the LMSR and Tilling & British was formed on 15 May 1930 to incorporate these concerns. Then on 1 May 1933 the Western Transport Co. Ltd was merged with Crosville, bringing a GW shareholding into that company, the common denominator being the Tilling & British interest in each.

The actual operation of buses by the railways was very quickly relinquished, the last Great Western services being transferred to another operator on 10 April 1932 when London General Country Services took over the GWR services round Slough. Last of all was the service operated by the GWR on behalf of the Southern and the Great Western Railways from Weymouth to Radipole and Wyke Regis which passed to the Southern National Omnibus Co. Ltd on 1 January 1934.

The railway companies appointed directors to the boards of the bus operating companies in which they had invested, usually from senior traffic officers; it was frequently the case that particular officers acted, as he was called in the case of the Southern Railway, 'road transport liaison officer'. The only case of a railway representative on a company bus board becoming chairman was that of G. S. Szlumper, assistant general manager of the Southern Railway, who became chairman of the Southern Vectis Omnibus Co. Ltd during the period when control was shared with the Dodson family, before the Tilling & British investment. It was customary for a railway member of the joint municipal committees to take the chair in alternate years. Thomas Hornsby, when divisional general manager of the North Eastern area of the LNER, served as deputy chairman of United Automobile Services Ltd. At a rather lower level, standing joint committees or liaison committees of railway officers with local knowledge and bus company officers were set up to investigate co-ordination of time-tables, publication of joint timetables, provision of interavailable return tickets, operation of combined road and rail excursions, replacement of trains by buses whether in emergencies or permanently, working of bus routes into station yards and the like and a remarkable degree of public benefit resulted.

Co-operation seemed closest to the author between the BET companies and the railways rather than with the Tilling-managed Tilling & British or the Tilling companies, and indeed I observed the Potteries Motor Traction Co. Ltd, a BET company in which there was no railway investment, to have the most well developed liaison with the LMS of any company I investigated. Under the influence of the British Transport Commission and its separate executives it is unfortunately not possible to say that there is any notable improvement in co-ordination or apparent public benefit.

6
Municipal Buses

In the nature of things bus operation could hardly get into the peculiar position that tramway operation did for municipal authorities – that under the Tramways Act they were allowed to own them so long as they did not work them. It was Huddersfield, unable to find a contractor to take on the lease of its tramway system, that eventually caused a breakthrough in 1882. Hatred of the idea of tramways and especially of electric tramways with overhead wires turned the thoughts of Eastbourne Corporation to investigation of the possibilities of the motor bus. An Act to operate motor buses in the borough and a mile beyond the boundary was secured in 1902 and operation began, with Milnes-Daimler single-deckers, on 12 April 1903. A double-deck Milnes-Daimler 34-seat vehicle was acquired the following year and by the time of my first visit to the town the blue and cream fleet of Leyland 34-seaters similar to the pre-war New Centrals in London was well established on the routes to Ocklynge, the Archery and the foot of Beachy Head. As late as 1916 a Milnes-Daimler and De Dions were returned as part of the fleet.

Not every municipality was so persevering with motor-bus operation as Eastbourne; Bournemouth Corporation obtained powers in 1904 and began a service from Boscombe Arcade to Bournemouth in April 1906. A loss was made each year from 1907 to 1911 and then bus running was suspended for some time in 1911 to 1915. In 1916 the loss was much reduced but eventually for a number of years the resort decided to operate mainly in the summer months, relying on the trams for business movement. As things settled down services were usually run during the summer months mostly with small vehicles, the rolling stock in 1928 comprising six conventional 26-seat buses, six Shelvoke & Drewry Tramocars (a vehicle on a refuse collecting chassis), six 16-seat Guy Runabouts and 12 W & G 26-seat buses as well as three 37-seat single-deck buses. In 1936 the trams were replaced by trolleybuses and later these in turn were replaced by buses.

Some towns, like Bolton, used buses while the tramway system was being completed. Here the buses were discarded and the capital written off after use between 1908 and 1911. It was 1923 before buses were instituted again. Haslingden, Lancs, was another intermittent bus user from 1907 and Hull operated from 1909 to 1912 and then left bus operations. On the other hand Liverpool Corporation entered the bus business on 1 January 1911 by buying the business of Woolton Motor Omnibus Co. Ltd for £1,000. In those places where the tramways had been company-owned, the associated bus company was often purchased: Stockton and Middlesbrough Corporations had to buy portions of the bus business of the Imperial Tramways Company in those areas. Cardiff Corporation began its own bus business on 24 December 1920 and thought it desirable to buy the motor bus undertaking of the Cardiff Tramways Company on 1 October 1922.

In Birmingham the Corporation began a motor bus undertaking on 19 July 1913 and in October 1914 purchased 30 Tilling-Stevens buses and Tennant Street Garage from Birmingham & Midland Motor Omnibus Co. Ltd. The Corporation buses served the area inside the city boundary, while the BMMO vehicles carried traffic from and to Birmingham at a small protective fare so that passengers were calculated to use the Corporation trams or buses to save their pennies. This protective fare system was adopted very generally in later years and enabled the bus to make journeys from city centre to city centre. Later on BMMO buses were hired by Birmingham Corporation to serve areas such as Sutton Coldfield for which it was not convenient for the municipality to provide all the buses it needed.

Many towns had hard struggles to get a bus undertaking standing on its feet. Dundee's original Order to operate buses (ponderously confirmed by Act of 1907) enabled the Corporation to run buses during construction or repair of the tramways, or to test the traffic; in 1920 and 1921 powers were sought to run beyond the boundaries but in neither year were they granted. In 1927 powers were obtained to run anywhere in the city but not in competition with the Dundee, Broughty Ferry & District Tramways. A 'traffic testing' route to Broughty Ferry was begun in 1921 and on the Tramway Company objecting the service was interdicted. On appeal it became possible to reinstate the service, but it was withdrawn in July 1922 because of the extravagant demands of the Harbour Trustees for the use of their private road.

For many years the municipal bus business comprised about 90 undertakings, but from time to time consolidations took place; Burnley, Colne & Nelson became a combined undertaking on 1 April 1933. The formation of the London Passenger Transport Board inspired the idea of other mergers, one mooted being the merger of eleven local authority undertakings in the Manchester area with a view to more efficient working. Many municipal concerns were too small to stand on their own feet – as a critic said at an Institute of Transport seminar, 'many municipal undertakings with general manager, traffic manager and engineering staff, have only as many vehicles to look after as a single depot of a large area agreement company'. In South Wales, for example, in 1937 the West Monmouthshire Omnibus Board (Mynyddislwyn and Bedwellty Urban District Councils) had 18 buses; Aberdare UDC, 25; Bedwas and Machen UDC, 3; Caerphilly UDC, 17; Cardiff, 142; Gellygaer, 12; Merthyr Tydfil Corporation, 27; Newport (Mon.) Corporation, 73, plus a tramway system; Pontypridd UDC, 25 buses and 9 trolleybuses. By contrast the area companies of South Wales had much larger fleets, such as 414 Red & White, 288 South Wales Transport and 432 Western Welsh; N. J. Young, when general manager of Newport Corporation, contended that if the council had followed his advice in the 1920s they could have extended their operations over much of the territory occupied by Red & White Services and its associates in subsequent years. Government attitudes towards local authority transport seem to have favoured the economies of scale to be derived from expanded boundaries or from deliberate formation of larger traffic areas, as effected under the 1968 Transport Act. Curiously, the South Wales area that seemed to so many observers ripe for action, has never been the scene of any move towards formation of a passenger transport executive.

Two municipalities formed companies in association with an area agreement company. From 2 October 1932 Keighley Corporation bus services were amalgamated with local routes of the West Yorkshire Road Car Co. Ltd as Keighley–West Yorkshire Services Ltd. Eighteen months later a joint committee was formed between York Corporation omnibus committee and West Yorkshire Road Car Co. Ltd to administer the services in and around York of that undertaking. This came into effect on 1 April 1934. Both have been dissolved since the war.

Many corporations leased their undertakings to the neighbouring area agreement bus operator. For example, Dover, which operated a tramway from 1897 to 1936, abandoned it on 1 January 1937 and from that date the East Kent Road Car Co. Ltd had operated buses on behalf of the Corporation. For some years it used to be said that you could tell the former Corporation drivers because they pulled up at stops like a tram in the middle of the road.

Bristol Corporation obtained several Acts giving it powers over the tramways undertaking of the Bristol Tramways & Carriage Co. Ltd and in addition had options under the Tramways Act (1870) to buy the tramways system in 1915, 1922, 1929 and 1936, but when the Tilling group obtained control of the Bristol Company in 1936 it initiated negotiations with the Corporation as a result of which a Parliamentary Bill was promoted by the Corporation and the company for the sale of the tramways (for £1,125 million) and the substitution of bus services under the company's management and the supervision of a joint committee of the corporation and the company.

Many municipal undertakings were worked jointly with the local bus company; Brighton Corporation from 1939 had an agreement with the Brighton, Hove & District Omnibus Co. Ltd by which trolleybuses were operated in place of trams and the two undertakings pooled mileage in agreed proportions. When after 21 years the agreement was renewed, Southdown Motor Services was also brought in. Plymouth Corporation has a pooling arrangement with Western National Omnibus Co. Ltd, Portsmouth with Southdown.

The areas at first chosen in 1969 for PTEs were Greater Manchester (originally South-East Lancashire and North-East Cheshire or SELNEC), Merseyside and Tyne and Wear (originally Tyneside) and the West Midlands. These first four passenger transport authorities, each of which had an executive to carry out the policy of the elected body, had a membership appointed by local authorities in the area on an electoral system laid down by the Minister of Transport; for example, the Merseyside authority had 29 members, 25 appointed by local authorities and 4 by the Ministry, but some of the PTEs had most complicated systems for the election of members. With the changes of local government boundaries it became convenient to make metropolitan counties correspond to PTE areas. The result is that several municipalities have been added to those originally absorbed in PTEs. Greater Manchester PTE took in Ashton-under-Lyne, Bolton, Bury, Manchester, Oldham, Rochdale, Salford, Stockport, Stalybridge, Hyde, Mossley and Dukinfield Joint Board, and to these Wigan was subsequently added. The Merseyside PTE was constituted from the Birkenhead, Liverpool and Wallasey undertakings and St Helens and Southport were, on 1 April 1974, added. The Tyne and Wear PTE was put together from the South Shields and Newcastle-upon-Tyne transport undertakings, but the area has been enlarged to take in that of Sunderland. The West Midlands area originally comprised Birmingham, Walsall, West Bromwich and Wolverhampton County and the South Yorkshire Metropolitan County were formed as a result of the local government changes of 1974 and each has a new PTE, one comprising Bradford, Calderdale (formerly Todmorden), Leeds and Huddersfield and the other Doncaster, Rotherham and Sheffield municipal systems. This came into operation in April 1974. Another of the new PTEs is that of Greater Glasgow, responsible to the Strathclyde Regional Authority.

Local government changes have taken place in all parts of the United Kingdom of recent years and there is a conscious effort to make administrative and transport areas coincide. Whereas the London County Council was restive at not being responsible for London's public transport, but only the tramways, and after 1933 not even that part of the business, from 1969 the Greater London Council has been responsible for the overall policy of the London Transport Executive. The situation thus roughly corresponds, although it is not identical, to that in the metropolitan counties. From 1 April 1970 Devon General Omnibus & Touring Co. Ltd took over the operations of Exeter City Transport; by 1975 it had been taken over by the Western National Omnibus Co. Ltd. Welsh changes of 1974 include the following: Aberdare UDC has become Cynon Valley DC; Bedwas & Machen, Caerphilly and Gellygaer merged as Rhymney Valley; Pontypridd UDC has become Taff Ely DC; West Monmouthshire Omnibus Board is now operated by Islwyn Borough Council. In England Darwen has joined Blackburn; Accrington has become Hyndburn; Burnley, Colne & Nelson has become Burnley & Pendle; Cleveland Transit represents the Langfaugh, Middlesbrough & Stockton-on-Tees Joint Transport Committee; Burton-on-Trent has been renamed East Staffordshire DC; Morecambe & Heysham has now joined City of Lancaster; Lowestoft has become Waveney DC; Lytham St Annes has become Fylde Borough; Swindon is now Thamesdown DC and Widnes is now Halton District Transport. Scottish changes include Aberdeen becoming Grampian; Dundee becoming Tayside; and Edinburgh, Lothian.

There are now only 51 municipal operators; formerly they were represented by the Municipal Passenger Transport Association, but in 1970 this reconstituted itself as the Association of Public Passenger Transport which in the end of 1975 decided to dissolve itself; many of the members had been represented for years in the Public Transport Association and its predecessors and in its successor, the Confederation of British Road Passenger Transport.

11 (*above*) Daimler KPL (Knight-Pieper-Lanchester) petrol-electric 34-seat bus, 1910. Two 12-h.p. petrol engines drove dynamotors, one on each side and an integral steel body was used. The project was brought to an end by a patent infringement action by Thomas Tilling Ltd

12 (*left*) A chain-driven Straker-Squire lightweight bus (afterwards LGOC Y-type) delivered to Great Eastern in 1911, in Great Eastern yellow livery with extreme destination on roller blind, route board in white on pink, and route indications in yellow on red and black on yellow—a colourful combination suppressed by the 'Generalisation' of route indications to meet police regulations

Over the years bus operation has become less glamorous – the West Monmouthshire Omnibus Board used to have a route that traversed the 1 in 4¼ of Aberbargoed Hill and was operated by a special fleet of Leyland Bulls, in succession to Saurer vehicles. With the maintenance routine laid down by R. T. Brown, the general manager, and overhaul at 10,000 mile intervals, a reliable service was provided. Long before the municipal owners of the board were amalgamated as Islwyn this route, with its confined railway culvert at the bottom of the bank and broken-surfaced winding incline, had been abandoned as a result of road improvements. Incidentally, I spent part of a day here in the early part of the war, having gone down to Bristol to see some producer-gas developments, and outside Newport station, having a few minutes before train time, decided to finish a roll of film in the camera and promptly found myself invited to go to the local police station by an enthusiastic war reserve constable, as a result of which I missed my train; a regular police sergeant did his best to set matters right by introducing me to a good establishment for a meal, telephoning home, and telling me of a train back that lumbered through the night via Gloucester. As a result of this and other incidents better means of establishing the identity of bona fide journalists were established. Needless to say, in the hard school of wartime technical journalism, with skeleton staff, I worked a full day the next day.

Unusual vehicles were the little 'camels' of Douglas Corporation Transport in the Isle of Man. These were 26-seat single-deck buses equipped with enormous indicator blinds front and rear that gave them a humped appearance.

Lincoln Corporation was the first operator to use Leyland Titan buses, these being low-height double-deckers that were able to pass under the Stone Bow in the middle of the city. The first of these vehicles had open staircases and obtained the height to the upper deck cover of 13 ft 1 in. by placing the gangway on the offside of the upper deck with up to four seats in a row on the left-hand side. The offside gangway made the lower-deck ceiling rather low. AEC countered this with a body used at Wallasey with a hummock over the centre gangway, but it was not of such universal application as the Titan when it came to country roads with low trees or low bridges. East Yorkshire Motor Services had used similar bodies for passing under Beverley Bar.

Largest independent bus operator in Britain until absorbed by Greater Manchester Passenger Transport Executive on 1 February 1976 was Lancashire United. In size it was nearly approached by West Riding Automobile and by Barton Transport of Chilwell, Nottinghamshire. The South Lancashire Electric Traction & Power Company was formed in 1900 to develop the St Helens, Leigh & Bolton Railways Syndicate of 1896, and the New St Helens & District Tramways Co. Ltd of 1898, the South Lancashire Tramways Company and the South Lancashire Electric Supply Co. Ltd of 1900. Lancashire United Tramways Ltd was formed on 29 December 1905 with a capital of £200,000 in ordinary stock and £700,000 in debentures. Several attempts were made to get bus services on a satisfactory basis. The first was between Leigh town centre and Westleigh St Pauls with three Scott-Stirling 14 h.p. wagonettes as used extensively in London at the time, on 23 March 1906. Failure quickly followed and the buses were sold in August 1906. When the general manager died in 1910 Mr Edward Henry (Ned) Edwardes, power station engineer to the South Lancashire company, was appointed as chief executive in his place and continued for the next 44 years. Three Dennis charabancs were obtained for experimental purposes in May 1914 and were quickly found unsuitable owing to the state of the roads so that they were sold in August of that year. The LUT suspension of bus service in that month was thus not for the usual reason – that the War Office had requisitioned the fleet. In 1919 the LUT made another attempt at getting off the ground with buses and this time with lasting success in a big way. A fleet of 25 Dennis War Department subsidy lorries (of which 7,000 were built) was purchased in 1919 and charabanc bodies were built for them and regular bus services began on 18 June 1920, using two second-hand single-deckers on a route from Lowton St Mary's to Haydock and then to Newton-le-Willows and Earlestown. Later in 1920 coaches were being worked to Blackpool from Swinton via Warrington and Wigan. Frequent buses on routes an hour long made links between Hindley and Walkden; Leigh and Worsley; Leigh and Haydock; Bickershaw and Warrington; Lowton St Mary and Haydock; Leigh and Warrington; Glazebury and Warrington; Swinton and Warrington; and Leigh and St Helens. By 1923 the elements of the LUT bus network can be discerned.

An interesting fleet taken over in 1925 was the three London S-types of Trafford Park Estates, Ltd. These AECs ran between Trafford Park Hotel and Patricroft for the workmen on the estate and looked very much as if finished in a livery drawn up by the London General Company, but with the fleet name 'Trafford Park'. In 1924 LUT went in for purchasing coach services in a big way; in fact from Arthur Robey and Avery & Roberts of Liverpool, from whom a fleet of Bristols was obtained. In 1925, jointly with Ribble, the business of Webster Brothers of Wigan was purchased. This introduced LUT to Leyland chassis. In 1928 arrangements were made with Leigh Corporation for through running of services – this undertaking was famous for many years for having a fleet of 29 buses and joint routes with everybody within range.

Tognarelli, a restauranteur primarily, who began buses in 1927, and worked up to a fleet of 21 buses in three years, was in competition with LUT from 1929 on a Bolton and Manchester service. Eventually Tognarelli sold out to LUT, Manchester, Salford, Bolton and Oldham Corporations (almost a predecessor in scope of the Greater Manchester Authority!) in December 1929. In 1932 LUT joined the Northern General's Limited Stop Pool service between Newcastle and Liverpool. In 1935 an Oldham to Blackpool route of M & H Motors was purchased, without any rolling stock; the last petrol-engined Dennis Lancet was purchased in 1936; a diesel-engined Lancet II was the first of the new era and the only one of the type in the fleet. Jointly with Ribble the business of A. Christy (Oldham) Ltd was bought in 1938 since when the LUT fleet has ceased to expand by purchase.

Ned Edwardes was good company at gatherings of busmen as well as being a shrewd bus operator. I used to see him at the Scottish busmen's conference at Turnberry. Any impression that he was not fully awake, despite his advanced years, was an illusion eagerly fostered by Ned.

7
London up to the First World War

Motorisation of the London horse-bus business began in a trickle in 1904. In Thomas Tilling, Ltd, formed in 1897 to take over Thomas Tilling's business after his death in 1893, Walter Wolsey, Thomas's son-in-law, was a believer in the possibilities of the new motor era. The first motor bus for *The Times* route ran from Peckham to the Green Man & Still, Oxford Street, on 30 September 1904. It was a Milnes-Daimler and continued the livery traditions of the horse bus, but roller blind extreme destination indicators were the first hint that a new age had begun. Motorisation of the entire route was soon Tilling policy and during the following year it was decided not to pursue the purchase of bus horses. Within a fortnight of the Tilling Milnes-Daimler appearing two Birch Milnes-Daimlers were at work from North Finchley to Oxford Circus and so this old-established company (in cabs from 1832 and in the motor bus business about the same time as Thomas Tilling) kept in the forefront of the new movement, although they retired in 1907 and did not re-enter until one of the next generation was a fully qualified automobile engineer.

The motor bus boom really began about the time the author was born. A helpful factor was that tyre makers had a better product and were prepared to make contracts to supply them at 2*d* a mile. The Motor Bus Trust decided to launch operating companies which got off the ground in 1905; and secured an option on a steady supply of Milnes-Daimler vehicles. A trial vehicle (probably for driver training) for the London Motor Omnibus Co. Ltd was seen in London on 16 March 1905 and on 27 March five went into public service. A line name, 'Vanguard', appeared on the side panels and the next line name selected was 'Victory', but Vanguard proved so popular as a fleet name that it was continued. There is evidence that the original livery intended for Vanguard was mainly blue, but very early on white Vanguards were appearing. What is important is that this was the first assault on the entrenched position of the associations because the Motor Omnibus Trust believed in the superior speed and greater productivity of the motor bus so that where the horse bus fare was 4d, the Vanguard fare was 2d. Early services included Brondesbury to the Law Courts, the lower part of Finchley Road to Victoria and from the Highgate direction towards Putney. The directors of the London Motor Omnibus Company Ltd included E. H. Bayley, with experience in coachbuilding and of the London Road Car organisation, Clarence Freeland, with experience at Hastings and St Leonards, and Thomas Ottey, a director of the Birmingham Motor Express Co. Ltd, which in 1904 had gone into the foundation of the Birmingham & Midland Motor Omnibus Co. Ltd. A. T. Salisbury-Jones was also prominent in the directorate and later the whole group of companies became known as Vanguard or the Salisbury-Jones group.

Besides the London Motor Omnibus Co. Ltd, there was the Motor Omnibus Co. Ltd which operated as 'Pilot' and had Mors chassis with United Electric Car bodies for its first dozen vehicles; the name of the company was set out above the fleet name as the 'London Bus Co. Ltd', an unusual use of the abbreviation; the intention was to serve the northern and eastern suburbs, and Elephant to Dalston Junction was definitely one of the routes worked by Pilot before its buses went on to Vanguard services. The London & District Motor Omnibus Co. Ltd which seems to have begun with a Straker fleet and had Provincial Motor Bus Co. Ltd and London & Provincial Motor Bus Co. Ltd as subsidiaries, took 'Arrow' as its fleet name and was going to distinguish its services by the colours of the arrows poised above the bonnets of the buses.

In 1906 George Samuel Dicks, traffic manager of Vanguard, had the brainwave which entitles him to a place in the hall of fame – the service number – and from 30 April these were used on the Vanguard fleet and spread to others of the Salisbury-Jones group. At first there was a liberal plastering of service number discs on a bus – two screwed on the front canopy on either side and two on the sides – but the display soon settled down to one at the front and one disc on the corner of the rear platform and ready detachability was soon discovered to be an advantage. Six years later illuminated opal plates behind stencils were adopted by the LGOC.

Then it seems to have come home to the LMO Co. that there was merit in Christopher Dodson's idea as a coachbuilder that route and destination boards could be made detachable and the extreme destination could be indicated on a board that could be turned over for the return journey. By the end of 1907 some 500 London buses carried Dodson's patent destination boards, in which a spring clip kept down the more noisy vibrations. Tilling and many other early buses had roller blind destination boxes like tramcars, although until electric light generators became universal on bus chassis they had some disadvantages at night. Until then acetylene lighting was the best expedient. By 1909 Dodson boards were in use practically everywhere.

The Vanguard fleet was not the first motor-bus fleet in London to be established without horse-bus antecedents. John Stirling, who had experimented with motor buses in Scotland in 1896, began operations as the London Motor Omnibus Syndicate Ltd between Cricklewood and Oxford Circus on 26 November 1902 with 12-seat Stirling vehicles probably best described as enclosed wagonettes. In February 1904 an enlarged fleet of 14- and 16-seaters was operating on Edgware Road under the name of the London Power Omnibus Co. Ltd of which the Scottish pioneer, Norman D. Macdonald, was a director. On 7 February 1906, with a Cricklewood garage for more than 100 vehicles, a fleet of double-deck Scott-Stirling 34-seaters (some also seated two alongside the driver) which numbered 67 at its maximum, was in service, the principal route being Cricklewood, Lord Palmerston, Maida Vale, Marble Arch, Oxford Circus, Regent Street, Piccadilly and Charing Cross. The side panels in 1906 showed the fleet name 'The Pioneer' in rather elegant capitals below the company's full name. The bodies were built by the Brush Electrical Engineering Co. Ltd at Loughborough, a British Electric Traction group subsidiary equipped for electrical engineering and tramcar building. At this time the Scott-Stirling chassis was built at Twickenham and the output was advertised as being 500 a year. There seemed to be some bottle-necks with the output, some at the Brush end of production, but suddenly the company seemed to be in difficulties and the Scott-Stirling Motor Co. Ltd was a reorganisation of the manufacturing side in May 1907. The LPOC vehicles disappeared from Edgware Road a few weeks later and energetic harrying by the police seems to have been the deciding factor in prompting the withdrawal; the last of the Pioneers disappeared on 20 July 1907.

By the end of 1905 the General had only just over 20 motors, whereas London Road Car, which decided at the beginning of the year to devote £116,000 to motor bus expansion, had 65. Even Thomas Tilling had acquired

20 motor vehicles in 15 months. Activity among motor vehicle salesmen, agents, emporia and consultants was intense and a dozen Continental makes, from France, Germany, Switzerland and Belgium, found places on the London streets. Milnes-Daimler was in the lead and the German Büssing next, some mildly disguised as Straker. Eventually Sydney Straker took in Squire as partner and the firm settled down to a fairly prosperous career as Sydney Straker & Squire Ltd. In view of the connection with E. H. Bayley, of London Road Car, that company acquired a large fleet of Straker-Squire vehicles. As the LGOC had had to turn that way, having missed the boat with Milnes-Daimler, by the second half of 1907 the London area Straker fleet was bigger than that of Milnes-Daimler. Third in numbers was De Dion and next were the English Wolseley, a second version of which proved very reliable, and Clarkson. Some of the foreign marques were very disappointing – so much so that Frank Searle had recommended one that turned out a failure and gave up consultancy to join Arrow's engineering staff. Many British firms supplied prototypes to London and found that the gruelling nature of Metropolitan service vanquished them. Among makers of one-off jobs were such firms as Armstrong-Whitworth, BTH, Bellis & Morconn, Hunslet and Thames Ironworks, respectively with interests in shipbuilding, electrical engineering, high-speed steam engines, locomotives and ships. Surprisingly, the number of Thornycroft buses in London remained fewer than the digits of one hand at this time. One of the frustrations of my youth was to see from the top of a passing bus a glimpse of a Stratford scrap yard where all sorts of colours, shapes and sizes of bus had gathered after the 1907 realisation of the hollowness of the motor boom had come home to some of the less successful operators.

France was later to launch two vehicles of original characteristics on the London market. One was by the Improved Electric Traction Co. Ltd and was operated by the London Electrobus Co. Ltd from 15 July 1907. The spokesmen of the builder were singularly vague about the 'improvements'. Accumulators of unspecified make provided 90 volts but the rating of the BTH motor was only 14 h.p. Progress was smooth rather than rapid. The capital cost was high and the fleet seems to have peaked at only 20. One was shown off in Victoria Station yard with a light canopy over the top deck, but one can be confident that the Metropolitan Police did not sanction the carrying of fare-paying passengers on a bus thus equipped. When it became necessary to give up London operation, the Brighton, Hove & Preston United Omnibus Co. Ltd that had some of the earliest Milnes-Daimler double-deckers on the South Coast, bought some of the Electrobus fleet and as late as 1916 was returning the number of London Electric chassis as 12.

The other French importation was the Darracq-Serpollet steam bus, which had a very efficient paraffin-fired flash boiler. Between October 1907 and May 1908 about 20 joined the service of the Metropolitan Steam Omnibus Co. Ltd which adopted an olive-green livery with a dove-grey band on the side panel and an elaborate coat of arms. A Hammersmith–Charing Cross service was provided from a garage at Downs Place, Hammersmith.

By 1907 it was realised that the motor bus had not fulfilled its early promise and that it indeed had accomplished several quite unintentional results. The association system of protecting horse-bus operators had broken down; the electrification of the old shallow underground railways had not benefited them to the extent anticipated; the new tubes found themselves unable to compete satisfactorily with the motor bus, which had not materialised when they were first thought of: and in some cases the losses motor-bus concerns themselves had incurred were stupendous. The Salisbury-Jones group was reorganised on 4 April 1907 as the Vanguard Motor Omnibus Co. Ltd and its capital consolidated at a time when 160 of its 260 or more buses were out of use. By July 1907 the London Power Omnibus Co. Ltd, which had lost 7d per car mile, seemed to have sunk without trace; the Tibbs family's Associated Omnibus Co. Ltd sold its 29 motor buses, mainly to the Great Western Railway, about the same time, having arranged a £50,000 debenture about the end of 1905 to buy motor rolling stock and build the Whicher Place garage in Camden Town, afterwards used by British Automobile Traction. The motor buses of the Star Omnibus Co. Ltd, associated with S. Andrews & Son Ltd of Cardiff, were withdrawn on 9 August.

This melancholy tale brought about the raising of the Central London fare between Shepherds Bush and Bank from 2d to 3d from 1 July 1907 as a result of a meeting between the railway interests concerned; and a wider-based meeting took place on 22 July with four leading bus companies represented as well as the underground railways. The result was a diminution of cut-throat competition, although my friend Dick Farmer has produced for me a 1907 photograph, primarily one of his family's Atlas Express parcels vans at the Bank crossing, showing a London Electrobus on the Liverpool Street to Victoria run carrying posters to announce that the Electrobus people were keeping to the old fares. In general, however, all the London operators began to pay more attention to the economics of the motor-bus business, although in 1910 the London Electrobus fleet retired to the sea air of Brighton, where some of them lasted another six years.

Out of the 1907 negotiations about fares arose some friendships and, indeed, some mergers. These at first were merely proposals. The Vanguard needed working capital and in 1908 held talks with the LGOC, only to be rebuffed by its debenture holders. The LGOC was losing money. The London Road Car held some talks with the Great Eastern London Motor Omnibus Co. By May 1908 an amalgamation between the LGOC, Road Car and Great Eastern companies was imminent when a legal and accounting snag about the value of the horse buses put the Great Eastern, which had suppressed its horse buses some time previously, out of the talks. Instead a formula which satisfied (temporarily) the shareholders of the LGOC, the Vanguard and the Road Car undertakings was arrived at and the merger took place as from 1 July. But neither shareholders nor debenture holders of the smaller companies were wholly satisfied and rumblings were still going on into 1910. This is possibly the explanation of why Vanguard and Road Car liveries were to be seen on buses in London long after 1908 – a matter which puzzled me as a boy when I learned of the merger. In July 1908 the LGOC fleet totalled 288 motor buses, the Road Car 225 and Vanguard 386; the capitals of the three companies were £1,323,592, £676,000, and £608,000 respectively. The enlarged LGOC took a good deal of know-how from the smaller concerns, expertise from men such as Daniel Duff of the Road Car, service numbers from Vanguard. It expanded its capital from £1,323,592 to £2,140,899. The first year the loss was reduced to just over £1,000, perhaps because it scrapped about a quarter of its fleet; to September 1910 the combined undertaking made £120,000.

With a prospect of greater economic stability in the bus industry the enemies of the motor bus rallied. Highway authorities, long active in hounding mechanised road transport, now found common cause with tramway operators, especially when they were one and the same body. While tramtracks for electric cars were being laid along Romford Road between Forest Gate and Manor Park, bus owners were compelled to use the waterbound macadam, laid on a thin foundation, of the parallel Sherrard Road and the surface proved unable to withstand the onslaught of the first generation of motor buses. The motor-bus companies ignored threats of legal action and it was widely believed that any lawsuit would be laughed out of court. Aubrey Llewellyn Coventry Fell, chief officer of the LCC Tramways Department, was assured of the rightness of the tramway cause and added weight to the case against the motor bus, although paradoxically, he believed in motor transport when it came to his department's permanent way maintenance. The Metropolitan Police came to believe in the need for stricter control of the motor bus and in April 1907, 120 Vanguards were stopped by the police without any reason being assigned. About this time 46 Clarkson steamers had to be withdrawn; the police looked on flash generation of steam rather as a mobile atom bomb might be regarded today. Of course, they had some reason for suspicion. Out of 521 buses licensed in the year ending in the summer of 1906, 37 showed serious steering defects and 22 had caught fire. Excessive noise troubled the police a good deal and appears to account for many of the stop orders issued on buses, as a result of which many Strakers in the Road Car fleet were withdrawn while quieter chains were fitted. Even the most respectable operators descended to filling a gearbox with oily sawdust when a chassis was submitted for its noise test, which usually took place in the then rural seclusion of Parkside, alongside Wimbledon Common. In November 1907 no fewer than 20 LGOC buses were stopped and the passengers were turned off to the disruption of an important trunk service. On 18 July 1907 the nine Orions of Victoria Omnibus Co. Ltd ('The Old Vic') were withdrawn; on 9 August Pat Hearn gave up his nine motor buses, and on the same day the Star withdrew 23 motors. On 3 November Birch Brothers Ltd took their fleet of 14 motors off the road. High repair costs were mainly responsible for the toll of 1907, but the constant nagging of police complaints drove many operators into scrapping the buses that were the subject of frequent breakdowns or stoppages for noise – an easy allegation for any thrusting police constable.

Cause for concern as to public safety must be admitted. On 30 August 1905 the London Motor Omnibus Co. Ltd began a service from Northumberland Avenue to Brighton. This came to an abrupt end on 12 July 1906, when a private party of tradesmen from Orpington was travelling in a Vanguard Milnes-Daimler to Brighton via Handcross Hill. The driver quite properly tried to change down near the top of the hill, but unfortunately in doing so disrupted the crash gearbox, most of which fell on the road. The transmission brake then had no connection with the rear wheels, the handbrake was too feeble to be effective and the bus began to gather speed. The driver tried to slow by rubbing the offside wheels on the high bank on the right of the road. The upper deck struck a stout branch of a tree, sweeping passengers and seats into the road, the remainder of the bus then charged the bank, shattering the rest of the body. The final toll was 10 deaths, many injuries and long-distance motor bus journeys in disrepute.

As a result of the various agitations new regulations were issued by Sir Edward Henry, Commissioner of Metropolitan Police, on 30 August 1909. Entitled 'Notice to proprietors as to conditions for obtaining a certificate of fitness for motor omnibuses', they were to come into effect in March 1910 and contained some 62 clauses, some of which were vague in the extreme, but allowed the police some flexibility and are alleged, by some of the smaller proprietors, to have opened the way to blatant bribery in the public carriage department when an applicant for a licence was told under which seat to leave the £5 note.

Some of the general remarks in the introduction to the regulations included 'no carriage will be certified fit for public use unless it is properly painted and varnished'. In effect this apparently meant twelve coats of paint and five of varnish in the days before synthetics were available but, like several matters raised in the regulations, chapter and verse is elusive. Condition 5 stated that if necessary an expert would be employed to advise; his fee would be deposited with the Commissioner by the proprietor and returned should the vehicle be passed without alteration being required. Under Condition 6 the routes on which the vehicle was to ply must be specified, and these routes must not be departed from without due notice, although if the vehicle was certified for several routes it could be changed from one to another as often as the proprietor chose. It was a note after Condition 62 that gave the public carriage department most scope for exercising conservatism: 'Though the above Conditions may have been complied with, yet, if there be anything in the construction, form or general appearance which, in the opinion of the Commissioner, renders the carriage unfit for public use, it will not be licensed.'

Other conditions were much more positive. Destination and route boards with black letters on a white ground, the destination at least 4½ in. high and the route at least 4 in. high and 'of a proportionate thickness' and in the geographical sequence according to direction were required, while no advertisement was to be allowed to interfere with the easy legibility of this information.

The number of passengers allowed on a double-decker was set at 34, 16 down and 18 up, but if fewer than 30 were provided for the number of passengers carried outside must not be in greater proportion than seven outside to six inside. The maximum weights were fixed at 3 tons 10 cwt unladen, or if the makers preferred, 4 tons on the back axle laden and 2 tons on the front axle laden. The total weight was not to exceed 6 tons when the vehicle was fully loaded and ready for service; 140 lb was to be allowed for each passenger and for the driver and conductor. The chassis, with platform, was not to exceed 23 ft in length; the ground clearance, fully loaded, was to be at least 10 inches; the spring base must be at least 38 in. at front and 45 in. at rear; the wheelbase was not to exceed 14 ft 6 in. and the wheel track was to be at least 5 ft 6 in. The vehicle was not to exceed 7 ft 2 in. in breadth. Regulations on brakes, steering and fire resistance were quite sensible but Condition 21 required the maximum speed to be 12 m.p.h. and an audible warning device to be fitted so that it should sound as soon as 12 m.p.h. was exceeded.

As the acceptable weight of a bus had, until the coming into force of the 1909 regulations, been 5 tons, the new 3½ ton limit caused some consternation among manufacturers. On rubber tyres a 5 ton bus had been eligible for the 12 m.p.h. speed limit. Prophets of gloom were quick to gather with forecasts of the demise of the motor bus or at least an attenuated existence with the weight limit bringing the capacity down to 16 seats, at which level it would be impossible to make it a paying proposition. Fell unhappily committed himself to the forecast that in ten years there would be no motor bus outside a museum.

Instead, the new ukase from Scotland Yard was the means of putting the motor bus at last in a state of viability. Techniques of construction had advanced and the new weight limits had persuaded every manufacturer to look for means of improving strength and cutting out unnecessary weight. The LGOC board had been about to place a further order for Wolseleys; they had had very good reliability from 120 of an improved type in their fleet, but the drive was still by chain and the wheels were heavy and of a clumsy wooden-spoked 'artillery' type. In 1907 the LGOC was fortunate in having Frank Searle enter their service. He was a steam locomotive engineer trained by the Great Western Railway at Swindon. He had set up as a consultant automobile engineer, in which capacity he was responsible for the importation of Turgan and Lacoste & Battman bus chassis from France. Upon these vehicles proving unsatisfactory (only after they were licensed!) Searle joined the engineering staff of the London & District Motor Omnibus Co. Ltd. Early in 1907 he became garage superintendent for the LGOC at Mortlake, where he pointed forcefully to the folly of spreading 28 different makes in small lots over practically every garage. He found only a quarter of the buses runners. The rest had been cannibalised with no provision to repair the defective units or to replace them. He persuaded the directors to segregate the makes, thus simplifying the keeping of spares and increasing the expertise of the mechanics who had a less variegated fleet to keep in order. Within three months he was appointed chief engineer of the company. About this time steel wheels, replacing the heavy and clumsy wooden-spoked artillery type, and aluminium alloy parts, together with other improved components, were beginning to become available.

When the new police regulations were mooted Searle persuaded the LGOC board to essay manufacture in the Walthamstow overhaul works they had inherited from Vanguard. The first cast was not entirely successful. Its rated horsepower was only 28, the spur gear change speed was noisy and the balance of the vehicle was not as good as it might have been, in addition to which it interpreted too literally the police specification of the 12 m.p.h. limit. The first was shown to the public carriage department on 12 August 1909 and was classified 'X1' by Searle – presumably x the unknown. He was disappointed by its reception from the directors. He thought it a very neat bus, calculated, because it contained all the longest-wearing components to be found in the fleet, to be more reliable than anything so far seen and he expected that, all glossy paint, it would be an object of great interest to the board. Instead, almost simultaneously, some horses came back from Army manoeuvres and his audience disappeared to talk to horsekeepers about their health and some superficial injuries. This showed how little some board members of the amalgamated company realised their future was now dependent on the motor bus. The first X did not pass the police until 16 December 1909; two more came out in March 1910 and 58 appeared in the next six months. The first worked on services 15 and 14 but eventually all the X-type were placed at Middle Row garage and special schedules were provided for all 61 of them on service 7 (Liverpool Street–Wormwood Scrubs) until their withdrawal in 1920.

Snide descriptions of Searle's bus called it a 'Daimler-Wolseley-Straker' and Searle admitted his indebtedness to other makes for durable components. But he did not care, because by this time his masterpiece, the B-type, was on the way. This had a 30-h.p. four-cylinder engine, a leather-faced cone clutch and a roller-chain constant mesh foolproof gearbox actuated by dog clutches. The underframe of the chassis was ash with nickel steel flitch plates, the track 5 ft 8 in. and the wheelbase 12 ft 10⅝ in. The ground clearance under the tie rod of the back axle was 10¾ in. Cast steel wheels of several types appeared on the front and at the rear with either eight circular spokes or eight Y-formation spokes; the swivel axles protruded less at the hubs than those on the X-type, which sometimes fouled obstructions to the dismay of drivers. The first B-type appeared on 7 October 1910 and was licensed on 18 October. It was a beautiful vehicle; at less than 10 m.p.h. it made a faint whisper from the carburettor, but otherwise only such noise as was occasioned by the solid tyres on the roads of the day. The first few B-types went to a former horse bus garage at Clay Hall, Old Ford, and I remember coming home from Victoria by a bus on 25 which at that time ran to Old Ford, in order to ride on the new 'silent motor bus' even though it meant a long walk home from the Old Ford route which father decreed for all the family. This is an indication of the generation of enthusiasm for the new bus even among the non-technical public. Production of the new buses was fairly rapid – 279 were turned out between October 1910 and April 1911 and 482 between then and December. It was already apparent that Searle and his assistant, Walter James Iden (a London, Brighton & South Coast Railway steam man) had produced a winner and that the General's financial future was assured. Increased manufacturing facilities were matched by a new programme of garage construction. The LGOC was very confident in 1911.

Early in that year this resulted in a renewal of negotiations with the

13 A new era dawned for the bus in London in 1912, when the Underground purchased the London General Omnibus Company Ltd. Our picture shows the District Railway staff at Hounslow Barracks station seeing the first bus to Windsor Castle on 14 July 1912

14 The Daimler Company's first attempt at a petrol-electric, using Automixte patents and very heavy construction. The 22 buses in the Gearless 1913 fleet had similar Daimler chassis to the British Automobile Traction fleet

15 The Central (London Central Omnibus Co. Ltd) Leylands had a lemon-yellow livery in 1913

Great Eastern London Omnibus Co. Ltd, which had previously been full of plans for pooling with the Road Car Company and other competition-reducing devices, especially since magistrates had been disapproving of dangerous driving resulting from Vanguard or LGOC-Great Eastern rivalry for passengers. The Great Eastern originated from the Lea Bridge, Leyton & Walthamstow Tramways, which operated some horse-bus services into other company's territory and then formed a subsidiary in 1897, the Great Eastern London Suburban Omnibus & Tramways Company, to keep the tramway company operating within its powers. The motor buses of this undertaking were transferred to the Great Eastern London Motor Omnibus Co. Ltd on 22 March 1906 and whereas the original company had a red livery, the new adopted a primrose yellow.

The motor fleet now comprised a considerable number of Straker-Squire, some Dennis, and 24 Arrol-Johnston vehicles, the last-mentioned a clumsy production with the driver in a semi-forward control position and an extraordinary rake on the steering column. There were garages at Green Street, Forest Gate and Leyton Green and, surprisingly, at West Kilburn, the latter with the insignia of the GE of LSO & TC, probably defunct before it came into service, incorporated in the structure. This company had 80 vehicles in 1911, according to Frank Pick, but the situation was fluid as during 1910 it had felt compelled to order some of the lightweight vehicles insisted upon by the police. Its choice had fallen on silent chain-driven Straker-Squires of which 100 were ordered. What drove the LGOC into purchasing the company outright was that the 5 per cent GE of L dividend in 1908–9 was increased to 6 per cent for 1910, and this example of the results of good management was deemed liable, with the obvious success of the B-type as a dividend-maker, to increase competition.

The GE of L confidence is shown by a pooling scheme in which it proposed 120 GE buses to 1,080 LGOC on 30 June 1911. But in the upshot the £115,733 ordinary and £20,444 debenture shares were purchased at par, by the LGOC. So only 22 Strakers were delivered in the Great Eastern of London's new livery of bright chrome yellow, with the fleet name in flossy gold lettering on a red band. The first few had red hand-painted destination boards, but in April what the *Commercial Motor* called 'Generalisation' took place and standard General route boards and service number discs were fitted. After 24 May the Strakers were delivered in General red livery and only another 29 appeared, as the rest of the order was cancelled. The financial transfer was 'as from' 1 January 1911, negotiations being finalised on 2 May. Sidney Straker never forgave the General for reducing his order and afterwards supported W. P. Allen with 15 shaft-driven Strakers for London in 1913 and had the idea of an ex-serviceman's bus company in 1919 for which he and his friends hoped to recruit 3,000 owner-drivers on the lines of the taxi trade.

The Great Eastern operated several services to the Elephant and Castle from Leyton, Seven Kings and the Barking Road respectively, from West Kilburn to Ilford and so on and service numbers 35, 36 and 37 were allocated, but the only survivor recognisable in original form is 35 between Lea Bridge Road and the Elephant. Route 36, still Liverpool Street and West Kilburn via Kennington and Victoria in the early part of 1912, was in June of that year cut back to Victoria and then projected south-eastward in conjunction with Thomas Tilling Ltd. The next new service in June 1912, from Victoria to the Lea Bridge Road and Leyton Green, took the number 38. The garage was a rebuilding of the Great Eastern premises at Leyton Green.

This period was truly a golden age of the bus for a youthful enthusiast. In June 1912 the eastern termini of 25 and 8 were swapped, so that they became Victoria and Seven Kings and Willesden and Old Ford respectively. The LGOC gained greatly in prestige from its new buses; from 1910 it published a list of services and from June 1911 it produced a monthly map and guide, such as Moore had long urged, and its boundaries of motor operation could be seen visibly to be expanding.

On 1 January 1911 there were 1,149 motor buses in London; by 1 January 1912 the number had expanded to 1,641 despite withdrawal of many doubtful runners, as a result of which the streets were quieter, less smelly, and no longer cluttered by thirsty buses queueing for radiator water at Aldgate Pump. Moreover the LGOC made £200,000 in 1911, declared a dividend for the first time in two years (at 8 per cent) and its shares rose in price to near £200, deemed by Stock Exchange pundits to be because of 'outside buying'. In fact, as became obvious in 1912, some element of this had entered into the enhanced price, because the Underground Electric Railways of London, Ltd had made a very good offer, announced on 20 January. For each £100 LGOC share £105 of UERL 1st cumulative preference debenture stock plus £105 of 6 per cent UERL income bonds, 100 UERL 'A' ordinary shares of 1s each and a cash bonus of £8 were offered; interest on the first two was to begin on 1 January 1912. The offer was estimated to be worth £227 per £100 LGOC share.

The benefits of the same holding company being interested both in the electric underground railways (the UERL controlled all of these except the Metropolitan, the Great Northern & City, the East London and the Waterloo & City by 1913) and the principal bus undertaking became apparent later in 1912. On 14 July 1912 the first fruits of the takeover were seen when LGOC buses began to operate from Hounslow Barracks Station on the Metropolitan District Railway to Windsor Castle. With bated breath an hourly service on Sundays was proposed, but the idea proved so popular that the 12-mile journey was soon being covered every 5 minutes on Sunday in each direction. The enormous growth of traffic produced a rapid revision of plans; the service, at first numbered 62, was revamped as 81 and ran every day of the week. It is interesting that old traditions died hard and it was felt desirable to start from a public house, 'The Bell' at Hounslow. At this time the nearest garage was at Turnham Green, over 5 miles from 'The Bell', where availability of radiator water was no doubt an inducement to call. By September several other country routes, designed for Sunday operation, were put on as a daily feature – to St Albans from Golders Green, on the Hampstead tube, and to Romford (Gidea Park) from Bow Road District station. Not only Golders Green, but Finsbury Park, Ealing Broadway, Highgate, Hammersmith and Barking underground stations were made railheads for services into nearby country and suburbs.

It is noteworthy that whereas the September 1912 issue of the *Railway Magazine* contained a moan about the loss of £14,000 more of suburban traffic by the London & South Western Railway to the buses which 'now ran alongside the line as far as Windsor', the October issue contained a short article praising the community of interests established between the Underground lines and the bus undertaking. No doubt this was owing to a good public relations service having been established by the Underground group.

During the next three years much visible progress was made. About 600 B-types were built in 1913 by a mass-production method, but on parallel assembly lines, perfected by Iden. Most of the bodies were turned out from the General's own body factories, of which the principal was at North Road, Islington. The B-type was so reliable that with 2,500 in service in 1913, 55 million miles were run and only 0·02 per cent of scheduled mileage was lost through mechanical faults. The output was so rapid that it was now possible to think of supplying other operators with B-type buses and in 1912 an agreement was made with the Tibbs family's Associated Omnibus Co. Ltd, which had been registered in 1900 to run horse buses, turned to motors in 1905 and relinquished them two years later. They showed a desire to buy 50 Daimler buses in 1912, which precipitated an offer from the LGOC. The LGOC arranged to let the company have 55 B-type buses for £50,000 (the chassis were reputed to cost £350 each!) and to operate and maintain them from 1 November 1912 for 20 years. Daniel Duff was appointed to the board, although Phillip Willing Tibbs remained managing director. The vehicles were in the General's dark red livery of the time and the fleet name was 'Associated' set out on the side panel in seriffed capital letters. They were worked at LGOC direction for 8·5d (just over 3·5p) a mile, plus a fluctuation to allow for the price of petrol and rubber. Of the Associated fleet 22 were allocated to Holloway Garage, where they began to operate on 4 October

1912, and 11 each to Albany Street, Palmers Green and Shepherds Bush. I saw one at the Bank on 43 a few days later. The company had issued £14,527, 5 per cent first mortgage debentures on its own Camden Town garage and in 1912 issued the LGOC in payment for its new fleet with £50,000, 6 per cent second debentures. It had parted with the garage to the British Automobile Traction Company and its earning power did not look a rosy prospect at the end of the First World War. So in 1918 over 80 per cent of the 5s ordinary shares were bought by the LGOC at 2s 6d each. The remaining ordinary shareholders received 2s 9d for each share when the voluntary liquidation was effected. This spelled out the fate of yet another of the London pioneer motor operators.

Next to be supplied with B-type was the Metropolitan Steam Omnibus Co. Ltd. It had to revise its ideas about its Darracq-Serpollet buses in the light of the 1909 Police Regulations and a much lighter design with steel wheels was produced (it is said in London, whereas Serpollet's factory was in Paris). By September 1911 52 of these improved buses were in service, 23 on the Waltham Green–Putney–Brixton route. A new garage was opened at Lots Road, Chelsea. The fleet totalled 65 when the LGOC began intense competition by means of its new route 37 between Herne Hill, Brixton, Clapham and Putney on 30 March 1912. The Metropolitan Steam company put in a big new paraffin tank at its Lots Road premises that summer but it not only faced a ten-minute interval on its principal route, but the possibility of a much more frequent service over this section. At the same time, it became clear that the supply of new buses and spares was very uncertain. A proposition that B-type buses should be operated in conjunction with the LGOC therefore seemed attractive to the company. It was arranged that the new 100-strong petrol fleet of the Metropolitan Steam company should be available from December 1912 at the new Willesden garage just built by the LGOC. I was delighted to see the olive green livery of the Steam company on my next school holiday when I accompanied my father on business to Hackney Wick. The green was relieved by gold lining; 'Metropolitan' appeared as a fleet name in gold on a black background and either side of the black strip was a dove grey panel; the whole was completed by a colourful coat-of-arms device in the middle of the side panel and white window surrounds. The green Metropolitans appeared on routes operated by Willesden, such as 6 to South Hackney from Kensal Rise, 8 to Old Ford, 18 to London Bridge (a Metropolitan on this service figured in a handbook of the advertising profession, showing the spaces available on a bus), 26 to Hackney Wick from Kensal Rise, 46 to Victoria from Kilburn, and 66 which at that time ran to Tooting from Willesden. They vanished after the summer of 1914 when the Metropolitan

Steam Omnibus Co. Ltd was acquired by the LGOC on 14 July and was wound up.

In the following year someone at Underground headquarters thought the excellent title of the company ought to be protected, which was done by registering a £100 company of the same name on 12 February 1915. Arrangements were then made for the fleet name 'Metropolitan' to be transferred to the buses of the Tramways (MET) Omnibus Co. Ltd. The story of this concern is a complex one, largely concerned with Frank Searle and the Daimler Company, which, in its 1904 formation, had hopes of entering the commercial vehicle market in a big way and as long ago as 1906 had produced a clumsy petrol-electric vehicle incorporating the Auto-mixte patents of Henri Pieper, the Belgian enthusiast for this form of infinitely variable gear and followed this up by registering the Gearless Motor Omnibus Co. Ltd on 23 May 1906.

In May 1911 the ambitious Searle, who had received £1,000 for his rights in his ingenious silent roller-chain constant-mesh gearbox, but probably thought he should have had more, faced by an adamant LGOC board, had parted company from them to join the service of Daimler, both to advise on bus design and to assist the Gearless company which had designed an original design of lightweight bus, the KPL or Knight-Pieper-Lanchester. J. H. Knight was the designer of a sleeve-valve engine which was notably silent – at the cost of oil consumption – and Dr F. W. Lanchester, the consultant, and in which the heavy features of the 1908 Gearless design were replaced by large diameter wire-spoked wheels, driven by a motor on each side of the conventional 34-seat body. The old allies of the LGOC, Thomas Tilling Ltd, hoping for favours to come, prepared to give evidence that this infringed their own petrol-electric patents. Their first S B & S (in which W. A. Stevens Ltd, electrical engineers of Maidstone, Frank Brown of David Brown & Sons of Huddersfield, builder of the final drive, and Percy Frost-Smith, their own chief engineer, were concerned) appeared in 1908 and was built for them by J. & E. Hall Ltd of Dartford, who had previously been associated with Saurer of Switzerland. The Hallford-Stevens was not pursued, but by 1911 a new petrol-electric, the Tilling-Stevens, was about to go into production. Giving up the idea of the KPL (it was probably a bit too freakish to attract the majority of conservative bus purchasers) Daimler, by now associated with the Birmingham Small Arms Group, got Searle to design a 34-seat gearbox transmission bus of 40 h.p. which closely resembled the B-type, but had a Silent Knight sleeve-valve petrol engine. These became available in 1912 and large numbers were ordered by the British Electric Traction group which by this time was disillusioned with the tramcar and had started a number of provincial bus undertakings, soon to be managed by a subsidiary, formed in 1905 as British Automobile Development Co. Ltd, and renamed in 1910 with more propitious initials than BAD as British Automobile Traction Co. Ltd.

When in 1911 the LGOC was obviously going to expand, the Metropolitan Electric Tramways Ltd, which had been hoping to profit by the expansion of the Middlesex suburbs they had helped to bring about, and which was fostered by the flow of tube trains to Finsbury Park, Highgate and Golders Green (as well as Metropolitan trains to Willesden Green), the BET tramway company thought, as a result of conversations with the LGOC, that it should acquire a bus fleet of its own and this was registered as the Tramways (MET) Omnibus Co. Ltd on 13 January 1912. The ink was hardly dry on the Board of Trade forms before it was realised that the LGOC had now become a subsidiary of the powerful Underground group. Salesman Searle cashed in on this situation. He had an order for 100 Daimlers for the Tramways (MET) and undertook to maintain them for three years at $3\frac{1}{2}d$ (1·5p) a mile. He then went to A. H. Stanley (later Lord Ashfield), managing director of the Underground, and disclosed what he was doing for the MET. Stanley countered by offering to buy 250 Daimlers, where upon Searle announced this to the MET board. By these 'Smart Alec' tactics he obtained an order for 350 Daimlers, but had to cut the maintenance contract to $3d$ a mile. In the upshot he succeeded in gaining the enmity of both parties who came together by one of Stanley's typical negotiations of peace. On 28 January 1913, when the MET buses began work, they operated at the direction of the LGOC from garages at Colindale and Tottenham. Moreover, MET only took delivery of 226 Daimlers: the remainder of the fleet was a batch of 124 B-types. The LGOC had already signed agreements not to compete with the BET undertakings (the first agreement signed was with the Greenock & Port Glasgow Tramway Company on 19 November 1912) and on 25 July 1912 had adopted new articles of association that fixed the LGOC operating radius at 30 miles from Charing Cross, in lieu of the previous 15-mile radius – incidentally eleven days after beginning an *ultra vires* operation to Windsor. Moreover, Stanley had taken the opportunity to settle with the Daimler company over its manufacturing susceptibilities and its operating ambitions. This took the form of compensating Daimler for its cut-down MET order by making them sole agents for the LGOC manufactured product, the building of which had been hived off by formation of the Associated Equipment Co. Ltd on 13 June 1912. Albert Stanley's skill and energy as a negotiator was at this time at its peak. He persuaded the British Electric Traction group to participate in a joint holding company, London & Suburban Traction Co. Ltd, formed 20 November 1912, which took in as from 1 January 1913 the Underground's

London United Tramways, with the BET Metropolitan Electric Tramways Ltd, the BET South Metropolitan Tramways & Lighting Co. Ltd and the Tramways (MET) Omnibus Co. Ltd, and he persuaded the BSA-Daimler group to entrust the shares of the Gearless Omnibus Co. Ltd to the L & S T as a holding company and its 22 buses to the operating direction of the LGOC.

The first Tramways (MET) bus entered service on 28 January 1913, the first Gearless (of necessity, a gearbox transmission Daimler) on 5 April 1913 and the first Southern, one of 10 B-types, on 1 August 1913. The MET buses bore the initials as fleet name in blue shaded gold on a dark blue ground. My delight at being overtaken by one on a morning in May while on my way to school was great; it was on a new service between West Kilburn and Ilford operated from the MET garage at Colindale. The MET had planned this before they were working in conjunction with the LGOC and it was really unnecessary. Not many months passed before the buses from Colindale were moved to the LGOC premises at Hendon. The Gearless Daimlers were at first in grey livery, but later adopted the dark blue of the MET which was also adopted by the Southern vehicles. Croydon Corporation objected to Southern buses operating through that town in view of their agreements with the BET tramway company about their tramway routes and so they were sent to the LGOC garage at Twickenham and I saw one on the Ealing and Surbiton service in the school holidays of 1913, a far cry from the Mitcham and Belmont extension of the SMET & L tramway route that the company had visualised when it contemplated owning buses, just as West Kilburn to Ilford or the running of services from Streatham, Putney or Plumstead garages was a long way from the contemplated MET services in extension of tramway routes in Hertfordshire or building up traffic along the hoped-for tram route out to Watford. In the autumn the grey Gearless Daimlers appeared on the new service 56 from Tottenham to Millwall Docks.

A fleet of Daimlers which appeared in 1912 was operated by British Automobile Traction Ltd. This originated through the promotion by the British Automobile Development Co. Ltd of the Amalgamated Motor Bus Co. Ltd. The BAD was the BET group's way of keeping abreast of motor bus developments and was formed in March 1905 to manufacture vehicles, sell or hire them to municipal or company operators and to promote operating companies in areas where there was no tramway undertaking. An assembly plant was erected adjacent to the BET's Brush works at Loughborough, Brush providing chassis and bodies and engines coming from such firms as Peter Brotherhood. A driver-over-engine vehicle was produced, the first made being known as 'British', but later batches appeared as 'Brush'. The

Amalgamated company was launched on 11 April 1906 and a prospectus was issued showing agreements to acquire the 'times' of certain horse bus proprietors in five of the associations, Atlas & Waterloo, Camden Town, John Bull, Islington & Old Kent Road and Kings Cross & Barnsbury. For each lot of three horse buses withdrawn, two motors would be provided, £200 being paid for each 'time'. But the year 1905 had clearly shown that the motor bus proprietor could easily succeed as a pirate and that paying for 'times' was not necessary. The investing public evidently held this view, judging by the meagre response to the £200,000 share issue, and C. W. French and the London Omnibus-Carriage Co. Ltd were evidently of the same view, as their horses and vehicles were withdrawn from service by 1907; during 1907–8 five Amalgamated 'Brush' buses appeared in London, very far short of the fleet of 120 intended. In the meantime the British Electric Traction group had discovered the facts about motor bus maintenance, and changed the name of British Automobile Development to British Automobile Traction Co. Ltd and on 1 April 1910 took over the somewhat meagre business of Amalgamated in London. In 1912 it began to take delivery of the new Daimler buses designed by Frank Searle and towards the end of that year signed agreements with the LGOC as a result of which 33 buses were operated in London at LGOC direction. They were finished in a dark green livery with silvery white fleet name 'British' and these Daimlers continued to give yeoman service until 1927 when a NS fleet replaced them.

We have already referred to the motorisation of horse bus services by Thomas Tilling Ltd, the founder of which was owner of a horse bus from 1849. The Peckham–Oxford Street route was completely operated by motors from 16 December 1905. From 1906 suburban routes were motorised, and in 1907 spare Tilling horse buses began competition with the LGOC in Western suburbs. This breach of a long-standing business friendship was soon repaired and in 1909 the first sharing arrangement concerning motor routes was agreed with the LGOC. The lightweight TTA1 petrol-electric 34-seat bus appeared on 2 June 1911 and went into public service on 11 June. A further sharing agreement took place in 1912 and from 6 October 1913 another limited the Tilling London fleet to 150. On 2 April 1914 general pooling in the London area began, and Tilling buses ceased to operate from Tilling garages at Elephant and Castle, Camberwell and Lewisham, which were given over to that company's commercial lorry fleets and began in the next two years running from the LGOC garages at Catford and Croydon and, after the war, Bromley. These changes determined the Tilling board to think in terms of provincial expansion, since London was no longer open to it for expansion of business. Later the number of buses in the Tilling London fleet was increased to 166 and then by another 166, some of which were purchased by the LGOC and were used as a pool between the two concerns according to the Tilling proportion of the total London fleet. When it exceeded 3,320, Tilling were entitled to 5 per cent of the pool. This was a supplementary agreement of 1923 and others of 1925 and related to particular routes and then were followed by a consolidation agreement in 1929. Tilling were at first inclined to a green livery for motors, and the first TTA1 with its cheese-dish bonnet and radiator behind the engine, is said to have been green, but the General red was adopted in 1911 and was in 1920 alleviated by a cream background to the name in script.

There are many remarkable rags to riches stories in the bus industry – that of William Benjamin Richardson is not only of interest as he was a horse-bus driver on a service to Surbiton of the London & Suburban Omnibus Co. Ltd, of which he became the managing director, but that he survived through several reorganisations and changes of location which demonstrated the flexibility and tenacity of early motor-bus tycoons. In 1895 the company became the New London & Suburban Omnibus Co. Ltd. To combat threatened competition from the London United Tramways it was decided to motorise the Surbiton–Kew Bridge service. The first bus ordered was a Dennis and it achieved fame as the first worm-driven bus in the country, the absence of chain clatter being commended. This vehicle was in service in April 1905 and was accompanied by the first Leyland bus, fitted by the Lancashire Steam Motor Co. Ltd with a Crossley petrol engine. But traffic on the Surbiton–Richmond–Kew Bridge route was thin in 1905 and Richardson withdrew from the route on 14 October. On 21 October with a plate to say 'way' screwed over the last syllable of the fleet name 'Kingston', four buses began service between Chalk Farm and the Law Courts via the new street, Kingsway. Some buses actually had interchangeable boards for weekday working as Kingsway and at weekends as Kingston. At this stage, early in 1906, the family behind Leyland Motors, as it now was, the Spurriers, took an interest, the London Central Motor Omnibus Co. Ltd was formed and the New London & Suburban company absorbed.

In the spring of 1907 the London Central company's route was extended to be Chalk Farm and Elephant and Castle and the depot was shifted from Shepherds Bush to Penrose Street, Walworth, where the London Central occupied the former horse tram depot and overhaul works of the London Tramways Company; during 1912 about 30 buses were kept there. J. C. Dean, when general manager of the West Yorkshire Road Car Company, told me he had grim boyhood memories of the garage superintendent's poky flat at Penrose Street. His father had some sort of argument with Daniel Duff, who had just become a member of the General board, and, as a result, was demoted from a large LGOC garage early in 1913 to be in charge of the New Central premises, a punishment which seems to have made more impression on the Dean family than upon papa Dean himself. In 1913, 12 primrose B-type buses, with dark blue or black bonnets, were added to the Central fleet, running on Whit Monday only on route 25a. They were then transferred to Kingston routes.

During 1909 a non-competitive arrangement was made with the London General company which agreed not to work services along Kingsway while the London Central company was not to use more than 25 buses or open any new route within 8 miles of Charing Cross. A further agreement to limit competition was made in December 1911 and then the New Central Omnibus Co. Ltd was registered on 3 January 1912 with a capital of £500,000 and a proposed fleet of 650 buses, to work in the suburbs and provinces. This issue was far from successful, only £58,000 being subscribed, no doubt owing to the Stock Exchange's appreciation of the commercial resilience of the LGOC as a result of its new B-type bus. The upshot of this faulty move was that at the end of 1912 the New Central Company made the same sort of pact with the LGOC that other operators had done. As a result from 1 January 1913, 66 buses at Penrose Street, Walworth Road and Ceres Road, Kingston, worked under a lease to the LGOC. In addition there were 12 buses operating from a depot at Bedford opened in May 1912 as the first instalment of provincial activities. Richardson had a 10-year contract with the LGOC but after six weeks he was paid substantial compensation for loss of office and had founded another operating concern at Wellingborough. The Underground Electric Railways of London bought the New Central Company in October 1913 and the assets were transferred to the LGOC on 30 June 1914. As a result the primrose and dark blue of the Central disappeared from the London streets and the Central Leylands were repainted in General red and classified L. This gave the LGOC a depot at Bedford, a business clearly in conflict with the agreements signed with the BET group in 1912, and as a result Theodore Thomas, then on the commercial staff of the Underground group, tried to sell the Bedford business to Sidney Garcke, but the latter, still resentful of the clipping of the wings of British Automobile and Tramways (MET) in London, refused to be interested. Had he been, it might have changed the bus map of England.

Because we now come to the story of the National Omnibus & Transport Co. Ltd. It will be recalled that Thomas Clarkson had made a successful impact on the London bus market with his Chelmsford-built steam chassis which were still further improved, like everybody else's, under the 1909 Metropolitan Police regulations and their stringent weight limits. Despite Frank Searle's interest in steam propulsion – he was enthusiastic for the

Bellis & Morcom bus and for the LGOC in July 1909 had a De Dion converted by Clarkson to steam operation complete with a Clarkson pattern of radiator with two ears such as appeared on that maker's lightweight models – the LGOC was not impressed and announced its intention of dispensing with all its steam buses and this, of course, included a fleet of over 70 Road Car Clarksons. Thomas Clarkson thereupon decided to muster his friends and form his own operating company in 1909. It was named the National Steam Car Co. Ltd to emphasise the founders' interest in the Territorial Army and other national service movements. He began to operate four buses on a Westminster to Shepherds Bush service on 2 November 1909. The garage was in Hercules Road, Lambeth. On 30 May 1910 the service was extended to Rye Lane, Peckham and on 20 February 1911 further extended to Peckham Rye. By 1 January 1914, when a working agreement was made with the LGOC, the National white fleet numbered 173 and besides the Peckham Rye–Shepherds Bush service a number of other original routes, such as Peckham Rye–Camden Town, Putney–Wood Green, Peckham Rye–Finsbury Park, were operated, with Sunday services such as Peckham–Petersham, Oxford Circus–Bexley, and Peckham–Hampton Church. National also provided hot competition with the Central London Railway with a Liverpool Street–Shepherds Bush service. At the latter point the terminal was the 'Princess Victoria', always referred to by Clarkson as the 'Victoria Tavern'. Some open ground here provided hard standing for buses taking layover. The London fleet was housed in two garages, at Nunhead and Putney Bridge, each with space for 120 buses. During the First World War the naphtha-fired Nationals operated the LGOC and Tilling peripheral service 37 between Peckham and Hounslow, thereby saving petrol.

But the effect of the war was severe; Clarkson was appalled at the increase in labour costs, brought about by the 8-hour day, and the price of naphtha was increased by 2,700 per cent. An arrangement was made for the National Steam Car Co. Ltd to relinquish London working, the last day of operation being 19 November 1919, and in return it took over the LGOC premises at Bedford. Steam buses were abandoned (Clarkson happily concentrated on producing a coke-fired steam lorry) and the bus company was reorganised as the National Omnibus & Transport Co. Ltd on 13 February 1920.

Some other operators were affected by high costs; one of these was the Allen Omnibus Co. Ltd. This was formed by W. P. Allen, an entrepreneur who began bus operations in numerous places up and down the country, including Clacton, Dartford and Farningham and Folkestone on 23 April 1914. He then acquired a fleet of Straker-Squire shaft-driven buses which were operated in London between Liverpool Street and West Kilburn. Allen's livery was a greenish yellow and he had distinctive bodywork with transverse seats, arranged one and two, in the front half of the lower deck, with longitudinal facing seats at the rear, with a deeper portion of the side panel on this section. The total seating capacity came down to 32. He also managed, after 1914, the fleet of what had been registered in 1912 as the Premier Omnibus Co. Ltd, but which became in May 1914 the London Premier Omnibus Co. Ltd, perhaps to distinguish it from the moribund company that Daimler hoped would use their KPL petrol-electrics. This Premier company imported De Dion petrol vehicles, but the first arrived in October 1913 and the maximum fleet was probably six. E. H. Bayley, formerly of the London Road Car Co. Ltd, appeared on the board of directors but although the authorised share capital was £250,000, only £22,000 appears to have been issued and paid up. Winding-up was decided upon on 15 January 1917 and the fun of yet another beetroot-coloured bus, but with the peculiar round radiator favoured by De Dion, was taken away from the enthusiast, although the only route I ever saw this Premier operating was Liverpool Street and Victoria. A receiver was appointed for the Allen Omnibus Co. Ltd on 1 December 1916, but a few days previously, on 27 November, the London business of the company had been purchased by the LGOC. For a few days into 1917 the service from Liverpool Street to West Kilburn and another route was maintained by the LGOC and then it was abandoned owing to restrictions on the use of petrol. The last I saw of the greenish-yellow Allen livery was in the railway strike of 1919 when a bus with 'Mersea Island' as fleet name appeared in Bow Road obviously bound for the 50-mile trip to West Mersea.

This brought to a close a picturesque period of London operation in which buses on General routes and bearing their route numbers might be of various operators' liveries, and though most of these were red, dark blue, dark green, grey and primrose figured, as well as the very different-looking TTA1 petrol-electrics of Thomas Tilling Ltd. The allocation clerks frequently changed these from route to route, there being a tendency to use Tilling and Central buses on the routes from Elephant and Castle; so Central buses appeared in the purlieus of Epping Forest and once when I joined my father in rowing on Finsbury Park lake and we journeyed thither by a 42, which pre-war ran from Finsbury Park over Tower Bridge to Camberwell Green, we purred all the way there by a Tilling petrol-electric. Tilling buses also figured at one time on the Epping Forest services; what intrigued me was the cost of boards and stencils; because, to assert their independence Tilling used non-standard sizes and new sets had to be supplied each time there was a change from Tilling to Central or vice-versa.

Whereas in 1911, with a fleet of about 1,108 buses, some 23 motor routes were operated by the LGOC, in the summer of 1914 a fleet of 3,100 buses was operating weekday and Sunday routes, including some as far afield as Epping Town, Bexley, Reigate, Dorking, Maidenhead and Burnham Beeches. Some of the Sunday routes were further refined by being run 'if fine', such as the extension of 171, Bow Road Underground Station to Epping Town back to Millwall Docks, which did not run in what the LGOC called 'inclement weather'. Incidentally at Bow Road, the police continued to permit backing to change direction, now used only at the Lower Sydenham Station terminal point. A little nearer town on the A12 reversal was by U-turn in Mile End Road near the Mile End Station terminus of 56 and this led to disaster as a City Leyland chanced to be passing a solid wooden-bodied LGOC B-type one day in 1924. The result was far more destructive than anything I heard of happening in a reversing incident. In 1914 there appeared to be many spare buses and spare crews galore; they worked long days and often presented themselves without much chance of paid-for work. I once met a conductor about 9 in the evening coming back from St Albans to Golders Green who had booked on at 6.30 in the morning at Forest Gate garage, many miles distant. Services were worked with great economy, despite the lavish resources; the 13 buses from Clay Hall garage on 98, Old Ford and Waterloo Station in the high summer of 1914 on weekdays, operated on Sundays on 174 from Aldgate to Hampton Court via Waterloo and West Hill. I last saw this service on a wet Sunday in July 1914 when the 13 were returning early from Aldgate to Bow Bridge to work to the garage in Old Ford. The First World War broke out on the first weekend in August and from then until 1919 Londoners had to put up with much-reduced bus facilities, although after 1916, as we have seen, there was only one operating policy.

So in just over eight years from the consolidation of the principal motor-bus companies in the Metropolis all the buses in London and the trams of the three companies were operating in collaboration with the Underground Electric Railways Co. of London. This highly desirable degree of co-ordination was to endure for a bare six years only. To understand what brought about its temporary end we must look at wartime and post-war conditions in London.

8
Between the Wars

The First World War dealt rather harshly with the London bus, as a great many were requisitioned by the War Office; the 1939–45 war was organised rather better from the civilian's viewpoint with a much greater appreciation of the part played by the motor vehicle in the life of the ordinary citizen. At the outbreak of war in August 1914, the LGOC and its associates owned a fleet of 3,071 buses, of which 1,319 went overseas. Neither the 173 National Steam buses nor the 175 Tilling petrol-electric vehicles in London service were similarly affected, as these types were not required by the War Office. By Armistice Day (11 November 1918) there were only 1,758 motor buses operating on the London streets. The total had increased to 1,905 on 1 January 1919, and to 2,044 by May. It was impossible in the prevailing conditions to secure new vehicles, and the LGOC hired from the Board of Trade 180 old AEC Army lorries, which were equipped with canvas hoods and garden seats. The first went into service on 2 June 1919 and these lorry-buses gave useful temporary help (although at an operating loss) until January 1920. On 18 July 1919 (the day before the official Peace Celebrations) 2,376 motor buses and lorry-buses were at work, an increase of 618 over the Armistice Day figure, but still woefully inadequate for London needs.

Several factors combined to accentuate the shortage of buses in 1919; one was the discarding of old vehicles by the LGOC itself. The X-type with 61 buses was being withdrawn (although the last survived until May 1920), and the 51 Y-type Straker-Squires all ceased their bus life early in the year. On top of these were 173 National steamers which had been taken out of London service in November 1919 owing to the National company's decision to adopt petrol vehicles and expand in provincial operation.

With remarkable foresight AEC post-war planning began in 1918 and the first bus produced after the war for the General took account of the eight-hour day, which made new police regulations essential. Accordingly the K-type, as this AEC model was designated, had rear-wheel arches inside the body although the overall width remained at 7 ft 2 in. The total seating capacity was 46, twelve more than the pre-war double-deck bus. I knew that the new bus was imminent and eagerly awaited the appearance of K1 upon Service 11 on 26 August 1919. I rode from Liverpool Street to Shepherds Bush and was surprised that this, to me, remarkable innovation, was received so calmly. About 500 B-type chassis were recovered from war service and met Metropolitan police requirements – some only with some difficulty so that they were licensed as 'traffic emergency vehicles' and were painted in a green livery described as 'khaki'. Their smoothness in traffic appeared unimpaired at least to one critical observer, so high is the standard imposed by the Metropolitan Police. That standard is, since 1931, imposed all over the country by the certifying officers of the 12 or 13 traffic commissions (there is one fewer than there were in 1930).

The LGOC increased its fleet as rapidly as it could, but only with the products of its own manufacturing unit, the AEC. The fact that other motor manufacturers were not contributing towards supplying a growing need in an era of rapid expansion in travel demand led to the encouragement of new proprietors to enter the field. Even before the war, the concentration of the London bus industry under LGOC guidance had resulted in various schemes for establishing new competition. Some of these were of the 'company promoter' type and proved unattractive to investors. Others were serious proposals by experienced busmen who saw opportunities for working with modern vehicles in greater freedom than the LGOC, which they regarded as 'shackled' by its financial and operating links with the Underground Railways and the company-owned tramways, and also by its manufacturing association with the AEC. A few who had been associated with the New Central Omnibus Co. Ltd and Leyland Motors Ltd formed the Alliance Motor Omnibus Co. Ltd, which was incorporated on 1 July 1914, but the outbreak of war prevented any immediate development. This group subsequently came into the picture as the City Motor Omnibus Co. Ltd, one of the best organised of post-war 'independents'.

After the war, Sydney Straker, who was still sore at the Great Eastern of London order being cut down to 52 (one of the Strakers rebuilt with a lorry body and carrying a big U and the spelt-out legend 'Upton Park Garage' gave me the clue to the lettered code of LGOC garages), endeavoured to start an owner-drivers' company for bus proprietors on the lines common to the taxi trade but later did get a number of entrepreneurs to buy or hire-purchase Straker-Squire 46-seat buses which were approved by the police. Unfortunately for Straker, Leyland and Dennis also produced models approved by the police. It is worthy of note that the Select Committee on Transport (Metropolitan Area), which was appointed on 29 May 1919, and began its sittings on 2 June under the chairmanship of Mr Kennedy Jones, reported on 25 July: 'Such evidence as they have heard does not convince them that the "Combine" in the last year of the war and after the Armistice might not have advantageously to a large extent supplemented its existing vehicles from other concerns than the Associated Equipment Company, which is really part of their own organisation. The principle of practically confining orders to this company may be mutually of benefit to both, though not necessarily helpful to the public.'

The LGOC continued to press the authorities to allow flexibility of weight limits and the next AEC model was the S-type, which weighed $8\frac{1}{2}$ tons and seated 54 passengers. Originally it had a bench seat facing the door and seated 57 passengers, but when the S-type emerged on 21 December 1920 the police ukase was that 54 seats were enough. In the meantime a vehicle with the front axle retracted to shorten the wheelbase, the T-type, was produced, but only experimentally. The T-type was specially designed for the turn at an acute angle from Oxford Street to Bond Street, and while matters were uncertain two Tilling-Stevens TS3A were allocated to service 25 (Victoria–Seven Kings) and worked for a month or two from Catford Garage to show that they could turn the corner without difficulty. It is suspected that the body of T1 was allocated to an S-type bus in the end. The TTA1 bus was a petrol-electric with 34-seat body and the radiator behind the engine; the bonnet was shaped like a cheese dish. There were a few normal-control front-radiator-fitted Tilling-Stevens in the Tilling London fleet even before 1914. In July 1921 Tilling-Stevens brought out a driver-behind-engine 48-seat vehicle, the TS3A. By the end of 1921 the LGOC and its associates owned a fleet of 2,972 buses, of which some 2,484 were in regular operation. This was still below the immediate pre-war total, and provided the incentive for an era of 'independent' or 'pirate' operation, with the backing of motor manufacturers and body-builders.

Effectively, the era of the 'independents' opened on 5 August 1922, when a chocolate-coloured Leyland bus with the fleet name 'Express' was placed in service. The proprietors were three ex-service men (Arthur George Partridge, David Francis Jermyn, Albert Sydney Griffin) who traded in partnership as the Express Omnibus Company. They had the financial support of Christopher Dodson, the vehicle body-builder of Willesden, who arranged 'easy terms'. Christopher Dodson died on 2 July 1959 at the age of 85. His activities in connection with the London independent operators, though important, were exaggerated in *The Times* of 3 July 1959, which credited him with running 'a fleet of 2,000 pirate buses in London'. A glamorised appreciation of Dodson by 'J.E.' (presumably Sir John Elliot), which appeared in *The Times* of 11 July 1959 attributed to Dodson a greater influence in regard to London buses than he really exercised. Partridge, who became a prominent and effective mouthpiece for the independents, was a taxi-owner who had been very impressed by crowds queuing for buses from Clapham Junction in the mornings and as a result he planned to do a morning trip on Service 19. All his plans were disclosed by a Leyland depot employee in the pride of delivering a new bus, so that when Partridge started work a General chaser was equipped with boards and fare tables for 19 as well as 11 and at the weekend it was no surprise to the General men that the Express went off on 33 to Richmond. At a public meeting of the London & Home Counties Traffic Advisory Committee, held at the Middlesex Guildhall, Westminster, on 22 June 1925, Partridge stated in evidence that, when he left the garage on the first morning of operation, three officials of the LGOC boarded his bus and 'paid their fares for a good many miles, as they never left us for three days'.

Shortly after the Express bus began working, the Thomas Transport Co. Ltd introduced an open AEC charabanc with cape cart hood, in regular service between Piccadilly Circus and Marble Arch at the fare of 1*d*, but this venture had a very short life. It provided one of the very rare cases of AEC chassis being used for independent operation. AEC vehicles were sold subject to the restriction that they were not to be worked as stage carriages within 30 miles of Charing Cross, or in any way in competition with motor buses operated by the LGOC, without the written consent of the latter.

Another early use of an open charabanc type vehicle was between Aldgate and Bow Bridge. East London Motors (J. W. Smith) maintained this service with an A-type Straker-Squire vehicle from 15 to 30 September 1922. This kind of working was exceptional, and of brief duration. Practically all the independent operators used conventional four-wheel open-top double-deck vehicles in the earlier stages, but later some single-deckers (usually for routes with low head-room) and also covered-top double-deckers were introduced. Latterly, a few operators had some six-wheel double-deckers, notably Guy and Sunbeam.

One operator, and probably the only one to do so, entered the London bus business in a modest way with an open motor coach, but quickly graduated into the ranks of an ordinary bus operator. This was the Samuelson Transport Co. Ltd, a motor-coach operator launched in a large way early in 1921, to which further reference is made later. At the end of the summer season of 1922, one coach was placed in bus service between Northfields Station and Ealing Broadway, beginning on 7 September. Early in October a double-deck bus was introduced, and later two others. The company had been placed in voluntary liquidation on 25 September 1922, and some of its assets (including the bus service) were taken over by the traffic superintendent, Sydney Harold Hole, trading as the Samuelson New Transport Company. The London bus operations were not extended, but the enterprise is worthy of mention here in view of its subsequent association with the LGOC in working the Straker-Squire vehicles acquired from other independents.

On 12 November 1922, Percy Frost-Smith, formerly chief engineer of Thomas Tilling Ltd, and one of the designers of the Tilling-Stevens petrol-electric chassis, began working between Lee Green and Liverpool Street with a revised form of petrol-electric bus assembled to his own design at the Dennis works. He traded as the F.S. Petrol-Electric Omnibus Company. Apart from this operator, all the London independents used vehicles of standard makes, mainly Straker-Squire, Leyland, and Dennis, but built to satisfy the requirements of the Metropolitan Police, then the licensing authority. Other makes used in small numbers were Bean, Daimler, Guy, Karrier, Maudslay, Sunbeam and Thornycroft.

Straker-Squire buses, seating 46 passengers, were much in evidence in the early days of the independent era, beginning with one bus called 'Primrose' which three ex-servicemen, all motor mechanics, placed in service on 25 November 1922. Then Bernard Cosgrove introduced the fleet name 'Admiral', an obvious counterblast to 'General', which became one of the best-known and most widely used of them all. Cosgrove worked from the Willow Walk premises of A. T. Bennett & Co. Ltd, and began operating with two Straker-Squire 46-seat buses. Bennett introduced the first of his own 'Admiral' fleet on 21 February 1923. Cosgrove withdrew from the group in July 1923 and thereafter the name 'Admiral' was peculiarly associated with Bennett; the fleet grew to some 40 vehicles. Alfred Temple Bennett, of Scottish descent, was born in Paddington in 1879, but his family moved to Wood Green in 1883, and much of his career was associated with that area. He served his apprenticeship with Richard Moreland & Son Ltd, where he was engaged on heavy pumping engines. In 1902 he began his own general engineering business at Willow Walk, Tottenham, specialising in the manufacture of automatic fog signals for Trinity House. He extended his activities to taxi cabs and garage work in 1909.

In the early months of 1923 many new independent operators appeared on the streets of London, mainly with single buses worked by ex-service men who had some Army experience of motor vehicles. They tended to run on existing services of the LGOC, or the heavy traffic portions of them, and to use the same route numbers. Both services and route numbers were within the exclusive province of the operator, as the Metropolitan Police responsibilities were confined to licensing the vehicles as Stage Carriages on satisfying themselves as to weight, dimensions, and structural and mechanical fitness; approving fare tables for reasonableness and consistency (but not for the basis of charging); and limiting the use of the buses to streets which were physically capable of accommodating such traffic, without discrimination between one operator and another.

In addition to the central London area, where the demand for bus transport was in excess of the capacity of the fleet owned by the LGOC and its associates (3,228 at the beginning of 1923), independent operators found a profitable field in the district northward of the London County boundary at Highgate, Finsbury Park and Stamford Hill. This was served mainly by the company-owned trams of the Metropolitan Electric Tramways Ltd. When that company became associated with the LGOC, from the beginning of 1913, as a result of a comprehensive agreement between the British Electric Traction Co. Ltd and the LGOC, working arrangements were made for all traction business within the London area. By reason of this traffic agreement, a co-ordinated service of trams and buses was operated, resulting in fewer buses than would otherwise have been used, and greater reliance on trams, which were losing their popularity. In 1923, the influx of a large number of independent bus services, working from central London over MET tram routes, gave greater speed, comfort and flexibility than the trams, and made it impossible to continue on the old basis. The LGOC found itself compelled to cover similar routes, and, to preserve the interests of the MET, a common area pooling agreement was made whereby traffic receipts in the MET area were pooled in agreed proportions.

A vivid description of this period was given many years later (in the *Financial Times* of 31 March 1959) by Harold Wincott, a respected financial writer, in a spirited article, of which the following is an excerpt: 'At certain times and in certain places there were more people than there were buses. A lot more. Now a chap called Bennett observed this and said to himself "I observe that there are more people wanting to travel between Finsbury Park and Cockfosters than there are buses to take them there. So I will be a public benefactor (admittedly I may in the process make myself a lot of lolly) and I will provide extra buses''. Now those were the bad old days of an uncontrolled economy and Mr. Bennett did put his buses on the streets, and he called those buses "Admirals". Well, you never saw such a state of affairs as resulted. The "Admirals" went thundering along hell for leather, beating the "Generals" whenever they could to the next bus stop and scooping up all the waiting passengers (if there were a lot) and sometimes not bothering to wait if there were only a few or none at all. The populace, of course, loved it. Not only did they not have to wait nearly so long at places like Finsbury Park. They got to where they wanted to go pretty quickly and had all the excitement of a race with the "Generals" (or the "Admirals") thrown in for free.'

Meanwhile, both the LGOC and Tilling were actively pursuing the production of improved types of bus, within the rigid restrictions imposed by the Metropolitan Police. In July 1923 Tilling introduced a modified form of the TS3A with driver-beside-engine petrol-electric chassis and a 48-seat body. It was called the TS7. In April 1923 Tilling had made a new agreement with the LGOC which facilitated Tilling continuing to own 5 per cent of the London Pool. Altogether, 166 of the TS7 type were built for Tilling and 166 for the LGOC. The latter, which the LGOC designated the O-type, were operated by Tilling on a fixed mileage basis, but ownership could be transferred if necessary to give Tilling 5 per cent of a growing fleet in London, and also the then-desired petrol-electric vehicles.

For its own operation, the LGOC produced its most remarkable post-war vehicle in the NS-type. This had many components similar to the S, but had the frame cranked down behind the driver's seat, making it London's first bus with a low centre of gravity and providing passengers with a single step from the ground. Its 52-seat body was designed to take a top-deck cover, but the police would not accept this, and insisted in adhering to their 'conditions' of 1909 that 'no canopy or similar superstructure will be permitted on the roof of an omnibus constructed to carry passengers on the top deck'. The NS classification was quickly interpreted as *Nulli Secundus*. As an open-top bus it entered service on 10 May 1923, and still on solid tyres. It was then intended to be a 'pirate basher' but unfortunately the police non-acceptance of the covered top until 1926 and gearbox troubles on the first day, prevented this being effective.

In general, this era of independent bus operation in London was singularly free from the company-promoter type of activity which had characterised the introduction of the motor bus two decades earlier, probably the only example being the Henslowe, if that was a culprit.

Some of the enterprises launched during 1923 were the nuclei of substantial businesses, and deserve separate mention. The group of former

Leyland men who had been concerned with the Alliance Motor Omnibus scheme in 1914 emerged as the City Motor Omnibus Co. Ltd. It was incorporated on 13 January 1923 and placed its first bus – a Leyland – in service on 9 March 1923. Its joint managing directors were Walter Crook and William Frederick Mallender, and they brought with them the benefit of many years of experience, both in engineering and in traffic operation. In its early days, its activities were limited to running on existing routes, but later the well-maintained 'City' buses, in a distinctive Spanish tan and brown livery, developed their own route with a fleet of some 40 vehicles.

During 1923 more than 60 new independents entered London bus operation, with some 184 licensed buses, or an average of about 3 vehicles severally. Of these, approximately 150 buses were in regular daily service. The LGOC fleet was increased by 1,060 during the year. It is impossible to give with precision the number of independent owners, as many of them were private partnerships of which the composition changed from time to time. In some cases, individual vehicles in a partnership were licensed to different partners, and an observer might have recorded these as separate businesses. Even when the undertakings were incorporated as private limited companies, the controlling shareholding sometimes changed hands, and it was not immediately obvious that two separate operators had effected a merger of interests. As the period was one of widespread unemployment, some ex-servicemen who had learned to drive during the First World War invested their savings in order to obtain employment.

Another personality who entered the London bus business at this period, and subsequently took a prominent place among independent operators, was Walter James Dangerfield. The company called Dangerfield Ltd was incorporated on 9 February 1923 and introduced its first bus in the next month, using the fleet name 'Carlton', which was derived, presumably, from the Carlton Window Cleaning Co. (1914) Ltd which had its registered office in the same premises. In May 1924 Dangerfield expanded his operations by introducing buses under the fleet name 'Overground', which were his personal property, but he continued as managing director of the Carlton fleet, and the two concerns worked in close harmony. The choice of the name 'Overground' was as obvious a contrast at that period to the familiar 'Underground', as the popular name of the group which controlled the LGOC, as was 'Admiral' to 'General'. The fleet name 'Carlton' was soon dropped and all the vehicles ran as 'Overground'.

The undoubted popularity with the public of the 'independent' buses attracted numerous motor-coach proprietors who were not parties to working agreements with the LGOC. A well-known early entrant was

Alexander Timpson of Rushey Green, Catford, who owned an old-established coaching business. He had pioneered a regular motor-coach service between Plumstead and Hastings in 1919 with a Karrier coach called *The Silver Bell* in striking silver livery, and expanded rapidly. For London bus service he adopted the name Timpson's Silver Omnibuses, and used Straker-Squire chassis. He began working on a Plumstead Common to Bromley Common service on 29 March 1923. This was extended on Sundays to Green Street Green from 15 April and later to Westerham Hill. Unlike most of the early independents, Timpson adhered to his own distinctive route.

A much-publicised motor-coach operator to be attracted to London buses was the Cambrian Coaching Company. Its founder was Athole Murray Kemp-Gee, whose previous business career had been with the Cambrian Catering Company. He established his coaches in the summer of 1921 on London-to-the-Coast service in competition with the Samuelson fleet. With its spring timetable of coach services in 1923, the Cambrian offered £100 in prizes to its passengers for suggestions as to the most suitable London bus route on which to operate. The first Cambrian bus went into service on 3 August 1923. Straker-Squire vehicles were used at first, and subsequently Thornycroft and Dennis. The fleet eventually exceeded 50 buses.

At the beginning of 1924, there were no fewer than 68 independent operators working in London, with 194 licensed buses, of which 159 were in daily service. The tendency to concentrate on central area routes undoubtedly contributed to street congestion in some places, and in February Lord Ashfield launched an appeal for some form of legal control. His campaign was received favourably by the Press, probably on grounds of public policy, although opponents suggested that there was some measure of prejudice, as the Underground Group (including the LGOC) placed a substantial amount of advertising, whereas the independents did not. The trade unions generally favoured such control, as they preferred to deal with large employers. Although trade unionism expressed itself against the small owner, and was prepared to do nothing to hinder his downfall, the London Labour Party was not in favour of the form of control envisaged, as it took the view that such control would confer a virtual bus monopoly on the LGOC and its associated companies. The London Labour Party, of course, considered that the proper solution of the problem was on the basis of public ownership.

On the other hand, the independents gained a considerable amount of public sympathy by their increased thought for the wishes and convenience of passengers, and by the improvement in motor-bus manners shown by their staffs. The private owner, anxious for return on his labour and investment, was on the look-out for the wayside passenger and welcomed him aboard, as another fare added to the takings: the employee of a large company, sure of his wage, saw no profit to himself in an extra fare and treated him as something of a nuisance. Moreover, the driver of a bus owned by a large company often turned a blind eye to the would-be passenger who hailed him. 'Not stopping when hailed' at one time figured in almost every traffic circular issued to LGOC staff. The driver was not entirely to blame, as the LGOC and its associates had been endeavouring for some years to persuade passengers to use specified stopping places, which was a privilege enjoyed by trams from the beginning of electrification. A motor-bus 'indicator post' in south-east London was illustrated in the *Commercial Motor* for 7 May 1914. Such indications were also used to a limited extent in the horse-bus era, but on private premises, such as public houses. In 1913 the LGOC began to experiment with queues (with staff to regulate them) at Clapham Common. The practice was extended, first at outlying points and then at town points, and by June 1919 there were 59 positions at 49 different points. On 10 August 1916 Herbert E. Blain, operating manager of the Underground Group, asked the consent of the police to establish fixed stopping points (to the exclusion of hailing), but he was informed on 18 August that this would mean special Parliamentary sanction, and that this was not advocated during the war. His renewed application on 16 May 1918 was also without success. However, the LGOC made experimental use of posts marking important stopping places, erected in 1918 largely as a wartime measure. A system of definite stopping places was adopted by the LGOC on 18 February 1920 when the first bus stop sign was erected in Grosvenor Gardens. The efforts met with only limited success, as Metropolitan Stage Carriages were required by law to stop at any point on being hailed (with a few safety exceptions, mainly in central London). In general, the independent operator gladly obeyed the law, as it added to his revenue and made a satisfied customer who was probably willing to support his case by signing a public petition!

On 22 March 1924 the London tramwaymen struck for better wages, and the bus workers came out in sympathy. The strike ended on 30 March after Ramsay MacDonald (who had become the first Labour Prime Minister on the previous 23 January) arranged with the London County Council and the Underground Group that higher tramway wages should be conceded. Although it was not officially admitted, Herbert Morrison stated that part of the settlement was that MacDonald agreed to pass legislation restricting bus operation in the London area. A Bill (which had been drafted under the previous Conservative Government, headed by Stanley Baldwin) was

16 (*above*) The Provincial Tramways Company used this Yorkshire Steam Wagon chassis for a bus in Grimsby during the petrol shortage of the First World War

17 (*below*) A Barton J-type Thornycroft running on town gas in the First World War

18 (*above*) The short wheelbase and retracted steering of the AEC abortive T-type, apparently designed for the acute turn from Oxford Street (westbound) into Bond Street

19 (*below*) The second K-type bus was allocated to Seven Kings garage in 1919. It seated 46 passengers

20 (*above*) A Straker-Squire 46-seat double-decker of 1920 in the service of Ortona of Cambridge

21 (*below*) Loading an express excursion to Llandudno in 1923, before the Seymour Street stand in Birmingham was transferred to Digbeth bus station

22 (*above*) The London Six, a 72-seat vehicle. It was licensed on 4 June 1927 but did not go into everyday service until September. One built for AEC works service seated 104 and one had petrol-electric transmission

23 (*below*) Red & White Albion and Bristol (Bristol 1 type) at the boundary between the two companies in Chepstow, 1927

duly introduced and became the London Traffic Act of 7 August 1924.

In an endeavour to deter passengers from boarding the first vehicle which presented itself, the London County Council Tramways introduced ordinary return tickets on 1 January 1924, and also reduced to 5d the maximum single ordinary fare within the County of London. The LGOC and associated companies adopted a similar policy by offering return tickets on sections of routes where the buses competed with the LCC trams, but did not reduce single fares. About one half of the LGOC fleet was affected by the new scale, and 75 routes were involved. The first British Empire Exhibition at Wembley was opened by King George V on 23 April 1924 and attracted additional traffic to London. During part of the year, independent buses were increasing at the rate of some 20 a week.

The London Traffic Act came into operation on 1 October 1924, and on 1 December routes were renumbered to conform with new regulations made by the Commissioner of Police of the Metropolis under the new Act. From that date all proprietors were required to work their vehicles during the following week on pre-selected routes only, with an alternative on Saturday and Sunday. All short journeys (except garage runs) were required to bear a separate number or suffix letter. Routes were classified as follows:

A—Routes for all types of buses.
B—Routes for buses with a smaller turning circle.
C—Routes for single-deckers.
D—Routes for buses with special equipment, such as sprags.
E—Low bridges.

Almost immediately, the larger independent operators began to plan their own distinctive routes and an outstanding example was the new service inaugurated on 7 December between Highgate Station and Peckham Rye and numbered 517. The City Motor Omnibus Co. Ltd provided the major share, with 16 vehicles, and there were also four buses of the United Omnibus Company. This lasted only until 21 January 1925, when it was altered to service 536a, working between Highgate and Brockley Cross, via Oxford Circus, Victoria and New Cross. At this time a new partner came into the enterprise with buses operating under the fleet name 'Archway'. The proprietor was Birch Brothers Ltd, one of the oldest family firms in the passenger road transport business. A William Birch, of Stoke Damerel, Plymouth, had been concerned about 1790 in operating a mail coach between Plymouth and Exeter. His farmer son (also William) migrated to London in 1810, and in November 1815 established himself as a dairy farmer in Horseferry Road, Westminster. The next generation (another William) began running cabs in 1832, but was killed by being thrown out of his gig in Broad Sanctuary, Westminster, when only 34 years old, in 1846. His widow, Elizabeth, continued the business and also furnished some capital to some friends who established a bus service between the 'Monster' at Pimlico and the Mansion House. She began running two buses in her own name on 1 May 1851, and thereafter the Birch family continued to operate horse buses in London until 1912. In addition, they worked motor buses from 12 October 1904 until December 1907, but with disastrous results financially. This was, therefore, a return to the London bus business of one of its oldest members and Raymond Birch followed an automobile engineering apprenticeship to prepare him for the role.

During 1925 two Restricted Street Orders were made under the London Traffic Act. The first, in February, declared some 200 thoroughfares to be congested streets, and in consequence no buses not already plying for hire in these streets were permitted to do so. This Regulation occasioned hardship to owners who had vehicles on order, but, through unavoidable circumstances, were unable to get them on the road in time. The matter was debated in the House of Commons on 12 March and the Minister altered the date of limitation from 1 January to 17 February, which satisfied most legitimate grievances. The second London Traffic (Restricted Streets) Order was made on 3 June 1925 and embraced some 600 additional streets (in the majority of instances those on which trams operated), and the third Order, made a month later, dealt with streets north and north-east of Finsbury Park Station. The result was that no buses might thereafter ply for hire on any tramway route, or upon any of the principal streets within the central area, unless they were so operating before the Regulations were brought into force.

According to a Return made to the House of Commons, the number of bus proprietors licensed to ply for hire in the Metropolitan Police District at 31 December 1924 was 188. This figure, of course, included the LGOC and its associates, and the total of independent operators would appear to be 174. The number of buses licensed on that date was 5,032, of which 4,533 were owned by the LGOC and the companies working in conjunction with it, and 499 were independent. Of the last-named figure, 459 were in daily operation, or 300 more than at the beginning of the year. The London & Home Counties Traffic Advisory Committee, which was established under the London Traffic Act (1924) held its first meeting on 18 December 1924, and its annual reports (the first of which was for the calendar year 1925) contain a large amount of statistical and other information about the development of traffic in the Greater London area.

Obviously, the first action of the independent operators was to challenge the Restricted Streets Orders, and a public meeting of the London & Home Counties Traffic Advisory Committee was held at the Middlesex Guildhall, Westminster, on 22 June 1925, with Sir Henry Maybury in the chair, when representations were heard. The contention of the independent proprietors was that they had entered the business during a period when existing facilities were inadequate, and that any subsequent traffic congestion had been caused by the competitive activities of the LGOC and its associates, and not by the independent buses. Despite a considerable amount of public sympathy, the Orders were enforced and the existing position was stabilised. Even with these limitations, the number of independents continued to grow, and the answer to a Question in Parliament in November revealed that 282 new buses had been licensed between 1 January and 31 October 1925, of which 47·9 per cent were to the LGOC and its associates and 52·1 per cent to independent owners. Some of the new vehicles may have been replacements, but these figures give the only available statistical information. At the end of October, the total of independent operators in the Metropolitan Area reached 199. On 31 December 1925 the independent owners numbered 197 with 646 licensed buses, of which 556 were in scheduled operation and carried 12·96 per cent of the bus passengers wholly or partly within a 10-mile radius of Charing Cross. In the period from 1 April 1923 the LGOC and its associates had increased their fleets scheduled for operation by 964 buses.

Until a position of legally-enforceable stabilisation had been achieved, the LGOC had shown no inclination to buy any of the independent businesses, but on 8 January 1926 it announced that it had acquired a substantial interest in the Cambrian Coaching & Goods Transport Ltd, which was working 52 buses in London. The Cambrian buses were operated under the control of the LGOC on and from 23 February. This was the beginning of a hectic period of acquisitions which continued throughout the year. In fact, the first independent fleet to come under LGOC operation was that of the Central Omnibus Co. Ltd with four vehicles, which was worked from 1 February. The directors of the Central company (who included J. Coventon Moth of Trent Motor Traction) had an interest in the Cambrian company, and are stated to have approached the LGOC immediately after the conclusion of the Cambrian deal. In all, 44 independent businesses passed to the control of the LGOC during 1926, and Timpson's Omnibus Services Ltd passed to Thomas Tilling Ltd. These deals reduced the independent buses by 208, of which 149 were in scheduled operation.

In the initial stages no licences were transferred. With those independent operators that were incorporated as limited companies the LGOC acquired the whole of, or a controlling interest in, the share capital. Many of the independents, however, were proprietory businesses or partnerships, and here the method was to form the business into a limited company to facilitate the sale by means of a share transfer. This explains why the dates of incorporation are often only a few weeks before those of the change in control. In numerous cases, agreement to sell had been reached already, and the formalities of incorporation were undertaken by Messrs Joynson Hicks & Co., the well-known firm of solicitors which acted for the Underground Group. Often this provided the first intimation that a sale was pending.

Meanwhile, the activities of the surviving independents were being affected by two forces. One was the rapid improvement in the type of vehicle being used for London bus services, and the need for replacement of vehicles by independent operators who had bought their vehicles under hire-purchase agreements and had not all made adequate provision for depreciation. When the independents began to work, the London motor bus was a four-wheel open-top vehicle with solid tyres. As already mentioned, the police were reluctant to licence any changes, but eventually the first covered-top bus was approved and was placed in service by the LGOC on 2 October 1925. It was an NS which had been designed for this purpose and weighed 9 tons 6 cwt. During the same year, the pneumatic tyre was also making its appearance in the central area. Barnet Motor Services had introduced a single-deck pneumatic-tyred Fiat bus in the Barnet area as early as March 1923, but the pioneer who convinced the Metropolitan Police of the suitability of the pneumatic tyre (at first only on single-deck vehicles) in the central area was A. T. Bennett of the Admiral Line in May 1925. Later (on 2 November 1926), Bennett also succeeded in introducing a four-wheel-braked bus, after many months of advocacy with the Public Carriage Department. Not many of the independents were able to show such enterprise. The first LGOC pneumatic-tyred buses were single-deckers that were introduced in the Slough area on 12 August 1925.

The other, and more immediate, influence affecting the independent operators was the announcement of the licensing authorities to reduce the number of buses working over certain tram routes, as from 29 March 1926. The Association of London Omnibus Proprietors (the representative body of the independents) immediately organised a protest petition for presentation to the House of Commons. Popular interest was excited by quoting the case of Cornelius Beattie, DCM, a comparative late-comer to London bus operation, who had begun working on 27 March 1925. By reason of the control then exercised, he was not licensed to operate any nearer to central London than Shepherds Bush, and the reductions now envisaged on the tram route thence to Hanwell would have meant his complete withdrawal. Of him Gerald Nowell, chairman of the Association, said: 'He has invested his war gratuity, his wife's savings, and everything else he had. He will be absolutely wiped out. In the war he won the Mons Star and the DCM.' In an atmosphere thus charged with sentiment, London was bombarded with leaflets about 'the most glaring injustice of modern times', and a public meeting organised at Cannon Street Hotel on 10 March 1926 by the London Omnibus Passengers Association was addressed by G. K. Chesterton and 'other brilliant speakers', which passed a resolution viewing with anxiety the proposed suppression of private buses.

Although the petition to the House of Commons bore more than one million signatures, the Ministry of Transport did not modify its Orders and at 7.30 a.m. on Monday 29 March Driver Beattie, wearing his DCM ribbon, drove his bus from Shepherds Bush to Southall, amidst cheers, along his then 'unauthorised' route. Legal proceedings followed, and summonses were issued against the drivers of various operators, but it was agreed that the case of Cornelius Beattie should be taken as a test case. In the outcome, the summonses were dismissed on 28 September, mainly on the technicality that the Minister of Transport, in making the regulations, had taken into consideration a matter outside his province. The London Traffic Act, for the purpose of 'facilitating and improving the regulation of traffic in and near London', did not authorise the Minister to take an action based on the economic position of the tramway companies. The matter ultimately reached the House of Lords, where an appeal of Beattie against a Ministry of Transport Order for a reduction in the number of buses along Uxbridge Road was dismissed. It may be added that Cornelius Beattie was afterwards provided with schedules on other (not very remunerative) routes.

Acquisition of control of numerous independents brought into the combined fleets of the LGOC and associated companies various types of vehicle which heretofore had not been represented. This posed problems of maintenance and stores of spare parts, and the LGOC adopted various expedients to bring vehicles of similar types under unified control. With acquired operators of sufficient size, such as the Cambrian, the vehicles continued to be worked from their own garages, which in some cases also took in vehicles of similar types. Two cases are worthy of separate mention. The first is that of the 'Batten group', consisting of various companies associated with Charles William Batten, and generally operating Leyland vehicles. Two of the Batten companies, namely Atlas Omnibus Co. Ltd and the East Ham Omnibus Co. Ltd, came under LGOC control in June 1926, and continued to operate as a unit from a garage in East Ham. In July various other independent companies were acquired by the LGOC and placed under Batten management. Some of these had been incorporated as limited companies a few weeks earlier, to facilitate such transfer, with registered offices at 41 Finsbury Square, EC2, where the legal formalities were effected by Mr H. C. Merrett (of United Counties), who also for a time acted as a director of them. The group thus formed included Atlas, Britannia, Cosgrove, East Ham, Grangewood, Invicta, Loveland, Tottenham Hotspur, Vivid, W & P, and White Star. This autonomous operation continued until the end of December 1927.

The other interesting example is provided by the arrangement made with Sidney Harold Hole (Samuelsons) whose independent buses in the Ealing area had been withdrawn in favour of the LGOC in December 1923. In August 1926 the LGOC handed over to Samuelson Motor Coaches a fleet of Straker-Squire buses taken over from various independents, which Samuelson's maintained and operated under contract until the LGOC disposed of them to outside buyers for uses other than in London bus service in the course of its policy of standardisation. The arrangement was not long-lived, as the LGOC had no wish to continue working Straker-Squire vehicles. Straker Squire Ltd had been placed in receivership by the first mortgage debenture holders in May 1925. A new company had been incorporated on 23 May 1925 to take over the business, but the arrangements which it made with a finance company had proved unsuccessful, and it seemed unlikely that spare parts would be obtainable in the future. Probably the most important fleet placed under Samuelson management was that of Edward Paul Ltd. These vehicles were replaced on 16 March 1927 by K-type buses working out of Nunhead garage.

In the latter part of 1926 the LGOC continued its policy of buying independents as opportunity presented, but most of the acquisitions were of single-bus companies or those with very small fleets. The one exception was provided by Redburn's Motor Services Ltd, one of the early operators. It had begun working on 5 May 1923 and had built up a fleet of 31 buses, working mainly on route 69 (Camberwell Green–Waltham Cross). Control was secured by the LGOC on 25 October 1926, but the organisation continued to work as an entity till 1 January 1928.

The year 1927 began with 395 independent buses still in operation, in the hands of 146 owners. Negotiations were in progress with four small proprietors, and these were taken over in January, but their fleets totalled only nine vehicles. There was then a pause, and the surviving independents showed little inclination to sell.

In March 1927, with Christopher Dodson as intermediary, Lord Ashfield made an offer on behalf of the LGOC to the Association of London Omnibus Proprietors Ltd for the purchase of a minimum of 350 buses belonging to members of the Association at £2,500 each. Sir Charles Cleveland, Secretary of the Association, replied that, at a very well-attended meeting of members, a secret ballot showed only seven members, owning 24 buses, in favour of acceptance. Although these overtures failed, they resulted in separate negotiations with two of the more substantial proprietors, namely, the Orange service of Haywood & Nowell Ltd, with twelve buses, which was acquired on 17 May, and the Overground fleet of about 37 buses, controlled by Walter James Dangerfield, but owned by various companies.

During this period there was parallel action in the form of a serious attempt to group the activities of the remaining independents into one company, under the leadership of Alfred Temple Bennett, the managing director of the Admiral fleet. As a result, the London Public Omnibus Co. Ltd was incorporated on 2 July 1927 with an authorised capital of £600,000, of which only half was issued. The Marquis of Winchester was chairman, A. T. Bennett managing director, and Sir Charles Cleveland director and secretary. The project was financed by a City group headed by Clarence Charles Hatry who was also a director of the London Public Company. A leading part in the management was taken by Philip Henry Roper Harris, whose business (the PHRH bus service) was absorbed. The first units were taken over in July, and, by the end of the year, no fewer than 68 undertakings with a total of about 190 buses had been absorbed. These were complete absorptions and the individual companies were not retained as subsidiaries. Eight further businesses, with a total of some 25 buses, were taken over in the early part of 1928.

As might be expected of a company formed in this way, the Public fleet initially comprised various makes of vehicle, although nearly 80 per cent of the rolling stock was of Dennis manufacture. A. T. Bennett had been rapidly replacing his Straker-Squires by Dennis buses, and, when the Admirals were taken over, only two Straker-Squires were left. These were withdrawn after a few weeks; two Daimlers were converted into lorries; and the Thornycrofts and Maudslays were sold. Before the London Public company had been formed, Bennett secured the approval of Scotland Yard in April 1927 to the introduction of rigid six-wheel double-deck Guy vehicles with covered tops, and the first of these appeared under the auspices of the Public company on 9 September, on route 529. The LGOC, however, had placed in service its experimental six-wheel LS 1, built by the AEC, on 4 June.

At the end of 1927 the number of independent owners had been reduced to 66, with 387 scheduled buses in operation, but the reduction from 146 to 66 in the number of owners was accounted for mainly by the merging of 68 undertakings into the London Public. During the year the LGOC itself had taken over control of only 13 independents, and of these only the Orange and Overground fleets (already mentioned) were other than small enterprises. On 1 January 1928, 52 of the 57 companies (formerly independent) in which the LGOC had acquired a controlling interest were absorbed either by the LGOC or by the Tramways (MET) Omnibus Co. Ltd. This involved the licences and schedules of 156 buses. Overground Ltd at the same time absorbed Dangerfield Ltd, Northern Omnibus Co. Ltd, and Nulli Secundus Omnibus Co. Ltd. From the same date, also, the fleet operated in the name of the South Metropolitan Electric Tramways & Lighting Co. Ltd was worked in the name of the Tramways (MET) Omnibus Co. Ltd. On 1 May 1928 the Cambrian licences and schedules were taken over by the LGOC. Since 25 January 1928 the passes of the LGOC and associated companies had been available on Cambrian buses.

While this rationalisation within the LGOC group was in progress, overtures were being made to the London Public, and it was announced on 26 March 1928 that the LGOC had acquired a controlling interest in that business. The immediate comment of the *Evening News* was that 'London's bus war has been reduced to a skirmish by the announcement'. At that time the London Public was stated to own 234 buses. Frank Pick, managing director of the Underground Group, told a Parliamentary Joint Select Committee in June 1928 that, during what he called the 'third period of amalgamation' of the LGOC, between January 1926 and December 1927, the LGOC had acquired the undertakings of 59 of the independent omnibus businesses established since the end of the First World War; they operated 234 buses. In addition, the LGOC had acquired control of the Cambrian, Overground and London Public companies, representing a further 273 buses. They had now absorbed, or obtained a controlling interest in, 75 separate companies. It is difficult to reconcile with precision these and other official figures which have been published, as it is not always clear whether the numbers of vehicles mentioned are those of buses scheduled for operation or the total fleets including spares. Also, closely-associated independents seem to have been treated at times as one unit although they comprised two or more separate limited companies. In addition, many of the statistics included in the annual reports of the London & Home Counties Traffic Advisory Committee are confined to buses operated on approved routes situated wholly or partly within a radius of ten miles from Charing Cross, an area which is not co-terminous with the Metropolitan Police District. Such variations, however, are slight, and do not affect the validity of the trends indicated.

At the end of 1928 there were still 201 independent buses in operation, owned by 59 proprietors, and this position remained substantially unchanged up to the time of the formation of the London Passenger Transport

Board. This may be explained by the stability of the situation which had been achieved, as this enabled a scheduled operator to make a good profit from the prevailing fare structure, and with a large measure of protection from competition. In the case of Birch Brothers, with its long experience of bus operation, and with a family tradition of playing an important part in the old horse-bus associations, this even extended to an agreement with the LGOC in August 1930 for a measure of co-ordination and withdrawal of competition. Odd workings which Birch had acquired from other proprietors were transferred to the LGOC, and the latter withdrew from service 214C (Hendon Central to Mill Hill) in favour of Birch. Joint operations were also established on service 526D (North Finchley to Wandsworth Bridge). In evidence before the Joint Select Committee on the London Passenger Transport Bill, Sir William McLintock, an eminent accountant, stated on 20 May 1931 that the profits of certain of the London independent omnibus proprietors during the years 1928, 1929, and 1930 ranged between 25·85 per cent and 64·72 per cent per annum on the capital employed. The London Traffic Act (1924) provided that in certain circumstances the Minister of Transport could order the reduction of bus fares, but this course was probably impracticable as it would have applied necessarily to all operators, and the LGOC profits (by reasons of that company's membership of the 'Common Fund') were being used to subsidise the tube railways, which would have been in financial difficulties without such help.

Coincidentally with these changes, the whole question of passenger transport services in London was under Parliamentary consideration. In August 1927 a sub-committee of the London & Home Counties Traffic Advisory Committee sent to the Cabinet a scheme for the co-ordination, joint management, and pooling of receipts of bus, tram and underground railway passenger transport services. There was no immediate response and eventually the Underground Group joined with the London County Council in promoting two enabling Bills during the 1928–9 session, providing for the common management and pooling of receipts of their respective transport undertakings, with authority for other parties to enter the proposed pool voluntarily. With a change of government in May 1929, the Bills were rejected, and it was announced that proposals for public ownership would be introduced. Further political changes, and delays occasioned largely by the desire to secure as great a measure of agreement as was practicable, prevented the proposals reaching the Statute Book until 13 April 1933, when the London Passenger Transport Board was incorporated by the Act 23 George V, cap. 14. It is enough here to record that provision was made for the compulsory acquisition by the new Board of all independent bus operators in the Metropolitan Police Area (and indeed in a larger area in which the new Board was given virtually monopolistic powers). Failing voluntary agreement, the terms were to be settled by an Arbitration Tribunal established under the Act. In all, 55 independent operators in the Metropolitan Police Area were involved, with a total of 278 buses; 54 such operators were scheduled to the Act, and one other (H. F. Phillips) had begun working after the schedule had been prepared. These acquisitions began on 1 November 1933 and were completed on 5 December 1934, when the eight buses of the Prince Omnibus Co. Ltd were transferred.

Within the period of slightly more than twelve years (5 August 1922 to 5 December 1934) the London bus attracted more interest with the travelling public, and indulged in more colourful and exciting operations, than ever before or since. If the London bus be regarded in isolation, the answer must be that there would have been little scope for the independent had the LGOC been more flexible. To give this facile reply, however, is to ignore the long-term value of the efforts made over many years to achieve co-ordinated transport, as envisaged as long ago as 1905 by the Royal Commission on London Traffic. The Underground railway system, which was vital to successful mass passenger movement, was uneconomic on the prevailing fare structure, and its subsidy by the associated buses has been mentioned already. Also, agreement with the company-owned tramways in the areas beyond the County of London gave a large measure of protection to such trams (as the first in the field in their area). When the activities of the independent operators broke through such arrangements, the travelling public showed a decided preference for the buses, which were more modern vehicles, were generally faster, and ran through without the necessity for changing. The resultant common area pooling agreement between the LGOC and the MET has been mentioned already.

After most of the independents had been purchased by the LGOC and its associates, this common area pooling agreement was cancelled on 1 January 1931 (coinciding with the new lease for 42 years from that date granted by the Middlesex County Council to the MET), but, to secure a measure of co-ordination where trams and LGOC buses worked on the same roads, arrangements were then established by which the traffic carried on such services was 'shared equitably' between the companies interested. This arrangement subsisted until the formation of the London Passenger Transport Board. (The financial interests of the British Electric Traction Co. Ltd in the London area tramways had been sold to the Underground Group in November 1928. An intermediate stage was formation of the London & Suburban Traction Co. Ltd jointly between Underground and BET, to consolidate the interests of Metropolitan Electric Tramways Ltd,

London United Tramways Ltd, and Tramways (MET) Omnibus Co. Ltd on 20 November 1912.) One result was that the intensity of bus services over the tram routes was reduced and on 22 March 1932 the through service between Winchmore Hill and Pimlico was discontinued. Residents and traders in the Winchmore Hill locality petitioned the Minister of Transport for the restoration of the service, but the Minister replied that he was unable to comply.

As indicated earlier, a noteworthy feature of the 1922–34 period of independent bus operation was that (unlike the earlier period of competition in 1905–12) the professional company promoter played very little part. Certainly, Clarence Hatry was concerned with the formation of the London Public company, but this was an exceptional instance. A company which attracted some attention by reason of its way of endeavouring to raise capital was the Henslowe Bus Co. Ltd. Various ex-servicemen were induced to invest sums in order to obtain employment, and this attracted the attention of the publication *John Bull* on 25 April 1925, particularly as the prospectus (bearing the name of Lord Rotherham as chairman) was circulated by a small issuing house after the first of the Restricted Streets Regulations had been made. This invalidated the assumption that what had been done could be continued and extended on a proportionate basis. *John Bull* characterised the proposal as a wild-cat scheme, and referred to the estimated profit of over 32 per cent per annum as the confident (but illogical) anticipation of 'this mug-hunting circular'. In the outcome few were misled, and the company expanded very little. It was in receivership from 31 May 1926 to 13 June 1927, and its business of five buses was acquired by the London Public on 19 December 1927. The affairs of this company are quoted to show that the professional company promoter did not overlook the independent buses, but his activities in this sphere were few and did not constitute a significant feature of the movement.

A fascinating side issue of this period of independent operation is that of the multiplicity of fleet names used. A distinctive word in large lettering was a feature of the horse bus for many years, but its purpose was different. Normally it was an indication of route rather than fleet, and often was used by numerous proprietors working in association. Names such as Atlas, City Atlas, Favorite, Paragon and so forth, gave an indication of route in an age when literacy was not universal. Many other names were exclusively indications of general direction, such as Putney, Paddington, Bayswater, Camden Town. The names of the 1922–34 independents gave no such indication of route, and the principal purpose served seems to have been to indicate that the vehicles were *not* General, thus appealing to popular sympathy with the 'small man' against the alleged 'monopoly'. Obviously

Admiral and Field Marshal were in contrast to General; Genial was a colourful imitation; and Overground and Overland contrasted with Underground (the name of the LGOC parent). Latin names appealed to some proprietors (was this because of the latin origin of the word *omnibus*?) and produced Nil Desperandum, Nulli Secundus, Peraeque, Pro Bono Publico, Regina, and Ubique. Patriotism may have accounted for the many words and combinations such as Britannia, British Lion, Dominion, Empire, Empire's Best, Monarch, Regent, Regal, Royal, Royal Blue, Royal Highlander, and St George. It is improbable that Earl, Gordon, Nelson, and the like, paid tribute to the peerage or to national heroes; the local hostelry or street name is the more probable. Street names certainly account for Henslowe and Scarboro', and a garage name for Claremont. Perhaps, surprisingly, the portmanteau word with humorous intent was not often adopted, although we had Havaride, Superbus, and Uneedus.

The last solid-tyred bus was retired on 10 September 1937. The last petrol-engined bus was withdrawn in 1950. The last of the famous open-top 34-seat B-type buses of 1910 was scheduled to be withdrawn from service on 12 October 1926; actually B-type were retained as spares and the last actual withdrawal of a double-deck B-type was made on 9 August 1927; the last single-deck B was sent to the scrap heap on 19 October 1927, over a year after the official date of withdrawal.

9
BET Companies

A German who made a comprehensive study of electrical engineering was Emile Garcke. He became secretary of Brush Electrical Engineering (at first known as Falcon Engine Works) in 1883 at the age of 27 and in due course became interested in and a recognised authority on electric tramway development. The British Electric Traction (Pioneer) Co. Ltd was formed in 1895 with city financial backing and the British Electric Traction Co. Ltd itself was registered on 26 October 1896. Emile Garcke had already given evidence on light railways on behalf of the London Chamber of Commerce to a Board of Trade committee, as a result of which the Light Railways Act was passed. This gave a fillip to the promotion of what were virtually street tramways by an easier means than the procedure laid down by the Tramways Act, which also had some penal clauses by which the tramway virtually had to be given to the local authorities after 21 years. This inhibited the process of investing in electrification of them and Garcke's campaigns for fairer treatment of investors in tramways caused him many disputes with local government. The British Electric Traction Co. Ltd set up tramway undertakings in many areas and electricity generating concerns in rather fewer, although before the grid system had been thought of any small traction concern had to have its individual power supply.

The Birmingham & District Investment Trust was registered as the Birmingham & Midland Tramways Ltd in 1883 and it was part of the network of Black Country tramways that British Electric Traction invested in for electrification after 1896. This company had a joint controlling interest in the Birmingham & Midland Motor Omnibus Co. Ltd, which was for some years the largest bus concern in the country with some 2,000 vehicles. Formed in 1904, it acquired the Birmingham Motor Express Co. Ltd and the bus undertakings of the City of Birmingham Tramways Co. Ltd and the Birmingham District Power & Traction Co. Ltd and Leamington & Warwick Transport Co. Ltd, Stratford-on-Avon Blue Motors Ltd and Kemp & Shaw Ltd. Operations began in May 1905 and motors ceased to work in October 1907, a reversion being made to horses for five years; when a start was made again it was with a fleet of Tilling-Stevens petrol-electric buses.

During the First World War the company took over operation of the Worcestershire Motor Transport Co. Ltd which began operation on 14 August 1914 and soon afterwards had its buses impressed by the War Office; the BMMO petrol-electrics were not eagerly sought by the War Department so that the BMMO was able to maintain skeleton services over the Worcestershire company's routes, with the aid of coal-gas fuel, carried in balloons, unmolested. The North Warwickshire Motor Omnibus & Traction Co. Ltd, formed to take over J. Thornburn's services round Tamworth and Nuneaton from 11 October 1913, came to be operated by Midland 'Red' vehicles for the same reasons. Rather curiously there always seemed to be reluctance to admit the connection with Stratford Blue and I remember one day when I was seeing the then chief engineer and in the course of our perambulations round the central overhaul depot he discovered a Stratford Blue vehicle which had been sent to Carlyle depot for some heavy accident repairs; he was most wrath that some underling should have misguidedly perpetrated such a deed.

Equally strong characters had occupied the chair of the chief engineer at an earlier date – the feud between the Irish traffic manager Orlando Cecil Power and fiery L. G. Wyndham Shire was well-known throughout the industry; the story of one celebrated occasion was that Power said in a report to the chairman that the capacity of the Rugby garage was 40 more than Shire thought reasonable. To prove his point Shire took the wheels off 40 of the fleet and next morning the traffic staff arrived to find 40 of the buses standing on barrels!

There was a green-baize-covered door between the traffic and engineering sides of the headquarters at Bearwood like the portals of servants' quarters in a Victorian country house and woe betide any junior member of the staff who essayed any liaison between the departments. Even I as a visitor from the technical press had to prove to Power the first time I met him that I had no intention (on that occasion at any rate!) of doing an article about those infamous engineers.

It all arose back in 1912 when Shire arrived as a brash young chief engineer from the Deal branch of the company. When he wanted to order some cigars and to prove he was credit-worthy told the tobacconist that he was chief engineer of BMMO and might even be made general manager before long. Power heard about it the next day, thought the worst, and never ceased to devise schemes to deflate Shire's self-conceit. It was not alleviated until the Second World War when Shire resigned and was replaced by Donald Sinclair, the brilliant Scot who had been assistant chief engineer of the Northern General group for whom he had designed side-engined vehicles. On Power's death in 1943 – literally in harness, at a meeting of the Public Transport Association – Sinclair became general manager.

Shire was not a bus engineer to accept conventional designs. In 1922, for example, he had 40 Tilling-Stevens double-deckers with front-entrance bodies and knifeboard seating on the upper deck, rankly ugly, but suited to what he was trying to achieve for the traffic department.

In one of his phases of co-operation with Power, in 1924 Shire designed a lightweight high performance pneumatic-tyred single-deck bus with driver behind the engine for 31 or 32 passengers and followed this in 1926 and 1927 by 34- and 37-seat driver-beside-engine front-entrance models which had the roof trimmed to use the minimum amount of material and minimise the weight which came out at 3 tons 15 cwt. These vehicles were known as SOS, but most of them had the names of their operators cast in the radiator header. Designed to combat jitney* competition, they were only available to BET associates and in practice this meant a big Midland Red fleet and 956 supplied to Northern General, Ortona, Peterborough Electric Traction, Potteries, and Trent companies. Under Donald Sinclair a few rear-engined buses built by Shire were converted to 40-seat under-

---

*The jitney had a great vogue in the USA from 1914 onwards, especially in Los Angeles where there were more than 700 at the end of that year. The name is said to derive from a negro jail trusty called Jedney who used to smuggle tobacco into prison for fellow inmates. For every dime he received he delivered a nickel's worth of tobacco; hence a 'Jedney's worth', later corrupted to a 'jitney's worth' came to be a way of referring to a five-cents' worth of anything. In England, of course, ordinary BMMO fares were undercut and the vehicles chosen were on pneumatic tyres and fast in acceleration, hence the good done to the company by the SOS which was light and could show a clean pair of heels to competitors.

floor engined vehicles, the engines being turned on their sides for wartime conversion.

The advantages of these vehicles becoming generally apparent, not only BMMO built large numbers of single-deck under-floor-engined and chassis-less vehicles, but two under-floor-engined double-deckers. While there were many imitators of the single-deck type among commercial chassis-builders, there were no commercial repeats of the double-decker, although it showed a fairly easy way to the 80-seat bus. The ability of the under-floor-engined bus or coach designer to get many seats in on a short-wheelbase single-decker (which could seat up to 44 and with length relaxations up to 52 or more) was remarkable and when I went for a ride with Sinclair's test driver, Ransome, in 1943 I was astonished by his ability to go past the doors of the garage at Bearwood before his wheels turned towards them.

In the 15 years between 1924 and 1939 this remarkable company built 2,960 buses. From 1930 a six-cylinder version of the SOS engine was produced and in 1932 a few double-deckers began to be produced, these having rather remarkable front-entrance bodies. The SOS version of the compression-ignition engine, that ran on cheaper diesel oil, appeared in 1935, and although from 1939 to 1945 the company had to make do with Daimler and Guy double-deckers to wartime specifications, from 1944 onwards it resumed making its own designs, if only to give the BET an insight into manufacturing costs. In the decade from 1944 no fewer than 750 mostly monocoque single-deckers – now to the designs of Seymour C. Vince, chief engineer, were added to the bus fleet and 270 more 'S14' type were on order in 1954; in 1954 75 coaches were placed in service and in 1954 373 63-seat buses of the 'D7' type were under construction.

Eventually, about 1962–3, British Leyland persuaded the company that there was merit in buying standard Leyland Leopard chassis with 53-seat bodies and Daimler Fleetline rear-engined front-entrance 77-seat double-deckers; construction of comparatively small numbers of BMMO vehicles at Carlyle works ceased. But it performed a valuable function for Midland Red and the bus and coach industry (I had the pleasure of pointing out the merits of the under-floor-engined vehicle to Pilkington of Leyland on one post-war occasion when he had cast doubts on it and was surprised to hear that BMMO had 400 such units in course of construction; Leyland Worldmasters and other under-floor-engined models followed almost within months) and the 1,700 or so BMMO vehicles built since the end of the war were by no means waste of money to the BET group. Valuable lessons in dealing with fibreglass bodies and their repair were among the benefits and BMMO passengers had comfort to be derived from independent front suspension at a time when it was an undreamed-of luxury on most public service vehicles.

The BMMO territory reached to Shrewsbury in 1918, Leicester in 1922; in 1934 some routes round Canon Pyon in Herefordshire were passed to the Yeomans family, a reversal of the usual process of aggrandisement supposed to be pursued by large companies.

The Northern General Transport Co. Ltd group of bus companies was founded by the BET on 29 November 1913 to consolidate the bus interests of the Gateshead & District Tramways Company, the Tynemouth & District Transport Co. Ltd and the Jarrow & District Electric Traction Co. Ltd and later it took responsibility for Sunderland District Omnibus Co. Ltd, Wakefield's Motors Ltd and it obtained a controlling interest in Tyneside Tramways and Tramroads Company. With a thin belt of territory on the north of the Tyne the Northern General group thus operated a roughly triangular area of County Durham, westward as far as Consett and south to the county town. Although fares in the area were below average the company had been relatively prosperous and was able to issue 138,000 ordinary shares as a bonus to shareholders by capitalising reserves. On 7 May 1913 the Gateshead company began bus operation in extension of its trams with Daimler buses and on 1 January 1914 it handed the services to Northern General.

The company produced some large capacity side-engined single-deck buses (with engines under the offside of the passenger compartment) to operate on routes where low bridges rendered a high capacity single-deck vehicle desirable. Some coaches were also produced on this pattern and I remember seeing one on several occasions on the Great North Road on an Isle of Wight tour from Newcastle. More recently the Northern General engineering department has distinguished itself by rebuilding a Leyland Titan PD3/4 72-seater for one-man operation with a driver-behind-engine layout and front entrance with 68 seats. This was a preparatory exercise before converting a number of London Transport Routemaster vehicles. The argument was the lower maintenance cost of the Routemaster – £800 at recertification overhaul, compared with £1,300 either for Atlantean or Fleetline.

In 1974 D. A. Cox, the current chief engineer of the Northern group of companies, made 32 modifications to a Leyland National single-decker which improved its performances. This demonstrates the co-operation between manufacturer and operator that has been beneficial to the whole industry and differs sharply from the suspicion that at one time prevailed, especially between regular manufacturers and operators who built their own buses, some of whom, notably Bristol and the London General (as AEC), joined the ranks of regular manufacturers after they became established.

Finally, it must be noted that Northern General Transport is in the category of operating companies that emulated the child that swallowed its parent in that it became the main company of the BET in the north-east and among its subsidiaries was the Gateshead company that originally gave it birth. The LNER also directly invested in this BET subsidiary.

Another BET direct subsidiary was the Potteries Motor Traction Co. Ltd, registered in 1898 as the Potteries Electric Traction Co. Ltd, the change of name having taken place in 1933. There was no railway shareholding in this company owing to the shares being unattractive to the LMS and LNER companies at the time of railway investment in bus undertakings, this situation arising from the burden of tramway debt with which the undertaking had been saddled. In 1896 the BET obtained control of the North Staffordshire Tramways, which had been steam-operated since 1881 and descended from an undertaking founded with horse haulage by the formidable American George Francis Train. The Potteries Electric Traction Company was formed on 28 June 1898 and electric operation of the tramways began on 16 May 1899; by 1905 there were over 30 miles of tramway route. Experimental operation of steam buses began in 1901 and in December 1904 three front-entrance open-top double-deck buses with stairs behind the driver were operated on Brush chassis, but permanent working of a bus fleet did not begin until 22 December 1913. In August 1914 half-a-dozen more were acquired, but the war made a heavy setback which was not overcome until the Armistice. Buses were looked on as feeders to the trams until after 1922, when there were 28 buses in the fleet.

The Stoke-on-Trent City Council wanted to be rid of the trams but could not reach agreement with the company, and tended to favour independent operators rather than the Potteries concern. The company then appealed to the Ministry of Transport and 70 licences for buses in the city were then granted to it in substitution for the tram services.

The last tramcar ran on 11 July 1928, but in Stoke-on-Trent by the time of the Road Traffic Act (1930) there were 55 operators licensed by the corporation, running 200 buses in competition with the 'establishment'. Under the 1930 Act and its impartial administration, the company was able to advance and it purchased some of its competitors. The name was changed to Potteries Motor Traction Co. Ltd in 1933 and it has become widely known as 'PMT'. Some of the more important rivals purchased included, on 20 April 1944, the ABC as the Associated Bus Companies Ltd running 60 buses, mostly on the 'main line', as the principal north and south route through the city is known; in May and June 1951 Raymond Birch, the then chairman, made a determined effort to absorb other big competitors; Mainwaring Brothers, Audley, 22 buses; Brown's Motor Company (Tunstall) Ltd, Burslem, 43 buses; Thomas Tilstone & Sons Ltd, Burslem, 32 buses; Stoke-on-Trent Motors Ltd, Stoke, 30 buses; Milton Bus Service Ltd, Milton, 24 buses; and Wells Motor Services Ltd, Biddulph, 20 buses, in February 1953. Later in that year a 126-vehicle garage in Clough Street, Hanley, was opened at a cost of only £500 a bus housed and the services were reorganised. The relaxation of the vehicle length restrictions was particularly valuable to PMT, as well as to Northern General, as it enabled a more economical capacity of single-deck buses to be operated on many routes, seating 40, and later over 50, passengers in one vehicle. The concession that many concerns were compelled to use was, however, the large capacity one-man bus. A few routes in the Potteries area have ultra-low bridges, requiring specially squat-built vehicles.

Potteries Motor Traction were early users of pneumatic tyres on its fleet. Its engineering was always maintained at a very high standard when its general manager, Warwick Wroth, was a genial and witty chief. He listened to a lecture on the design of bus stations in which the author advocated a design in which buses should park on an island site, reversing away for a few yards to resume their onward journey. Wroth's contribution to the discussion consisted of one sentence only: 'My silly buggers run into things when they are going forwards.' On another occasion, when we were looking round the overhaul shops, a youthful engineer's mate tried to hide from his general manager that he had been out for refreshment for his senior in mid-morning. The wind was taken out of the boy's sails by Wroth's saying: 'All right, boy, don't fall over yourself by trying to keep your tea bucket from my sight.'

The South Wales Transport Co. Ltd also originated in a BET tramway undertaking, the Swansea Tramways, and it began operation on 2 May 1914, no less than 107 years after the first of its railed undertakings, then known as the Oystermouth Railway or Tramroad, began public operation. It had some legal aspects of a railway, but from 1929 was operated by 106-seat electric tramcar type of vehicles. As I wrote in *The Golden Age of Tramways*, everyone must be indebted to Charles E. Lee for his book *The Swansea and Mumbles Railway*, in which the complicated relationships of the Oystermouth undertaking and the Swansea & Mumbles Railways Ltd and the Swansea Improvements & Tramways Company are set forth. The latter's bus-operating subsidiary, like the Northern General, eventually swallowed its own parent and so on 17 September 1929 was assigned the remainder of the 999-year lease of the Swansea & Mumbles Railway which it now electrified from 2 March 1929. The South Wales Transport Co. took over the Swansea Improvements & Tramways, incorporated in 1874, the Swansea Corporation tramway powers of 1902 and Glamorgan County Council's tramway powers of 1905. Replacement of Swansea trams by buses took effect under the Swansea & District Transport Act of 1936. So, as Sidney Garcke once recounted to me, his father laid down the electric tramways in Swansea between 1898 when Emile Garcke and the BET obtained control and 1900 (BET obtained almost the entire share capital of SI & T in 1930–1) and the son took them up once the go-ahead was given, so fast that the whole operation was completed on 29 June 1937. For the same reason as the Potteries undertaking, the complications of tramway share capital, there was no railway shareholding in the South Wales Transport Co. Ltd. A Bill for the abandonment of the Swansea & Mumbles concern was passed in 1958–9 session of Parliament and provided for the vesting of the undertaking in the South Wales Transport Company for the unexpired remainder of the 999-year lease and for the winding-up of the former owners. The offer was made in September 1958, after 156 years of operation, in anticipation of a further fall in the railway receipts. The last day of railway operation was 5 January 1960 on which morning a local daily paper published a note 'Last night in the rain the Mumbles Railway died'; any historian who slavishly believes the local press beyond all else might easily record this abandonment as 4 January. To those to whom such things matter, it may be important; this particular record came about through a decision to make the changeover on a Tuesday after the morning peak and is certainly a lesson to historians.

The first SWT bus garage in Swansea was the yard of a builders' merchant. The South Wales Transport Company's bus undertaking made rapid progress; by 1924, a decade from the start, there were some 16 services. At Neath the depot of the gas-engined Corporation trams became an early SWT garage and there was an hourly service to Neath and Margam. Two central Swansea housing estates are Mayhill and Townhill, both up steep banks, and Saurer buses were purchased for them, equipped with sprag gear as a safeguard against running back. In 1952 the Balfour Beatty Llanelli trolleybus system, which began as a tram undertaking, was replaced by SWT buses and in 1962 the business of J. James & Son Ltd of Ammanford made one of the most notable purchasers of fleets for South Wales Transport, which now has 497 buses and coaches. Up Swansea Vale to Ystradgynlais – nearly a 2-hour run – there was a 40-minute headway and as far as Pontardawe buses every 20 minutes. Swansea was linked to Llanelli and there were connections from Llanelli to Pembrey, Pontardulais, Ammanford and Cross Hands, the two last-mentioned by GWR bus; the GWR also advertised an ambitious series of connections between Neath Station and Carmarthen Station. As the South Wales Transport undertaking has expanded it has gradually grown to link Brecon with the Gower;

in fact I travelled from Brecon to Rhosilli and back in a day while staying in the former town as far back as 1946. Pembrey was reached in 1915 and Gowerton by 1916.

Almost parallel with the BET and purchased by it in 1931 was the development of the National Electric Construction Co. Ltd which was registered on 16 July 1897 as the National Electric Free Wiring Co. Ltd and changed its title in 1899 to National Electric Wiring Co. Ltd and again in 1903. It became a holding company with a controlling interest in several concerns. Among these were Mexborough & Swinton Traction Co. Ltd, which originally operated, from 1907, a surface contact tramway undertaking in Yorkshire; overhead wires were rapidly installed in August 1908, the conventional system being found more reliable; in 1915 two short trolleybus routes expanded the tram service, using solid-tyred 28-seat Daimler-Brush trolleybuses, and the local authorities exacted a payment of 3s 8d per car mile as a contribution towards the maintenance of the roads. Along the tram route these trolleybuses took their power from the overhead and completed the circuit by a skate in the tramline, except when it jumped out, the task of returning it keeping the conductor fairly busy. In 1922 AEC trolleybuses, also with Brush bodies, replaced the original rolling stock. AEC motor buses (petrol-driven) appeared in the same year, a service being inaugurated from Mexborough to Bolton-upon-Dearne and Goldthorpe; other services in the nature of feeders to the trolleybus and tramcar routes being begun in subsequent years to 1927, at which time powers to replace the trams with trolleybuses were obtained and in 1929 bus powers over the trolleybus route were obtained.

Although these gave a monopoly to the renamed Mexborough & Swinton Traction Company, a joint running agreement was made with the Yorkshire Traction Co. Ltd in the interests of providing through services. The last tram ran on 20 March 1929. The 1929 rolling stock was 32-seat Garrett trolleybuses on pneumatic tyres and in 1950 the last rolling stock change brought Sunbeam 35-seat vehicles on the streets of Mexborough and Swinton. In 1950, 38 vehicles carried over 16 million passengers whereas in the 22 years of tramway operation 82 million passengers were carried. Some trolleybus service was abandoned in 1954, but with higher capacity diesel buses being available (the largest trams were 72-seat double-deckers, 80 passenger capacity with Weymann bodies on Leyland Atlantean chassis) the trolleybuses were abandoned as a whole on 26 March 1961. The day was an occasion for some junketing locally and Harley Drayton, the chairman of the company, and of the BET, made a ceremonial drive of one of the last trolleybuses in service.

Another NEC investment was the Oxford Transport Trust Ltd, which embraced the interests of the Barnett and Phillips families and the rather complicated structure under which the five 4-ft gauge routes of the City of Oxford & District Tramways Co. Ltd of 1879 were to be electrified by the NEC as a 4 ft-8½ in. gauge system extending as far as Upper Wolvercot, Iffley, Cowley and New Headington. For this purpose a new company, City of Oxford Electric Tramways Co. Ltd, was formed on 6 December 1906. Overhead wires were unthinkable in a city of the calibre of Oxford and, as we have seen, the Dolter surface contact system that had been sponsored by the NEC had turned out to have some considerable defects. To safeguard its position the tramways company began negotiation with the Corporation of Oxford, but the citizens became very impatient as the ancient horse trams appeared out of date and the tracks became more and more decrepit. On 30 December 1913 one of them, one William Morris, afterwards Lord Nuffield, put a Daimler bus to work in the city, mainly to show what was being missed by the failure to modernise local transport. This brought matters to a head; the horse trams came to an end, but faded out so gradually that nobody seems to have recorded a precise date. In February 1914 the bus fleets of Morris and the City of Oxford Electric Tramways were merged and the Corporation and the company made an arrangement for the purchase by the corporation of the track and its removal from the streets. In addition the company was to have a bus monopoly of the city services for 42 years.

During the First World War the fleet continued largely to be composed of Daimler vehicles, unlike London where the War Office seems to have made a point of requisitioning Daimler chassis. There was also a resemblance to Cambridge, where the Ortona Motor Company also relied during the years of the First World War on McCurd and Austin 3-ton chassis for the maintenance of its 34-seat double-deck bus fleet.

At one time the City of Oxford company had the reputation of not trusting its buses more than a radius of 25 miles from the headquarters garage, which rather cramped its style on private hires; maybe it was a canard intended to explain why it did not develop any long-distance services. Certainly coach trips from London to Oxford were provided by vehicles of the London General company; the Great Western Railway Cheltenham and Oxford service was passed to Bristol Tramways & Carriage Co. Ltd without the co-ordination of the coach and train service that was such a prominent feature of its GWR administration, and the express coach services between London and Oxford were operated by others. Two Varsity undertakings were purchased through Thomas Tilling Ltd, the service from London to Oxford operated by Varsity Express Motors Ltd passing to United Counties Omnibus Co. Ltd in the beginning of 1934. The operation missed by City of Oxford is stressed by the fact that in 1922 South Midland

Touring & Transport Co. Ltd was set up with headquarters in Oxford itself and was a 60-vehicle company served in the metropolis by London Coastal Coaches Ltd in a little over a decade. In the meantime Black & White Motorways was jointly purchased by Midland Red, Bristol and City of Oxford, thus giving the latter undertaking a third interest in an important coach operator if not a direct share in operation. City of Oxford thus had an interest in the exchange of coach traffic that took place at the Black & White Cheltenham coach station.

In South Wales the NEC in 1920 took an interest in South Wales Commercial Motors Ltd which operated between Newport and Chepstow, on routes between Cardiff and Penarth, Cardiff and Bridgend and from Bridgend to Porthcawl, Maesteg, Pontypridd and Blaengarw. The company was a subsidiary of Rhondda Tramways Company, which leased its tracks from the Rhondda UDC, began operations in 1908 and completed the system in 1912. Through services with the tramways of Pontypridd UDC began on 14 July 1919, and were unique in Wales. The company made an endeavour towards rubber-tyred vehicles by initiating trolley buses between Williamstown and Gilfach in December 1914, but owing to the terrible state of the roads the service had to be suspended in March 1915 and was not resumed until motor buses were brought back on the route in January 1921. On the previous 4 August the company began operation of lorry buses on ex-WD chassis (bought from the LGOC in 1920 after London service) on a Clydach Vale and Tonypandy route. Despite the uncomfortable vehicles and a capacity of only 27 seats the receipts per bus mile were 26.79d. The Rhondda trams were abandoned altogether on 2 February 1934 after which the bus business continued to develop; in 1937 the fleet totalled 131, mostly AEC double-deck oil-engined vehicles. The numbers rose to 161 by 1969.

When the Great Western Railway invested in South Wales Commercial Motors, that company had 300 buses and was renamed Western Welsh Omnibus Co. Ltd. Previously, on 11 July 1927 the Newport–Chepstow area, which had been somewhat remote from the main body of routes based on Cardiff and Bridgend, had been separated as the South Mon Motor Company and taken in by Gloucestershire Transport Ltd; it became known as Red & White Services (South Mon Section) to indicate its association with the J. H. Watts group. By 1969 the Western Welsh fleet strength was 576. The headquarters offices and garages of the NEC companies had a style of architecture which can only be described as 'distinctive'. Like other companies which have committed parenticide Western Welsh, under the direction of National Bus Company, has absorbed its Rhondda parent. Other important absorptions include on 1 November 1933 Lewis & James Ltd, and in the same month Bassetts (Eastern Valleys), June 1935

Pontyberem Transport and in November 1935 Thomas White & Co. (Cardiff & Barry) Ltd from the family owners of which management material has been derived by the BET.

National Electric Construction characteristics observable in the Devon General Omnibus & Touring Co. Ltd included the one-time presence of a Dolter surface-contact tramway as its nucleus in Torquay. Here the Dolter surface-contact system lasted until 1911 and the bus undertakings of Devon General founded in 1919 by John Mill and of Torquay Tramways were merged on 1 June 1922. The Devon General fleet, which had contained some AEC B- and K-type buses, settled down as a Daimler, ADC and Albion fleet, with a few Leyland coaches and took in as a separate entity Fleet Cars in 1924, the Torquay Chelston Car Ltd in 1926 and B. G. Babington of Ashburton in 1927. The DGO & T fleet totalled 147 in 1929 and 239 in 1937. Under the National Bus Company the Devon General fleet has been merged with that of Western National, although most of the former DG rolling stock continues to bear the Devon General fleet name and the light red livery favoured by the National Bus Group – instead of the rich red employed by DGO & T under BET auspices – while Western National is green and white, so some variety is still discernible.

A BET subsidiary especially intended to deal with bus operating was created in 1905 and named British Automobile Development Co. Ltd. The less inauspicious title of British Automobile Traction Co. Ltd was adopted in 1910. There were three ways of forming BAT operating companies; some were formed as branches of BAT such as Thames Valley or North Western Road Car; others were amalgamations to gather a concern with enough know-how and weight to get into business. East Kent and East Yorkshire were in this category. Others were existing businesses, such as Maidstone & District Motor Services Ltd.

The East Kent Road Car Co. Ltd was registered on 11 August 1916 and was the first to combine the interests of the Tilling and BET groups when owing to the circumstances of the First World War five undertakings with headquarters close to one another had more to gain from co-operation than from going their separate ways. The agreements Thomas Tilling Ltd had made with the LGOC had caused it to seek expansion in the provinces after 1914 and one of these outlets was Folkestone & District Road Car Co. Ltd. In 1908 the British Automobile Traction Co. Ltd established a branch at Deal. The reason was the abandonment of motor-bus operation by the Birmingham & Midland Motor Omnibus Co. Ltd becoming persuaded that the motor bus was too unreliable to be tolerated. Through the enterprise of Sidney Garcke, the son of the managing director, who was then 21, the motor buses did not get banned from Birmingham out of hand; it had occurred to him that in the more level area of Leamington and Warwick the motors might give a better account of themselves and three of them were moved to the new location. Six others were sent on a longer voyage (Sidney Garcke himself driving one of them) and travelled the best part of 200 miles, in the course of which they picked up new bodies from Birch Brothers of Kentish Town, five of them receiving Birch charabanc bodies with a light canopy suited to a holiday area and the sixth, Q-1283, a new double-deck body by the Brush Company after overhaul to make them as reliable as they could be in their new sphere.

L. G. Wyndham Shire and Arthur Twidle were the engineering assistants to Sidney Garcke, whose judgment about the traffic potentialities of Deal and Kingsdown was fully justified. Service with three of the fleet began early in April 1908 and the other three vehicles, Garcke records, were necessary as spares. London & South Coast Motor Services (1915) Ltd brought W. P. Allen as a director to East Kent in November 1933 and represented pioneer interests in long-distance operation dating from 1905 with large-diameter rear-wheel vehicles. In 1928 it acquired Co-operative Transport of Folkestone.

Walter Flexman French had formed a company called Margate & District Motor Services Ltd, and two other small firms were Ramsgate Motor Coaches (Griggs) Ltd and Wacher & Co. Ltd who were primarily coal merchants, but who ran buses between Canterbury and Herne Bay and Canterbury and Whitstable. Two fundamental reasons for the formation of the combined company were in the minds of the constituents – dissipation of resources in wartime and difficulties in finding spares. The rolling stock totalled 80 vehicles in the first year, but the difficulty of running a bus undertaking at that time is seen when it is realised that only 40 were runners at the end of 1916.

In the first 25 years of the company's existence it purchased 41 other undertakings, notable among which were the Folkestone area of A. M. Kemp-Gee Ltd (trading as Cambrian Coaches) which had acquired W. Buck & Son in 1928. At this time a dramatic find of coaches hidden in caves under Dover Castle to hide them from repossession by the hire-purchase financiers was made. The Hastings–Fairlight–Pett Level service of A. Timpson & Sons was bought in March 1934. On 1 January 1937 the Isle of Thanet Electric Supply Co. Ltd and Dover Corporation tramways were both taken over, the Thanet trams being abandoned on 24 March 1937. The M T Co. Ltd, a pioneer London–Margate coach operator, was taken over in May 1937. This was a company which had been very unfairly refused licences, despite its early appearance on the road, by the first south-eastern traffic commissioner and issued a very dramatic pamphlet on the

25 (*above*) The Mascot, a country carrier's Ford, at Gloucester Green, Oxford

24 (*opposite*) The 1928 Guy trolleybus restored by the Hastings Tramways Company and decorated for the Coronation in 1953. Probably the only open-top trolleybus in service

26 (*below*) The length of Loch Ness by bus in 1935

matter under the title *And the first shall be last.* Like all British Automobile Traction undertakings East Kent was highly individual in its management. Alfred Baynton, secretary and joint general manager, for example, did not see the purpose of service numbers until I advocated them to him on a visit on behalf of *Modern Transport.* There was, of course, no pressure on him to introduce them. Sydney Garcke was the chairman for over a quarter of a century and Thomas Wolsey, Tilling's son-in-law, at an early stage became deputy-chairman after the Tilling group demanded representation on the board.

Maidstone & District Motor Services Ltd was registered on 22 March 1911 and was one of several country-town bus concerns started up by Walter Flexman French, mentioned in connection with Margate. He had a wagonette service in the suburbs of south-west London and then began services at Aldershot, Guildford and the Maidstone, Gravesend & District Omnibus Service in 1912, 1914 and 1908 respectively. He secured British Automobile Traction backing for the Maidstone & District venture in 1911 and after then success was assured. It is interesting that later Tilling was represented on the board of M & D by Walter Wolsey, showing a Tilling investment in the Maidstone company, after that budding combine had become convinced of the rightness of provincial investment.

The Maidstone company provided an unusual father-and-son succession in general management when George Flexman French became General Manager. In 1917 the business of E. Neve of Sutton Valence was absorbed. Neve had begun with a steam bus about 1908 but operating difficulties became acute in the First World War. The BET-owned Gravesend & Northfleet Electric Tramways Ltd ceded its non-local bus business to M & D in 1920. This was trading as North Kent Motor Services Ltd formed in August 1913 and the remainder on 1 March 1929, the trams having ceased on 28 February.

One of the first tramway abandonments in England was that of the Sheerness & District Electric Power & Traction Co. Ltd, to replace which the Sheppey Motor Transport Co. Ltd was formed on 25 May 1917. It began operation on 2 July 1917. The Sheerness trams ceased on 7 July 1917. The motor-bus company which replaced them had members of the Standen family group until towards the end of the war, when owing to the isolation of the Isle of Sheppey it was taken over by T. Standen & Sons, through the severance of the King's Ferry bridge.

The Chatham & District Light Railways Company obtained its first light railways order on 17 August 1899, the last line opened being to Borstal in August 1908. It was a Balfour Beatty subsidiary company. The system closed on 30 September 1930 and was replaced by Leyland Titan buses, which were operated as a separate concern by Maidstone for the Chatham & District Traction Co. Ltd because of the statutory obligations, a brown band being added to the green livery. A. Timpson & Sons Ltd in 1925 bought West Hill Services at Hastings and also acquired Skinners of Ore in 1933. Weald of Kent of Headcorn was taken over on 1 November 1933. This company, managed by Captain C. E. E. Palin, had 13 vehicles, including two Thornycroft Cygnets and four 14-seat Bean buses. Only a chance putting off of an appointment with Palin, who had advertised for a traffic manager, saved me from being on the fatal train from Cannon Street on 24 August 1927, which came off the track near Polhill Tunnel. As things developed, I stayed in the haulage business until I was ready to make the change to technical journalism in 1935.

In February 1934 A. Timpson & Sons, the London business of which had passed to Thomas Tilling Ltd by arrangement with the LGOC, sold its Hastings business to Maidstone & District. As a Catford firm the coach service to Hastings began as a seasonal service in 1919. By 1923 the Timpson Hastings coaches called at the Cambrian Coaching & Goods Transport Soho Square office twice daily, in exchange Cambrian carrying Timpson Thanet traffic, but this operated only until 2 June and for a time in the summer of 1929 Timpson pooled receipts with Orange Luxury Coaches (Keith & Boyle (London) Ltd). In 1924 West Hill services ran 26-seat Vulcan runabout buses on two short routes from Hastings Memorial to Manor Road and Priory Park. By 1926 they were running under the fleet name of Timpson's West Hill Services in a cream livery instead of the silver or aluminium livery associated with Timpson's in Catford. In 1928 ADC/416 and Leyland Lion vehicles were bought. Skinner's, who had begun a Station to Top of High Street Ore service with a 34-seat Leyland in 1914, replaced by four Leyland Leviathan in 1925, were acquired in 1933. Besides the local routes, which extended to Bulverhythe, Wishing Tree (on the Crowhurst Road) and Pett Level, the London–Hastings coach services were transferred to Maidstone & District on 21 March 1934.

Through the formation of the London Passenger Transport Board on 1 July 1933 the Maidstone Company took over the operations of both bus companies centred on Tunbridge Wells. These operated in strenuous competition in the roaring twenties and then in what the journal of the Omnibus Society termed 'unfriendly co-operation', dictated by economic circumstances and after 1931 by the Traffic Commissioners. After some promoters' efforts to secure a tramway system in this hilly residential and spa town Spittles Tunbridge Wells Omnibus Company with iron-tyred horse buses began working to Pembury, Langton and Penshurst and the business was then bought by E. & A. P. Aubin, who developed it as the

Tunbridge Wells, Southborough & District Omnibus Co. Ltd, who had over 100 horses, stabled in villages surrounding the town. It is an interesting comment that 24 horses had to be destroyed and replaced by purchases in London owing to an attack of mange. When motor operation first made its appearance in the metropolis in the form of 10-seat wagonettes the Tunbridge Wells and District Motor Company was organised and was followed in October 1909 by the Autocar Co. Ltd, with Oscar Pritchard as general manager; it began with three ABC vehicles, built in Glasgow by the All British Car Co. Ltd, which worked between the LBSCR Station and Southborough Common. In March 1910 Pritchard was made managing director and reorganisation included use of three new Leyland 32-seat 40-h.p. buses; the ABC vehicles were second-hand from London where they were introduced in 1907 and as an advanced design had for a short period given good results for that period of the history of the petrol bus.

A new workshop and running shed, plus a railway parcels delivery service, were other innovations of 1910, and by 1914 connecting services with neighbouring companies were inaugurated, one to Hadlow, for example, linking with the Maidstone & District service into Maidstone. Autocar made agreements with M & D and Southdown as the local British Automobile Traction companies for exchange of traffic at other boundary points; in 1920 for a short time Autocar ran right across what became East Surrey territory to Farnborough, until exchange of traffic at Sevenoaks was agreed. In 1921 Ashby Motor Services Ltd brought competition between Tonbridge and Tunbridge Wells until in November 1923 Autocar bought a controlling interest. More lasting rivalry than Ashby was shown by Redcar Services, inspired by Major J. B. Elliott and his friends. They began operating a Napier car to Goudhurst and Cranbrook and then bought seven 18-seat Clement-Talbot buses, which could outpace the by this time elderly Autocar fleet.

In a pamphlet dated 18 July 1923 Redcar stated that Redcar Services Ltd ran their buses on country routes strictly to time. When they began running they wanted to give an increased and better service to the public and their timetables were fixed so as to *avoid clashing* with Autocar times. The Autocar company immediately put on charabancs at the Redcar times with the apparent intention of running Redcar off the roads. Mauve Autocar coaches thus ran between the advertised times and close on those of Redcar. The small man made the usual appeal to the man in the street against the 'monopoly' but, of course, did not mention how Autocar had provided a bus service in thin country areas over 14 development years, having several financial reconstructions in that time.

Apart from the speed of the Clement-Talbots the Redcar routes were often short extensions of Autocar services; thus, where the Autocar service ended at Goudhurst, Redcar went on to Cranbrook; where Autocar terminated at Hawkhurst, Redcar was extended to Sandhurst; Redcar opened a new cross-country connection to Edenbridge. Feuding between the companies reduced fares to $\frac{1}{2}d$ a mile; passengers on one 8d stage were able to ride for 1d. Books of tickets were issued at a discount of 2d in the 1s and conductors who purchased books were thus able to make a personal profit of 16 per cent on each short journey ticket they sold. In April 1928 East Surrey purchased a controlling interest in Autocar and altered the articles of association so that any resolution of the Autocar board had to have East Surrey approval. An agreement for three years from 1 May 1928 was then made with Redcar Services for working services at equal fares in an agreed area on a joint schedule with Autocar working 55 per cent and Redcar 45 per cent of the total mileage with receipts pooled and divided in the same proportions.

On 16 September 1927 Redcar broke out in a direction where the agreement did not limit them with a limited stop service from Tunbridge Wells and Tonbridge to the London Coastal coach station in London. Autocar and Maidstone & District thus had a working agreement about competing but Redcar and Maidstone & District used the same London terminal facilities. I well remember using the Redcar limited stop service as a means of reaching London on Sunday nights from the Tunbridge Wells direction and found it satisfactory and speedy, but not everybody was pleased with the riding of the rather spartan Clement-Talbot coaches and in the severe weather of the 1928 winter the Redcar London service was withdrawn from the beginning of January until early in April; the situation was ameliorated by introduction of Leyland Tiger coaches in February 1930.

In June 1929 the London General Omnibus Co. Ltd obtained control of the East Surrey Traction Co. Ltd, and thus of Autocar. A co-ordinating scheme for the country south of the Thames outside London was at the time contemplated in the form of Southern General Omnibus Co. Ltd, which would have included a Southern Railway shareholding, the East Surrey, Autocar and Redcar interests, but in view of the imminence of the London Passenger Transport Board proposal to cover the area in question this was dropped and as the title had not been protected in the usual LGOC method, it was taken up by an amalgamation of small Devon proprietors which passed into the Red & White group. While the Redcar service required pre-booking by the usual London Coastal method, Autocar set up a service from Oxford Circus to Tunbridge Wells, plying for hire along the route at selected stops, and operated by LGOC AEC T-type (Regal) coaches on 6 June

1930; this became a Green Line service shortly after the formation of that concern on 9 July 1930.

Under Section 99 of the London Passenger Transport Board Act (1933) the London Passenger Transport Board had to sell to the Southern Railway so much of the undertaking of London General Country Services Ltd as was represented by working public service vehicles outside the LPT area except on those specified roads such as Tonbridge to Sevenoaks where unlimited service could be given and Tunbridge Wells to Tonbridge where limited-stop service by LPTB was permitted. The Southern Railway then sold its interest in Autocar to Maidstone & District, which had to maintain it as a separate entity because of the agreement with Redcar. These transactions were completed immediately after the passage of the London Passenger Transport Board Act on 13 March 1933. After much negotiation the sale of Redcar Services Ltd took effect from 1 January 1935 to Maidstone & District at an extraordinary general meeting on Saturday 2 February 1935. Formal transfer took place on 22 February 1935. The following month M & D applied for the Autocar licences. Besides £83,928 paid for Redcar shares £13,350 was paid to Redcar directors and some employees for loss of office and some restrictive covenants on their bus operating activities in the next five years.

In April 1934 M & D consolidated its position in Tunbridge Wells by purchase of Tunbridge Wells Victor Motor Transport Co. Ltd with 21 vehicles operating five bus routes, and in November of that year purchased the Hastings Tramways Company, which had converted to trolleybus operation (50 single-deck and eight 56-seat double-deck) beginning in April 1928. The trolleybuses were replaced by a fleet of Atlantean diesel front-entrance rear-engined buses in 1959.

The Aldershot & District Traction Co. Ltd was formed on 24 July 1912 to take over the Aldershot & Farnborough Motor Omnibus Co. Ltd, a pioneer concern, in business from 1 June 1906, and to adopt an agreement with the British Automobile Traction Co. Ltd who installed members of the Foster family as chairman and managing director. A peculiarity of its arrangements with Southdown was the Aldershot operation via Midhurst to Chichester and Bognor right across Southdown territory. After purchasing the L & SWR Farnham–Haslemere service in 1913 and that of B. Chandler between Hindhead and Haslemere the Aldershot company seems to have made less expansion by purchase of other operators than most BAT companies, one of the most notable being Blue Coaches of Farnham which provided a limited stop service from Kings Cross to Farnham; after merger with the A & D service from London Coastal to Whitehill a thirty-minute headway was maintained from October 1934.

The Garcke family home was at Pinkneys Green, Maidenhead, so it is not surprising that an early site of British Automobile Traction operations, from June 1915, was Maidenhead and Reading, and a fleet of Belsize buses was gathered, this being a make not sought by the War Office. As from 1 July 1920 the services were transferred to Thames Valley Traction Co. Ltd which was registered on 10 July of that year. For a time the company operated Uxbridge garage of the London General Omnibus Co. Ltd. From 1933 Marlow & District Motor Services Ltd was maintained as a subsidiary company. In 1936 Ledbury & District Transport Co. Ltd, named after a Westbourne Grove mews, not the West Country town, with the fleet name of Thackray's Way, and operating a London to Reading and Newbury coach service, and part of the Penn Bus Co. Ltd was also acquired. Under the aegis of the National Bus Company the Thames Valley Traction Co. Ltd with 379 vehicles and the Aldershot & District Traction Co. Ltd with 285 vehicles, both rather small undertakings, were managed together under the trading name of Alder Valley, thus returning to fanciful names such as Ortona.

Very complicated histories were encountered by East Midland Motor Services, including a change in 1942 from the Tilling side of British Automobile Traction to the BET side. As will have been gathered earlier in this chapter Tilling and the BET first found themselves joint investors in British Automobile Traction concerns when they both supported the East Kent Road Car Co. Ltd in 1916, after which each of the holding companies made separate investments in a great many of the operating companies, this involving Thomas Tilling Ltd in making direct investments in 22 BAT operators. An exchange of shares was carried out and in acknowledgment of the position the title of the company was changed to Tilling & British Automobile Traction Ltd in May 1928. The TBAT chairman remained Sidney Garcke, but John F. Heaton was made vice-chairman and after 1936 Heaton was chairman in alternate years. The chairman of each operating company was derived from the management according to whose philosophy the company was controlled; the Tilling group set out specific lines of management which Heaton wanted followed, whereas the British Electric Traction style of management left much more to the discretion of the individual general manager. Some of the companies managed direct by Tilling were fortunate in having managers bold enough to confess that they threw away what they considered unreasonable directives from Tilling headquarters and admitted to objecting to the spying on staff or management that the Tilling methods induced; some of these were justified by the rigorous police enforcement of the 30 m.p.h. limit on buses and coaches, especially on the Great North Road where, however, drivers took a pride in running mile after mile at 29·9 m.p.h.

East Midland Motor Services Ltd was first registered as a subsidiary of United Automobile Services Ltd as W. T. Underwood Ltd with a nominal capital of £5,000, on 23 November 1920. Operation started that same day, the undertaking being managed from Clowne and indeed being known at first as Clowne & District Motor Services. As late as August 1923 Clowne & District was shown in the *TBR Guide* as operating ten services; there were two from Clowne to Mansfield (via Bolsover and via Worksop); to Intake (change for tram to Sheffield); Killamarsh to Intake; Dinnington and Worksop to Handsworth; Worksop to Chesterfield; Eckington to Chesterfield and Chesterfield to Barrow Hill. Worksop depot was opened in 1924 and a site known as the Empire garage which had been a skating rink was purchased against future developments. In 1926 a town service was begun in Worksop with 20-seat buses at 40-minute intervals. By 1957 six town services in Worksop (where the traffic and secretarial offices were from 1926 to 1930, when the head office moved to Chesterfield) operated on 4-minute headways in the peaks with double-deck buses. By 1957, when a new bus station was built in Worksop with night garage space for 68 buses (out of a fleet of 224), the town council and the company were jointly engaged in housing projects.

In 1927 the company was renamed East Midland Motor Services, and on 28 March 1930 it was reincorporated as a TBAT limited company with LMS and LNER participation at 34 shillings (£1 70 pence) a share. The railways arranged for it to be managed by Tilling & British Automobile Traction Ltd; so the registered office was at 88 Kingsway, traffic office at Worksop and the engineering department at Clowne. The purchase was completed by the T & BAT on 28 February 1931. For many years the livery of East Midland vehicles was beige, similar to the original United Automobile colour, but is described as red for buses and red and cream for coaches in 1969. The current description is green.

Notable undertakings acquired included in 1922 Lincolnshire & District Automobile Services and East Derbyshire Motor Co. Ltd, in 1925 Enterprise & Silver Dawn (dating from 1924), in 1928 Retford Motor Services (jointly with Lincolnshire Road Car Co. Ltd, 1930), Underwood Express (another Underwood Express was incorporated by W. T. Underwood and his wife and worked coaches on the Portsmouth road until purchased by Southdown in 1935), the Retford–Nottingham service of Retford Coaches; April 1936 saw G. C. Corbridge of Chesterfield taken over and January 1937 J. R. Godley of Darfoulds, Notts, absorbed who operated a Worksop to Steetley Colliery service. In 1951 Portland Coachways was purchased and the businesses of G. P. Glover and O. Bates Ltd; in 1955 Major's Coaches Ltd was acquired.

The East Yorkshire Motor Services Ltd was one of the last British

Automobile Traction concerns to be formed, apart from concerns invested in by the railways, being registered on 5 October 1926. It was also the company on which Sir John Spencer Wills, as he was to become, cut his bus-operating teeth. He came to it from being confidential clerk to Emile Garcke, founder of the BET, at the latter's Maidenhead home. Salaries just after the First World War were low and even allowing for the fact that Wills was living in, £50 a year and provide your own bicycle does not seem the sort of remuneration to cause a long queue to form. The East Yorkshire Company was formed to adopt an agreement with British Automobile Traction and to take over as going concerns the businesses of Hull & District Motor Services Ltd and Lee & Beaulah Ltd. J. S. Wills was the first secretary and E. J. Lee the first general manager. As is to be expected from its formation as an amalgamation of several undertakings, the original fleet was rather mixed, at the end of the first year comprising 84 vehicles, all but one of which was on pneumatic tyres and including 60 Leyland, 12 Dennis, 5 Tilling-Stevens, 1 Lancia, 2 Chevrolet, 2 Straker-Squire, 1 Napier and 1 AEC chassis. Of this fleet 13 were double-deckers; it was only after the use of the covered-top vehicle became general that problems of negotiating Beverley arch necessitated use of the roof domed in the centre that became a feature of the East Yorkshire fleet. In the early days of the company the largest garage was at Driffield, with accommodation for 27 vehicles, followed by Lister Street Hull (22). A garage for 100 vehicles was built at Anlaby Road, Hull, and a headquarters repair works at Anlaby Common.

Today East Yorkshire is still one of the smaller area agreement companies with 223 buses and coaches, of which 138 are double-deck. The fleet is mainly on Leyland chassis (90), with 70 AEC, 55 Daimler and 8 Bristol. Some of the notable acquisitions during the years have included Hull Road Motor & Electrical Engineering Co. Ltd and Fussey of Cottingham, absorbed even before the first balance sheet was completed in 1927; in June 1932 H. C. Motor Works Ltd was absorbed. This was a substantial undertaking and some of the incidents connected with its components show the difficulties under which local authorities laboured when they endeavoured to establish services beyond their boundaries in earlier years. Towards the end of 1922 Hull Corporation spent £8,000 on acquiring the goodwill of the Owbridge Grey Motor Bus Company's service on the Hessle road. The Ministry of Health refused to sanction this expenditure on a service beyond the borough boundary and the corporation was therefore obliged to dispose of it early in 1923 to Hull City Garage Ltd. This concern changed its name on 17 January 1923 to H. C. Motor Works Ltd and began an expansionist policy, buying Swift Motor Company in 1924, Wakefield Motor Services in 1925 and Newington Motor & Engineering, incorporated in 1919, in 1927. In June 1932 H. C. Motor Works was operating 45 buses as Kingston Services.

Some of the Newington services themselves had much interest, as had those of the Kingston group, the earliest operation of which dated from 1906. A motor-bus service between Hull and Hessle was begun in 1914. The Beverley–Brandesburton service, which the North Eastern Railway began on 7 September 1903, was the scene of quite a lot of competitive activity in the early 1920s; in May 1923 a Newington service was on the route and then the Wakefield company worked from Beverley to Hornsea via Brandesburton and on 1 October 1925 the London & North Eastern Railway, by now disenchanted with buses and deeming the prospect of obtaining universal road powers as pretty remote, sold the Newington undertaking the Beverley service, together with the right to run into Beverley station yard, and a regular connection with the train service was made. In May 1933 Hale Garage & Coachways Ltd, coach operators, were jointly acquired by East Yorkshire in conjunction with Yorkshire Traction, Yorkshire Woollen District, and West Yorkshire Road Car Co. Ltd. In 1932–3 the businesses of R. H. Sherwood of Hornsea and Binnington's Motors of Hull became part of East Yorkshire and were integrated with it. In 1935 Sharpe's Motors, dating from 1925, operating a Hull and Hedon service, was taken over jointly with Hull Corporation. EYMS and Hull Corporation made a sharing agreement in 1934 rather like the railway and municipal arrangements of 1929, dividing the city into zones, the centre of which was served by the Corporation, a middle zone jointly and the outer by East Yorkshire services. Incidentally in December 1929 the London & North Eastern Railway acquired a shareholding equal to Tilling & British Automobile Traction (79,605 shares) at £1 25 pence a share.

The North Western Road Car Co. Ltd began as a branch of the British Automobile Traction Co. Ltd which was opened on 10 November 1913 at King Edward Street, Macclesfield, and at Buxton and was equipped with a fleet of Belsize single-deckers. This make had a tendency to chassis trouble and soon the Buxton fleet was Daimler 34-seat double-deck vehicles, more or less standard with the London fleet of the company; soon afterwards a garage was opened in Stockport. Administration was then carried out by the picturesquely-named Peak District Committee, to be succeeded on 23 April 1923 by the formation of the North Western Road Car Co. Ltd. George Cardwell, who learnt his trade on tramway management at Hartlepool and Devonport, became general manager at Macclesfield in 1918 and of the new company in 1923. There he made an outstanding success of getting buses into Stockport, Manchester, Oldham and other tram-strewn local authority areas where at the time there was no independent means of persuading the issue of licences. It was common knowledge in the industry about 1930 that Uncle George, as he was affectionately known, was about to leave the BET company as a general manager and hoped for higher things with the Tilling group which saw administrative difficulties now that it had persuaded BET in 1928 to reconstitute the BAT as Tilling & British Automobile Traction Ltd. Cardwell took on the task of guiding the destinies of several TBAT companies that were allocated to the Tilling group. Later the differences in management produced recriminations between the BET chairman, at that time R. J. Howley, and J. F. Heaton of Tillings and a determination to separate the structure of the combined company between the principal partners. But this was to come upon them in 1942.

Early in the career of North Western the administrative skill of Cardwell showed to advantage in purchasing some of its principal rivals; thus in November 1924 the bus business of Mid-Cheshire Motor Co. Ltd of Northwich was acquired; on 1 January 1926 the business of Altrincham District Motor Services was taken over and in 1928 through running into Manchester came into effect.

10 More BET Companies

Just as William Percy Allen appears in the annals of so many early bus ventures, so the bus historian becomes accustomed to recording the name of Walter Flexman French in one concern after another and so it is no surprise to find the Sussex Motor Road Car Co. Ltd was one of the pioneer concerns of Southdown and that French conducted much of the pioneer correspondence from his Worthing home in 1904. In July they took delivery of two Clarkson steam buses and put them to work between Worthing and Pulborough. Furring-up of the boilers by the chalky water very soon put them out of action and collection of rain water in underground tanks at the White Horse Hotel, Storrington, was an attempt to overcome this difficulty. In March 1905 the struggle was given up, the Clarksons being disposed of to the Vale of Llangollen Engineering, Bus & Garage Co. Ltd and two petrol-engined Milnes-Daimler buses bought in their place, and three more added; with these a service from Worthing to Littlehampton and Arundel was introduced. Novelty riding was still part of the delight of going by bus and front seats commanded extra fares.

At this time the Worthing Motor Omnibus Company, formed in November 1904 by H. Gates and D. Brazier to compete with the horse-bus services in the town of Town, Searle and Jinks, began its rivalry with the Sussex Motor Road Car Co. Ltd, and being fortunate in getting licences from Hove they began a service to Palmeira Square on 27 June 1905, as well as their previously-established three local routes. The Worthing Motor Omnibus Co. had five Milnes-Daimlers and bitter struggles ensued for the Worthing–Brighton licences. In this the BET was rather unwillingly joined, since it had purchased the Brighton & District Tramways Company in 1898 with a view to electrification. Authorised in 1882, it was opened on 3 July 1884 and ran from Aldrington boundary to the neighbourhood of Shoreham where the line ended at Swiss Gardens. In 1885 the terminus was reached by a battery vehicle, but by the time the motor buses had appeared horse traction was used if it was used at all. The Worthing bus drivers had the reputation of putting a spoke in the tramway men's wheels by placing stones in strategic spots in the light 3 ft 6 in. gauge tram tracks so as to derail the cars before they reached the goal of the pleasure gardens.

When the rivalry was at its height there was a certain amount of tale-telling by the men and when the WMOC had a garage or parking plot at a place called Ivy Arch, it transpired that an illegal stock of petrol was stored there and there was a row with Worthing Urban District Council. The Brighton, Hove & Preston Union Omnibus Co. Ltd had been formed as a merger of horse-bus concerns in Brighton in 1884 and had experimented with motor buses as early as 1901; it then introduced a number of motors from December 1903 onwards upon Brighton Corporation considering its own motor bus service. The BHPU constituted a third contender on the Brighton–Worthing road.

On 20 August 1905 the Sussex Motor Road Car Co. Ltd took over the WMOC business, but its Worthing–Brighton route made a heavy loss owing to the Brighton licences being framed with conditions that acted strongly in favour of the United company. The Road Car Company at this stage appointed Alfred Douglas Mackenzie, a consulting engineer, as general manager from April 1907 and Alfred Cannon, of the 70-vehicle strong Pioneer Company in London, as chief engineer. These two were to become the most skilled and best-known busmen in the south of England.

The company introduced some Thornycroft charabancs in which the rows of seats ascended towards the back. Mackenzie also inaugurated services based on Portsmouth, including a lodging turn from there which spent the night at Hambledon – actually in a farmyard, whence it picked up and carried away a stowaway cockerel! Newhaven was another piece of new territory. As a boy spending family holidays at Bognor I was somewhat perplexed by the erratic appearance of motors there and later knowledge attributes it to the financial troubles of the SMRC Co. Ltd, which in 1908 could not pay its modest garage rent in Portsmouth and to prevent foreclosure on the vehicles drove them off after dark and stored them at quiet roadside spots in Worthing. In the beginning of the 1908–9 winter things looked very black and the company went into voluntary liquidation.

Mackenzie attributed this to the partisan attitude of the local councils' licensing committees, by which the Brighton Council licensed the United company and the Worthing council the Sussex Company, each then being compelled only to bring back return ticket holders and maintain a ticket office in the other terminal town. The Worthing–Storrington route was maintained all the winter as a source of revenue, Worthing Motor Services Ltd was formed and the route extended to Pulborough, so demonstrating Mackenzie's belief in the avoidance of 'thin ends'.

The licensing regulations became more stringent and WMS buses could not ply for hire east of Portslade. The WMS drivers used to make a parade of their bus from Royal Mews, Steine Street, to call attention to the fact that they were about to start off. New sources of revenue included a trip to the Derby (by the time they reached Epsom top-deck passengers were liberally sprinkled with tar, the roads en route having just been sprayed). On another occasion when the Storrington road had been tarred Mackenzie was driving a bus on a moonlit night and found he had driven straight off the road into the middle of Findon pond, the reflecting surfaces being indistinguishable.

The trading name Sussex Tourist Coaches was now adopted to indicate the wider scope that the WMS was adopting in its search for revenue. On 14 June 1913 a tour to the West Country was organised, followed by trips to Wales and the Lake District. At this stage Walter Flaxman French formed a new goods transport company, the London & South Coast Haulage Co. Ltd, with himself as managing director, which began with two lorries and a van as rolling stock, but did not prove very remunerative and consequently applied for some passenger licences – which it did not get – for the Brighton–Lewes road. He then bought a coach business, unbelievably called 'Jolly Jumbo's', from a small family business run by the Ecclestones, and secured the transfer of their licences. In 1914 a route to Hurstpierpoint was begun and extended to Burgess Hill.

The difficulties of the war brought the United company, London & South Coast Haulage and Worthing Motor Services to see that co-operation could be a good thing, and French enlisted the aid of Sydney Garcke to ensure that British Automobile Traction money should be put into a new BAT company, combining the excursion department of Brighton, Hove & Preston United, and the undertakings of Worthing Motor Services, and London & South Coast Haulage, as Southdown Motor Services Ltd, which was incorporated on 2 June 1915 with the energetic Walter Flaxman French as its first chairman. Among the directors was A. Douglas Mackenzie, also traffic manager, who personally owned some of the buses used by Worthing Motor Services, and Alfred Cannon, who had served WMS as chief engineer and continued to act in that capacity to Southdown. To these two may be attributed the company's instant success.

Mackenzie's abhorrence of 'thin ends' has already been mentioned and he also had some good workable rules about timetable design, one of which was that if an hourly service would not bring the potential customers off their bicycles a 30-minute headway should be tried. How sound this was can be seen from the success of Wilts & Dorset Motor Services Ltd, founded as a private venture by Cannon and Mackenzie, registered on 4 January 1915 with offices at Amesbury and frankly formed to cash in on the wartime stationing of troops on Salisbury Plain, with the aid of the Lephard family, the paper merchants, and a few friends. Where Wilts & Dorset ran half-hourly services every day, in almost exactly similar territory the National group very often ran once or twice a day on market days only and, with the spread of the use of motor cars, has lost the chance of ever developing the bus business profitably.

Southdown started its career with 31 vehicles, some of which, on Scout and Caledon chassis, were wartime makeshifts, and the skill of the board in obtaining vehicles during the continuance of wartime difficulties is shown by the fact that the fleet had become 65 by 1917. A characteristic of early Southdown buses was the goods or milkchurn compartment which many of them had built in to them, behind the driver. Major H. E. Hickmott was the first area manager at Brighton and was soon after the war appointed general manager of Ribble Motor Services by BAT. To obtain licences Mantell's horse-brake business was purchased in Brighton and a coach business in Bognor was bought from A. Davis, who was made the Bognor area manager. The rather long and narrow territory of Southdown was divided into five areas, each area manager with powers of 'life and death' over his staff, and as Michael Carling told me when he was area manager at Portsmouth, was expected to go to see the run-out at his most distant garage at four on a winter's morning more than once a month.

Some of the principal concerns purchased include Chapman & Sons Ltd of Eastbourne whose coaches I well remember seeing more numerous than Southdowns with gas balloons above their roofs filling with town gas at standpipes in Pevensey and other spots convenient to their tours when I was on holiday at Bexhill in 1917. William and George Chapman were in coaching with motor vehicles as early as 1909 and the limited company was formed in 1921; the purchase consideration was £78,000. Southdown bought it in February 1932 and simultaneously Southern Glideway Coaches Ltd. An early purchase by Southdown was, in 1925, the Southsea Tourist Co. Ltd.

After the Road Traffic Act of 1930 came into force and operators could be certain that if they paid for the goodwill of a business the traffic commissioners would see to it that they had value for money, purchases became more numerous. In March 1932 Southdown took in G. B. Motor Tours Ltd, in February 1934 the London–Portsmouth coach service of North End Motor Coaches Ltd, and in 1935, also with Portsmouth Road coaching in mind, Alexandra Coaches, Imperial Saloon and the well-run service of Underwood Express, operated by the founder of East Midland Motor Services, whom I knew very well. He ran a rather attractive service from Kings Cross to Southsea at the day return fare of 7s 6d (37½p), giving 11½ hours in Southsea, and with the Isle of Wight Aviation company provided an air connection with Ryde. A Jersey connection was in negotiation with Jersey Airways.

From 1 April 1924 through trams ran from Portsmouth to Horndean on to the Portsdown & Horndean Light Railway, induced by the competition of the Southsea Tourist Company, purchased by Southdown the following year. In view of the impending change by Portsmouth Corporation from trams to trolleybuses the Portsdown & Horndean Light Railway ceased to operate their trams on 9 January 1935 and the company, the Hampshire Light Railway (Electric) Ltd, was fortunate to persuade Southdown Motor Services Ltd to purchase the goodwill, signified by an increase in the Southdown service from South Parade Pier, Southsea, to Petersfield, from 10 January 1935. This inspired later that year Southdown's purchase of the Denmead Queen service on the Sussex–Hampshire border in the forest of Bere.

Ribble Motor Services Ltd was registered on 6 June 1919 with a capital of £20,000 to begin in a very modest way by acquiring the business of J. Hodson of Gregson Lane, near Preston, and less than a year later, in April 1920, it had taken over the Preston branch of the British Automobile Traction Co. Ltd. In the 1920s a number of bus business was absorbed; in 1925 the Chorley Autocar Co. Ltd and the KCR Buses (Kenyon, Coleman & Robinson Ltd of Blackburn); in 1926 the Blackburn firm of Lancashire Industrial Motors Ltd, known as Pendle Services; also in 1926 Pilot Motors Ltd, Preston; Collingwood Motors (Liverpool) Ltd; and Skipton Motor Co. Ltd, Loynds & Co. (Darwen); Wiseman's Motors (Skipton); Lancashire & Westmorland Services Ltd, Armstrong & Siddle Motor Services Ltd – all were acquired in 1927–9.

On 13 March 1929 the Merseyside Touring Co. Ltd began local operation between Liverpool and Bootle (Watts Lane) and by June 1930 a fleet of 35 vehicles was working 10 separate routes, despite the handicap of having licences only from Bootle and Litherland, Liverpool Corporation adopting an extreme policy of tramway protection. The Merseyside Company now acquired an interest in Nor' West bus services of Liverpool and distinguished its buses by service numbers between 50 and 60, with a series of As and Bs and a purple light at night, made of a blue glass screen and a red bulb. In mid-1930, although retaining separate identity, these services came under Ribble control; St John's Lane, the Liverpool terminus, was changed to Pier Head in peak.

In 1930 two other distinctive undertakings were acquired by Ribble. The Furness Omnibus Co. Ltd was an owner-driver concern incorporated on 9 January 1926. Business began on 1 June 1926; the principal road was Barrow–Ulverston, where their chief depot was at Newlands. The headquarters were at Dalton-in-Furness and subsidiaries were the Barrow Bus Co. Ltd and the Lonsdale Pullman Bus Co. Ltd. Furness vehicles were distinguished by a large red F on the front. Rather earlier in the post-war motor-bus boom was the Kendal Motor Bus Co. Ltd, which began in April 1922 and marked its fleet by a white K. There were nearly 30 vehicles in the Kendal fleet which was kept at Longlands Garage, Penrith Road, Kendal, except for two Thornycrofts stationed at Lancaster. Kendal vehicles were on pneumatics as early as 1923.

When in 1930 the Ribble fleet totalled 666 vehicles, operating over 1,430 route-miles, the subsidiaries, Rishton & Antley Motor Co. Ltd, Merseyside Touring Co. Ltd, Waterloo & Crosby Motor Services Ltd (successor of a tramway which extended the Liverpool Overhead Railway from 1900 to 1926 and was replaced by London NS-type AEC buses), and County Motors (Lancaster) Ltd, numbered a fleet of 185 in all. In January 1931 the Ribble company replaced the Waterloo & Crosby fleet with Leyland Titan covered double-deckers.

In 1931 Freeman's Silver Star services of Chorley was absorbed. In Carlisle R. Percival Ltd was taken over in preparation for tramway replacement. In June 1931 the agreement between Ribble and Liverpool Corporation made the services of Merseyside Touring Co. Ltd and 200 men redundant; the London express service had a few weeks previously been transferred to Crosville. At the annual general meeting in June 1931 W. S. Wreathall, the chairman, explained that Merseyside Touring Co. Ltd was the only subsidiary company continuing in existence and that was because of a hitch in Liverpool Corporation obtaining licences from the traffic commissioners, Litherland and Bootle objecting. Merseyside ceased operation in Liverpool on 30 September 1931, it having begun with five vehicles on 13 March 1929. This illustrates how short and sharp was the peak of operation before the Road Traffic Act 1930 stabilised the industry.

Trams in Carlisle ceased on 21 November 1931. The city authorities had

27 (*above*) This 14-seat Bean, on a local route at Pinner, was probably the smallest bus ever operated by London Transport or its predecessors

28 (*below*) The Scottish Motor Traction Company began operations with this Maudslay 34-seater on an Edinburgh local route

29 (*left*) An open staircase Leyland Titan in the service of Western National

30 (*below*) A Clarkson steam bus of the National Steam Car Company at Peckham Rye (or Nunhead) garage

had in mind running the bus system themselves and actually ordered 59 buses for the purpose. In the meantime the Northern Traffic Commissioners decided that the local services should be divided between Ribble and United companies, Ribble taking the west side of the city and United the east (which they reached through acquisition of Emmerson services). Forty-four buses were taken over from the existing operators and Ribble built an extensive bus station in Lowther Street; United also built a bus station; in 1970 it became redundant as Ribble's area was extended to cover the western area of United to the mid-point of the Pennines.

From 1929 onwards the London Midland & Scottish Railway owned a proportion of shares equal to the holding of the Tilling & British company, purchased at £1 87½ pence a share.

In 1934 the coach business of Kenyon, Coleman and Robinson Ltd, with services from Blackburn, Darwen and Great Harwood to Blackpool was transferred to Ribble.

In 1931 Ribble invested in W. C. Standerwick Ltd the Blackpool coach operators and Wright Brothers (Burnley) Ltd, both of which were established as subsidiary companies. Another Blackpool firm in which an interest was taken was Scout Motor Services Ltd, set up in 1932 to take over the business operated from 1919 onwards by James Watkinson. Standerwick was begun in 1925 and its business was directed mainly to the Blackpool and Colne to London services, calling for over 90 vehicles before the Second World War. In 1969 the fleet had come down to 82 vehicles, but it was only in the turmoil after 1970 that Standerwick ceased to be worked as a Ribble subsidiary.

I knew Ribble affairs best when Horatio Bottomley was in charge; I was entranced by the way (when he wanted) he could produce facts and statistics galore about the company, accurately recite agreements (on one occasion I had lunch at Frenchwood Avenue headquarters in Preston and after a game of snooker heard the arrangements with every local authority between Manchester and Carlisle recited from memory), and statistics about the state of traffic on many routes. I was fascinated by what he had to say about Pennine. Pennine Motor Services was the Simpson family business centred on Gargrave. In 1926 it had two stage-carriage vehicles and a dozen coaches, but in 1937 Ribble was prepared to lend them staff to ensure that they could continue their role in maintaining communications in the Skipton area. The part Ribble plays in sustaining Pennine still continues, although undefined.

Trent Motor Traction Co. Ltd was registered on 31 October 1913 and had a most unusual start. Commercial Cars Ltd was formed in September 1905, but after four years a falling-off of orders for new vehicles brought about a sales promotion scheme in the form of a vehicle hire company, Commercial Car Hirers Ltd, which was registered 18 June 1909; the secretary was J. Coventon Moth.

From these activities Commer Cars Ltd emerged as a very successful manufacturer of commercial vehicles and as a result of Commercial Car Hirers advertising an inquiry was received for a 2-ton vehicle which could be adapted to serve shooting parties on a Scottish estate. A 14-seat vehicle went on hire to the Scottish landowner concerned. One of his guests at that time owned Osmaston Manor near Ashbourne; he thought a similar vehicle would serve to convey staff and guests to and from Ashbourne and Derby and he got in touch with W. L. T. Arkwright, the chairman of Commercial Car Hirers Ltd, to rent such a vehicle for a year. Neighbours with similar needs wanted to borrow the vehicle so that a second one was soon needed.

The result was a regular timetabled service between Ashbourne and Derby; arrangements were made to stable the buses at Green Man Hotel, Ashbourne. It was decided to form a local company to facilitate expansion under Alderman W. Hart, a former mayor of Derby, as chairman. About this time W. S. Wreathall of the British Electric Traction group had noticed the remarkably brisk business being done by the Commercial Car Hirers vehicles and sought a meeting with Coventon Moth. The result was a joint British Automobile Traction and Commercial Car Hirers company, Trent Motor Traction Co. Ltd, formed on 31 October 1913 and in business on 1 November as such, although it will be realised that the 14-seat Commers had acted as forerunners some months earlier. Derby to Ashbourne and Alfreton and Alfreton to Clay Cross and Chesterfield was the scope of the new company in 1913. Ten years later the link with Commercial Car Hirers was severed, although Coventon Moth, who was promoted to the Trent board in 1915, was a director until his death in 1963 and was a specialist in BET laundry affairs.

Expansion began soon after the First World War; in 1919 the Loughborough Road Car Co. Ltd was taken over; in 1923 Clayton of Nottingham; in 1925 Clarke's Bus Service with a Nottingham–Ilkeston service; in 1928 Retford Motor Services (a complex purchase in which East Midland and Lincolnshire were associated); 1929 District Motor Co., Horsley; 1929 Chapman of Belper and Higgs & Walter (Melbourne) Ltd; 1931 Reynold's (jointly with Nottingham Corporation), Wagg's Super Service and Bayliss & Sons of Ashbourne. In 1932 Mrs L. Green's Blue Glider Service was acquired and the operations of J. W. Longdon.

Small businesses absorbed in the next five years included C. W. Rhodes, Derby (1933); J. W. Taylor, Whatstandwell (1933); Blue Bus Services (Derby)

Ltd, a favourite title in this area (1934); Haywood Brothers (1934); Kingfisher Services Ltd (1935); Eagle Services (S. O. Stevenson) (1935); T. Pollard, Derby (1935); Dutton's Unity Services (1935); Pippin Services, Ripley (1935); R. E. Horspool, Loughborough (1935); C. E. Salt's Red Star Service of Duffield (1936) and R. J. Walters & Sons Ltd (1936). Many of these marked consolidations of service. For example, Haywoods ran Derby, Ilkeston, Cotmanhay; Blue Bus had a Derby–Morley–Ilkeston service and this was extended to Cotmanhay and the two merged.

In 1919 Trent began a daring experiment in providing charabanc services to Skegness – 75 miles – and these were a great success, netting £500 in the first season. It was in 1924 that the livery first chosen for Trent buses – green – gave place to red. Extended tours began in 1925, the theme chosen being a five-day excursion to North Wales, which was repeated several times during the summer. During the intense competition with small proprietors a Trent driver followed one of these newcomers on a service and eventually traced his quarry into a residential street where it pulled up by a private house. To his dismay the jitney driver proved to be an extremely burly bruiser type and when he came over to the Trent bus the worst was feared. Speech, however, proved disarming. 'Mate, yer've been following me about all morning, would'st yer like to come and 'ave bite o'dinner wi'me?' They ended up firm friends.

On 23 May 1930 an important sequel to the London Midland & Scottish and London & North Eastern investment in Trent Motor Traction shares (equal to that of Tilling & British and taken in this case at 26 shillings a share) took place; this was the first meeting of the Standing Joint Committee of Trent and railway company representatives and they have continued since to ensure co-ordination between undertakings with different physical characteristics and methods of approach as in all the railway-associated undertakings, and, as has been mentioned, even in the case of some, like Potteries, that are not formally connected.

Originally registered on 3 March 1902 as the Barnsley & District Electric Traction Co. Ltd, the name of this company was changed first in July 1919, by dropping the word 'electric' and then in November 1928 to Yorkshire Traction Co. Ltd; it is usually known in the area as 'Tracky'. The tram services were abandoned on 31 August 1930 and those of the municipally-owned Dearne District Light Railway on 1 October 1932, on a profit-sharing arrangement with Yorkshire Traction Co. Ltd. During the next few years a number of undertakings was purchased owing to the strengthening of the position of the purchaser under the Road Traffic Act (1930). A number of these were joint acquisitions. In May 1933, for example, Hale Garage Co. Ltd and Coachways Ltd were taken over jointly with East Yorkshire, West

Yorkshire, Yorkshire (Woollen District) and Yorkshire Traction and also in 1933 the Fawdon Bus Co. was a joint acquisition of Northern General, West Yorkshire, Yorkshire (Woollen District) and Yorkshire Traction. Then in 1934 London Midland & Yorkshire Services, begun the previous year by B & E Coach Services, F. C. Wiles Parlour Car Services and South Yorkshire Motors, was taken over jointly by East Yorkshire, West Yorkshire, Yorkshire (Woollen District) and the Yorkshire Traction Company. In 1934–6 the Yorkshire Traction Co. Ltd took over the Doncaster–Skellow service of B & E Coach Services, which had been left out of the previous amalgamations, Wilson Haigh Ltd of Holmfirth, C. Wray of Barnsley, T. S. Camplejohn and J. Marsen & Sons, both of Bentley, Reuben Wilson of Hemsworth, George White of Great Houghton and E. L. Tiler.

Public road transport in the Spen Valley originated back in 1873 when the horse-drawn tram system of the Dewsbury, Batley & Birstall Tramways Co. Ltd was established modestly from Dewsbury Market Place to Combs Hill, Thornhill, 2½ miles distant. Later steam traction was introduced on various of the company's lines, which extended as far as Gomersal. The Yorkshire (Woollen District) Electric Tramways Limited was registered on 19 November 1901 and after negotiations with the local authorities took over the rights and duties of the British Electric Traction Co. Ltd and the Spen Valley Light Railway Orders. The Dewsbury–Thornhill section of the electric tramway opened on 18 February 1903. By 1905 there were 69 tramcars in stock, operating over 22 miles of route, including lines leased from Batley Corporation. These tracks were of 4 ft 8½ in. gauge, whereas Huddersfield had 4 ft 7¾ in. gauge, Bradford 4 ft gauge and Halifax 3 ft 6 in. gauge tramtrack; this was a direct incentive towards through services between West Riding towns being by bus, no matter how justified the choice of gauge seemed in the first place, such as the haulage of railway coal over one of the Huddersfield routes. A further tramway, sponsored by the National Electric Construction Co. Ltd, was the Dewsbury, Ossett and Soothill Nether system; this was standard gauge and was abandoned in 1933 after which Yorkshire (Woollen District) buses were used in replacement. The fleetname of the company was always 'Yorkshire' without qualification. In the meantime the London Midland & Scottish and London & North Eastern Railway companies had aquired ordinary shares in the company equal to the holding of the British Electric Traction Company in December 1929 and a co-ordinating committee was set up.

Motor services began to be operated in December 1913; a linking service with the Huddersfield tramways was established between Ravensthorpe and Bradley at a time when the company owned four vehicles. In 1913–15 the British Electric Traction Company was strongly tramway-orientated, as well as being in a somewhat difficult financial position. At this time Major Frank J. Chapple was Woollen District general manager, and he conducted a vigorous correspondence with head office urging the case for buying a fleet of buses which had stopped development early in the war at six vehicles. Between 1914 and 1920 tram traffic had increased by two-thirds and his advocacy was not falling on very fertile ground. In fact, bus services were suspended during February 1921 and Chapple's arguments included the threat of starting a bus service on his own account before the BET yielded and restarted Yorkshire operations with nine buses in April 1922. By the end of 1926 there were 51 buses in service and $4\frac{1}{2}$ million bus passengers were carried that year. The company obtained a tramway abandonment Act in 1931 and began closing the system down from 19 March 1932. The last tram ran on 31 October 1934.

Even before the Road Traffic Act (1930) the process of buying competitors had begun; Ideal Bus Services was absorbed in May 1929. In May of the following year the combined business of Hale Garage and Coachways Ltd was taken over jointly by East Yorkshire, West Yorkshire and Yorkshire Traction undertakings and in October 1933 Overland Service (owned by Tyne & Mersey Motor Service Ltd) was absorbed by five companies – Northern General, West Yorkshire, North Western, Lancashire United and Woollen District. The Fawdon Bus Company was taken over by Northern General, West Yorkshire, Yorkshire Traction and Woollen District and in November 1934 a quadripartite sharing of London Midland & Yorkshire services took place when East Yorkshire, West Yorkshire and Yorkshire Traction shared with Woollen District in its purchase. E. J. Slater & Son of Elland was acquired in April 1934 and in June 1935 the Morley and Leeds Service of H. V. Barker was taken over. A. Wallis & Sons, operating on a Leeds and Birstall service, was acquired in October 1935 and in March 1936 the services of Edwin Box & Sons of Dewsbury were acquired. G. H. Kilburn & Sons was then taken over. The buses had been carrying more passengers than the trams since 1930. A different combination of West Riding operators had acquired County Motors (Lepton) Ltd of Waterloo, near Huddersfield, which was maintained as a separate entity with two dozen or so vehicles. The partners were Woollen District, Yorkshire Traction and the Yorkshire (West Riding) Electric Tramways Ltd.

11
Tilling Group Companies

Thomas Tilling Ltd was a late starter as a holding company and in fact it was not until the effect of the 1913 agreement with the London General Omnibus Co. Ltd, which limited the company's activities in the Metropolis to a rigidly-laid-down number of vehicles, dawned on the management that any endeavours were made to start businesses outside London. Towns that were investigated included Folkestone, Ipswich, Yarmouth and Lowestoft, and Harry Webb was entrusted with far more decision-making than his title of London traffic superintendent would imply. As a result, the northern part of the Suffolk coast was left to United Automobile Services Ltd, which had established itself firmly with the local authorities and police there and in Norfolk; eventually the Tilling choice fell upon Folkestone when Folkestone & District was begun in April 1914; its merger has been recorded in a previous chapter where the development of the East Kent Road Car Co. Ltd has been described.

The next point of attack was the twin towns of Brighton and Hove, served since 1884 by the Brighton, Hove & Preston United Omnibus Co. Ltd, which had begun motor-bus experiments as long ago as 1902 and was operating Milnes-Daimler double-deckers on regular services in 1904. The same difficulty that had been found in Tilling's London operations was disclosed when it came to initiating horse-bus drivers in the mysteries of clutch and gearbox operation, and as a result a petrol-electric Hallford-Stevens bus was acquired and was fitted with the body from the 1902 Milnes-Daimler. Three electric accumulator buses were also purchased because their silent operation would appeal to the inhabitants of Hove, who were rather up-in-arms about the noise of petrol vehicles. These were of the London Electrobus model which had been running there since July 1907 and subsequently the Brighton company purchased eight more of the London fleet when the owning company ceased to do business in the Metropolis. This was no surprise to students of bus economics because the London Electrobus Company set its face against raising its fares in 1907 when other operators agreed upon increases. The Brighton fleet thus totalled 39 vehicles by 1910, 23 being petrol-driven (one with electric transmission) and 16 battery-electric.

The Brighton, Hove & Preston United Company now prepared plans for electric operation from wires – in other words trolleybuses – which were beginning to serve Bradford, Leeds and rural routes round Rotherham with rather clumsy vehicles. At the same time one appeared in London labelled for the Golders Green Road and rested awhile in the MET depot at Colindale. The BH & PU company actually obtained trolleybus powers in 1911 for various routes and in 1912 it put up a further scheme which included reinstatement of the roads on which the Hove and Shoreham Tramway ran. Brighton and Hove Corporations both obtained trolleybus Acts in 1912 and a novel feature was that the east–west route was to be operated jointly. Parliament agreed in 1913 to the BH & PU powers of 1911 being transferred to Brighton Corporation.

In 1914 the BH & PU ordered a fleet of Daimler buses as the ex-London Electrobus vehicles were showing signs of wear, but the new buses were requisitioned by the War Office on the outbreak of war and in 1916 the fleet at Brighton was of a very miscellaneous composition – there were still 12 London Electrobus chassis, 8 Tilling-Stevens petrol-electrics had been acquired, there were 23 assorted Straker-Squire, 2 five-year-old LGOC X-type, a couple of British Ensign chassis and there was one Daimler which had apparently been overlooked by the War Office and three ancient Milnes-Daimlers. It was a fleet to gladden the heart of a museum curator. There were also at this time, before the First World War, the Cedes demonstration trolley vehicle which had performed on Goldstone Terrace, Hove, before being sent to Keighley, and a Railless intended for Brighton. All these trolleybus powers in Brighton and Hove remained unexercised owing to the intervention of the First World War and the powers lapsed without revival. With part of its fleet worn out and the remainder of vehicles that BH & PU would not have operated if it used vehicles of its own choice, Thomas Tilling Ltd now applied for licences in Brighton and Hove, but there was a strong tendency to protect the BH & PU company, such as manifested itself when the pre-Southdown rivals sought to establish themselves. In 1915 some of the 'country' BH & PU routes were disposed of to Southdown; in fact, this really constituted the excursion business out of Brighton.

In February 1915 Hove Corporation issued 12 bus licences to Thomas Tilling Limited and 12 TTA1 petrol-electric buses were drafted to the Hove-based fleet. Brighton Corporation was adamant in refusing issue of licences and buses operated from points in Hove to the Brighton–Hove boundary, thence running to Castle Square to set down their passengers. On the return journey, as had happened with Sussex Motor Road Car journeys under these conditions, the return tickets which had been issued in Hove were accepted until the boundary was reached again. Thomas Tilling Ltd purchased the Brighton, Hove & Preston United company on 28 November 1916 and took over the BH & PU's territorial agreement; this protected Tilling in the Brighton and Hove area from Southdown competition and satisfied both municipalities so that ordinary tickets could be issued throughout all the Tilling and BH & PU services in the towns. The purchase arrangements included an agreement that BH & PU should not be wound up for two years. As this first provincial purchase only involved a company with 51 buses and £21,000 issued capital, the Brighton transaction did not cause much strain on Tilling's finances, which in 1916 were represented by £475,000 issued capital and £275,000 debentures, and this was counted as part of the London business.

During the next few years developments of bus services was not encouraged and there were acute fuel difficulties, overcome in the case of Chapman of Eastbourne, Southdown and others, by use of town gas carried on single-deck vehicles in a balloon mounted over the roof and in the case of the Tilling Brighton fleet by use of benzole made at the Turberville works in Dyke Road. At this time 'Thos. Tilling, London & Brighton' appeared cast on their radiators. In December 1935 the Tilling business in Brighton and Hove was formed into a £400,000 subsidiary company which was created as from 1 January 1936 under the name of Brighton, Hove & District Omnibus Co. Ltd. The Brighton Corporation at this time determined to recommend the conversion of the tramways system to trolleybuses and so some 25 years after the intention was first formed it was decided that trolleybuses should be introduced instead of tramways and on certain other streets. An interesting feature was that 11 trolleybuses were provided by the company to operate on the trolleybus system of the Corporation. The experts selected by the Corporation, A. R. Fearnley of Sheffield and

C. Owen Silvers of Wolverhampton, notable municipal managers, recommended co-ordination. The new set-up was on a 27½ per cent–72½ per cent pooling arrangement, the mileage to be provided by the summation of trolleybuses and motor buses, and there were complicated arrangements for provision of the quota of mileage by each party. This was a considerable contrast from the arrangement that had prevailed from 1919 when Tilling paid Brighton £40 each for the first 50 buses a year and £20 a bus a year thereafter to compensate the Corporation for wear and tear to the roads. The scheme came into operation on 1 April 1939 and was to last for 21 years in the first instance. An advisory committee was appointed to supervise the scheme, with three representatives of the company and three of the elected members of the Corporation (or permanent officials) for formal purposes. Fred P. Arnold, although a director of the Tilling company, was given as general manager of the company. The two towns were provided with transport from the site of the former tramway depot (trolleybuses and motor buses), and from the motor bus garage at Conway Street, Hove, of the former Brighton, Hove & Preston United Omnibus Co. Ltd and a new motor-bus garage at Whitehawk. The traffic manager remained Bertie Baker.

Various housing estates were established on fringes of Brighton with little reference to the 1915 agreement between the companies. The logical co-ordination of the Brighton area gave the public a much wider choice of service from all three undertakings. The six-minute trolleybus service was replaced by twelve Southdown buses an hour on Lewes Road going to a variety of destinations. A much more logical service is now established throughout the urban area. The tripartite pool began on 1 January 1961. The proportions were BH & D 50·5 per cent, Southdown 29 per cent and Brighton Corporation 20·5 per cent. The Brighton Corporation fleet is now in a blue livery and the BH & D buses are in Southdown green. The Brighton trolleybuses were withdrawn in mid-1961.

Tilling buses next began service in Ipswich and neighbourhood, in response to a request to link the town with the outlying districts. The holding companies, BET and Tilling, came together through the British Automobile Traction Company sponsoring in 1916, under stress of wartime maintenance problems, the East Kent Road Car Co. Ltd. Tilling buses began service in Ipswich in response to a local request. Thomas Tilling petrol-electric double-deckers were reported as being seen in Ipswich on the Shotley road at the return from school holidays by a school friend in 1919. The Tilling services had begun in June 1919. Within a few weeks it was decided to hive it off as a new British Automobile Traction company, the Eastern Counties Road Car Co. Ltd, an unusual concern, the interest being preponderantly a Tilling one. It was formed on 30 August 1919 and operations began on 1 September. A chain of small garages and dormy sheds, based on a repair shop in Ipswich, was established and included Bury St Edmunds, Woodbridge, Framlingham, Hadleigh, East Bergholt, Saxmundham, Eye, Ardleigh and Sudbury. By 1928 some 78 buses on 500 miles of route were operated.

Tilling investment in East Kent, the first company in which it participated with BAT, had taken place by amalgamation and in Maidstone & District and other concerns by investment, and in 1922 a holding was established in British Automobile Traction itself. The situation was regularised by a change of name in May 1928 to Tilling & British Automobile Traction Ltd. Although J. F. Heaton (later Sir Frederick) became a director of the company on 30 April 1928 it was not until 1936 that Heaton became chairman in alternate years. Before that Sidney Garcke had been managing director or chairman for many years.

Some of Eastern Counties' characteristics, including the comfortable person of J. Worssam, the general manager, were transferred to the Eastern Counties Omnibus Co. Ltd when that company was made out of the East Anglian section of United Automobile Services Ltd. This concern had been a bone of contention between the Tilling and London & North Eastern Railway chairmen in the June of 1929 but it was all settled amicably with the shares in United Automobile being divided equally between the LNER and Tilling & British. This result was arrived at, although one feels that Heaton handled the matter with a brashness that was strange to the suave business world of the BET. It is notable that Heaton shared shareholdings with the railways only in the case of the National Omnibus & Transport Company's subsidiaries, formed two years before the Tilling interest was taken, and the Tilling & British companies where the BET had determined the course of events and this acrimonious United transaction.

Different management methods in Tilling & British companies, according to whether they were Tilling-dominated or BET had the say, led to sharp personality clashes between J. F. Heaton, George Cardwell, S. E. Garcke and R. J. Howley and thus to a split in 1942 between the elements. After 1942 Tilling-managed companies included Caledonia Omnibus Co. Ltd, Crosville Motor Services Ltd, Cumberland Motor Services Ltd, Eastern Counties Omnibus Co. Ltd, Eastern National Omnibus Co. Ltd, Hants & Dorset Motor Services Ltd, Lincolnshire Road Car Co. Ltd, Southern National Omnibus Co. Ltd, Southern Vectis Omnibus Co. Ltd, Thames Valley Traction Co. Ltd, United Automobile Services Ltd, United Counties Omnibus Co. Ltd, West Yorkshire Road Car Co. Ltd, Western National Omnibus Co. Ltd, Wilts & Dorset Motor Services Ltd. The division of Tilling & British was different from what it had been because East

Midland and North Western were now back under BET management whereas companies newly under Tilling management were Crosville, Cumberland and Lincolnshire. When the assets of the new holding companies, BET Omnibus Services Ltd and Tilling Motor Services Ltd were assessed, it was seen that the Tilling group operators had more of the 'green fields' areas than the BET. The split of assets involved much less tension between the two groups and the two new companies were formed on 26 June 1942 after the adoption of the scheme at an extraordinary general meeting on 17 June.

United had begun in a modest way at Lowestoft, commencing operations in May 1912. The company was registered on 4 April 1912. The initial capital was £9,000 in £1 shares. The original fleet was of Halley and Commer vehicles; in the autumn of 1912 four more Commers began services in County Durham, locally from Bishop Auckland. In 1913 the fleet expanded by 8 more Commer and 6 LGOC B-type. By that year the services operated on the East Coast by the Great Eastern Railway had been purchased.

The fleet total rose to 64 in 1919, when the capital had risen to £46,000. Len Balls was responsible for developing the UAS services in Northumberland after 1920; Blyth–Newcastle routes were established from headquarters at Blyth. Other centres of development were at Ashington, Seaton Delaval and Morpeth. By this time UAS occupied much of the East Coast, from Suffolk and Norfolk to south Lincolnshire and then from Durham to Northumberland; on 1 June 1922 a depot was opened at Ripon and between 1922 and 1926 services were extended to cover the whole of North Riding. In 1928 UAS was operating 619 buses and the capital stood at £460,000. In 1931 the company disposed of its East Anglian assets for a proportionate allotment of shares in the new Eastern Counties Omnibus Co. Ltd, this step having been rendered easier by the purchase of UAS by Tilling & British Automobile Traction and the London & North Eastern Railway Company jointly in the summer of 1929. The holding company determined to localise UAS activities to the North of England.

Scarborough Corporation purchased the local tramways system for £20,000 in 1931 and abandoned it on 30 September; it had previously made an arrangement for the operation by UAS of local bus services in the town, thereby modernising the facilities. When UAS covered the East Coast it had seemed expedient to the Hutchinsons, who controlled it, to manage it from a central point at York and headquarters were established at Kilburn House in 1926. In 1932 the head office was transferred to Darlington to correspond with the new scene of the company's activities.

Following the Railway (Road Transport) Acts of 3 July 1928 the LNER acquired through its cartage agent Thompson McKay & Co. Ltd a

31 The first enclosed staircase bus in the London fleet, ST1. The staircase took a straight path from loading platform to upper deck

32 The London Midland & Scottish Railway had this Karrier Ro-Railer built; it is seen on trial at Redbourne (hence its registration in Hertfordshire) and was employed on a service from Euston via Blisworth and Stratford-on-Avon to the Welcombe Hotel, the last part being by road. The change to road wheels took $2\frac{1}{2}$ minutes. The designer was John Shearman, road motor engineer of the LMS

33 An AEC Regent 52-seater in the service of Bassetts of Gorseinon in South Wales

considerable interest in many minor bus undertakings including Blumers Bus Service of Greatham, Stockton-on-Tees, operator of a Hartlepool and Middlesbrough service with Crossley double-deck vehicles which were taken into the United fleet in November 1933. Other fleets taken over were Robert Emmerson & Co. Ltd, purchased by UAS on 1 January 1930. The Newcastle–Carlisle route, operated with AEC Reliance buses, was one of Emmerson's services and gave United access to Carlisle. Eastern Express Motors Ltd was another Durham area railway associate to come under United control on 1 January 1936; it had operated from West Hartlepool and had a fleet partially of lightweight American vehicles and of single-deck ADC '416' chassis. Services ran to Newcastle, Sunderland, Chester-le-Street and Darlington. Reliance Express of Darlington also acquired by UAS at the same time made a total fleet of nearly 100 vehicles to add to the United fleet in the beginning of 1930. An interesting feature of the UAS in 1930 was that the chairman, Thomas Hornsby, was north-eastern divisional general manager of the LNER; he constituted a co-ordinating feature of the early days of the railway group's interest in bus companies.

Coach companies under UAS control included Glenton Friars, National Coachways, Leeds–Newcastle Omnibus Co. Ltd and Majestic Saloon Coaches (Newcastle & London) Ltd. Express parcels were carried over all the territory from Scarborough to Carlisle and from Leeds to Berwick. For this purpose a fleet of Albion vans was provided. The localisation of UAS to the north of England and the creation of Eastern Counties Omnibus Co. Ltd as a strong East Anglian entity were two improvements in the structure of the bus industry. To round off the Eastern Counties business two small Tilling & British undertakings were contributed from the BET side. These were the Ortona Motor Co. Ltd of Cambridge and the Peterborough Electric Traction Co. Ltd.

The Ortona Company began in 1906 as an undertaking local to the town of Cambridge. It was set up by James B. Walford who was cruising in the North Sea when he saw an Italian steamer which had the name *Ortona* displayed on it – a town on the Adriatic coast of Italy. He liked the sound of the name and thought that it would serve for the bus company he was thinking of setting up. For a number of years the company enclosed its fleet name in inverted commas, thus, "Ortona". The limited company, the Ortona Motor Co. Ltd, was formed on 28 March 1908 out of the business of Walford and his son, John Berry Walford, who became managing director after the British Automobile Traction Co. Ltd took an interest in the business. When I first knew Ortona in 1916 its wartime fleet contained some 34-seat double-deckers on town services with Austin divided-drive $2\frac{1}{2}$-ton chassis and similar wartime substitutes from the McCurd stable. At that time the BAT investment was small and the total fleet only 19 vehicles.

Most of the fleet was in 1925 kept in Hills Road garage in Cambridge and the private hire fleet in St Pauls Garage in Hills Road. A small garage was built in 1925 at Newmarket and there 31-seat SOS buses obtained for operation of Newmarket–Ely and Newmarket–Cambridge services were kept. Another development of 1925 was provision by Cambridge Corporation of Drummer Street bus station, a more convenient terminus than the Senate House. In 1927 the fleet totalled 60; new paint shops were built in 1928 and the Hills Road garage enlarged. In this year covered-top double-deck buses (long advocated by J. B. Walford, but he was awaiting the compact Leyland Titan) appeared in the fleet. On 1 October 1928 the first Sunday service to be operated from Cambridge was to Bedford jointly with the National Omnibus & Transport Co. Ltd.

The 5·31 route miles of 3 ft 6 in. gauge track of the Peterborough Electric Traction Company's tramways were opened on 24 January 1903; the system was operated with 14 cars of 48 or 50 seats: it was financed by the British Electric Traction Company. Motor services were begun on 20 April 1913; in May 1928 when BAT reorganised as Tilling & British the controlling shareholding passed to T & BAT. The fleet in 1930 comprised 14 Leyland Titan, 50 SOS vehicles and a number of miscellaneous vehicles. In 1928 J. B. Walford of Ortona joined the Peterborough board and a through Peterborough–Cambridge service was the result. A joint railway offer at £1.17½ pence per share was made in December 1929, compared with a £2.25 pence offer at the same time for Ortona shares. With the four fleets that went to make the Eastern Counties Omnibus Co. Ltd that company had a total of 538 buses and coaches.

Under a mainly Tilling management (with J. F. Heaton as chairman) UAS continued to be as individual a company as before. The Hutchinson interests turned to freight and parcels undertakings, but Arthur Henry Hawkins of the East Surrey Traction Co. Ltd remained on the board as did (Sir) William J. Thomson, chairman and managing director of the Scottish Motor Traction Co. Ltd. The long through services operated jointly with the SMT from Newcastle to Edinburgh and to Glasgow were matched by English through routes to London (two routes), to Blackpool and to Lowestoft (for holiday traffic and seasonal workers in the fishing industry) and the company later joined others in the maintenance of the Limited Stop Service between Newcastle and Liverpool.

In 1975 United operated 1,056 buses and coaches, 270 double-deck and 674 single-decker buses and 111 coaches, with 1 minibus. Chassis included AEC, Bedford, Bristol and Leyland.

A company that had an unusually interesting career was Crosville Motor

Services Ltd. It started off as a motor-car manufacturer, and turned to the provision of bus services; then was purchased by the London Midland & Scottish Railway in 1929 to give the railway company experience in operating a bus undertaking, although at one stage the Crosville directors nearly walked out of the meeting owing to disparaging remarks by the LMS accountant. Subsequently a new company was formed to divide the interest of Crosville between Tilling & British Automobile Traction and the LMSR and then three years later an enlarged company was formed to take in the Western Transport Co. Ltd and Great Western Railway interests and to share them with Tilling & British Automobile Traction. The 1930 and 1933 Tilling & British companies were originally managed by the BET, but on the split in 1942 Tilling took over Crosville management.

Few companies have been described in such detail as Crosville, owing to the two excellent books, *Crosville – the Sowing and the Harvest* and *Nationalisation without Tears* by W. J. Crosland-Taylor, MC, F.C.Inst.T.

George Crosland-Taylor was born into the woollen business, but was greatly attracted by the electrical industry and as a result was a founder of the British Insulated & Helsby Cable Company in 1882 and then became interested in the early motor car and at the Paris Motor Show of 1904 met Georges Ville with whom he went into partnership to manufacture cars; he rented Crane Wharf, Chester, from the Shropshire Union Railway & Canal Company for the purpose. Only five cars were manufactured, however, and the name 'Crosville' was coined for them; although they built at least one motor boat the firm took up a suggestion in 1910 they should run a 'motor passenger service' from Chester to Ellesmere Port – a journey not possible by train without changing. So Crosville began to trade about January 1911 with a fleet of one Albion vehicle, although it had tried a Herald and a Germaine unsuccessfully. The car business had produced the registration of the company on 27 October 1906. By 1917 the Crosville fleet consisted of Daimler vehicles with Hora bodywork.

From 1909 to 1913 Crosville made substantial losses each year, although that in 1913 was only £21. The first year that a profit was shown was 1914 when £1,302 was recorded; this was attributed to running buses, and by 1918 traffic receipts were over £27,000. Early Crosville buses were named; *Royal George* was a Lacre, *Alma* was a Dennis and *Flying Fox* was a Daimler. A further peculiarity later on was that there was no number 13 in the stock; the vehicle that should have borne that number was lettered 'AC' instead.

George Crosland-Taylor died in January 1923; Claude Crosland-Taylor, his eldest son, took on the chairmanship until the railway purchase in 1929; from then until Claude's death in March 1935 he was managing director. The chairmanship passed to W. S. Wreathall, of Tilling & British. In 1939 (Sir)

John Spencer Wills became chairman and with the split of the Tilling and BAT partnership, Sir Frederick Heaton took the chair of Crosville.

Joey M. Hudson, who had spent the First World War in the Royal Navy, started some Crossley pneumatic-tyred buses between Ellesmere Port and Chester. He arrived at the Watch Committee hearing in Chester, and was introduced by his advocate to Claude Taylor and a sharp verbal exchange took place. 'What the hell did you want to start a bus service for?' said Taylor. 'You will not get a licence in Chester and even if you do I intend running you off the road.' These attempts at intimidation amounted in the end to Crosville painting a Crossley Tender in Hudson's colours, running just ahead of Hudson's times and keeping Hudson talking on the stand in Chester so that he missed a journey. Claude then offered Hudson the management of the newly established hire department. Freight haulage figured in Crosville's activities until after the First World War, when the four Foden steam wagons were sold.

Before the Road Traffic Act a firm called S. Jackson & Sons started a Crewe–Nantwich service and reduced the fare for the distance of over 10 miles to 4d. As they had been established before the dates set down in the Act they were able to carry on – although at a fare approved by the Traffic Commissioners – until 1934.

The first Crosville Sick Club was begun at Nantwich in 1922 at 6d a week and Nantwich also had the first staff mess room on the system. In 1927 a club room of a more elaborate type was opened above Burtons in Foregate Street, Chester, but it was 1937 before club rooms and garages came together.

In 1929 on February 5 the meeting was held at which it was agreed Crosville should be bought outright; from 1 May it belonged to the London Midland & Scottish Railway, the agreement for its purchase mentioned the sum of £398,750. The purchase was agreed in a ground-floor room at the old Euston Hotel. Just before the directors yielded to the LMS offer, the price of Crosville shares was 23s, although the official stock exchange quotation was 26s; the LMS offer was 27s 6d. They wanted to gain some experience of the road passenger business and they paid for it without regard to the cost, paying much more than they need have done for other businesses in North Wales as they purchased them. During 1929 Crosville buses were painted Midland Red and were known as LMS (Crosville); a few buses were repainted with the LMS crest.

The account given by W. J. Crosland-Taylor in *The Sowing and the Harvest* differs materially from the facts as generally known; perhaps this is due to the Great Western Railway withdrawal at one stage of the proceedings – a withdrawal that lasted some years, when the GWR recovered lost face by merging its Western Transport Co. Ltd with Crosville. According to an announcement of 5 August 1929 the GWR jointly agreed with the LMSR to buy Crosville for £398,750. The Crosville Motor Company was placed in voluntary liquidation and Claude Crosland-Taylor, the former chairman and managing director, was named as general manager. As stated, the purchase was carried out by the LMSR alone at the same price.

On 4 November 1929 Sir Robert Thomas, chairman of the Seaside Resorts and Development Co. Ltd, sold the Mona Maroons Saloons bus services (Holyhead Motor Services, working in Anglesey) and 18 buses; the concern was apparently on its last legs and was put under the control of Crosville on 4 November 1929, but the LMS paid £26,500. The following year it would probably not have been acceptable to the Traffic Commissioners. UNU (You Need Us!) Motors of Llangefni was bought from W. Webster of Wigan on 1 January 1930 for £32,000. For some years Brookes Brothers of Rhyl (White Rose Motor Services) had had a working arrangement with Crosville; on 1 May 1930 its services and 89 vehicles were purchased by LMSR for £125,000 and transferred to Crosville.

The LMSR made offers to the shareholders of Tilling & British Automobile Traction Ltd in respect of holdings of the requisite number of T & B shares to equalise its interests on 1 November 1929 and also made one of 25s (125 pence) per £1 ordinary share for the Llandudno Coaching & Carriage Co. Ltd, a T & BAT undertaking whose territory was entirely surrounded by Crosville routes. The agreement between T & BAT and Llandudno Coaching & Carriage was actually dated 28 December 1929. When LMSR bought UNU Motor Services (You Need Us) owned by W. Webster of Wigan, it added about 12 buses to Crosville stock. A company entitled Crosville Motor Services Ltd, incorporating LMSR and T & BAT shareholdings, was formed on 1 May 1930.

From 1 May 1933 Crosville took in the Western Transport Co. Ltd, a company with headquarters at Wrexham. A very small horse tramway was built in 1875 and 1876; its headquarters were at Johnstown, the rendezvous for carriers' carts centred on Wrexham. On 8 August 1900 the National Electric Traction Co. Ltd purchased the track and sold it on the following 22 December to British Electric Traction Co. Ltd, which began electric working on 4 April 1903. The name was changed to Wrexham & District Transport Co. Ltd on 19 March 1914, the first motor-bus service having been begun on 23 September 1913. At the end of the First World War the bus fleet comprised 10 single-deckers. The tram services at Wrexham were discontinued on 31 March 1927, buses being used to replace them. Although Viscount Churchill announced at the GWR annual general meeting in 1930 that the GWR was taking over the Wrexham & District bus services jointly with the LNER, the promised joint shareholding did not materialise; in June 1930 the Great Western bus services in the area were transferred to Wrexham & District operation and it was November 1930 before the change of name was made to Western Transport Co. Ltd, incorporating the word 'Western' like all other bus companies in which the GWR had taken an interest. The amount spent by the GWR on Western Transport shares was just over £87,710 for 76,916 shares. Two services round Corwen were begun in 1904 and 1907 respectively; 13 others and six former Corris Railway services (before which the Corris Railway had provided a number of horse-coach services) had begun between 1923 and 1926. The Western Transport merger eventually took place on 1 May 1933, holders in Western Transport receiving £1 share in Crosville for each share. Crosville shareholdings then were 50 per cent Tilling & BAT, 37½ per cent LMSR and 12½ per cent Great Western Railway.

Most of the Western Transport staff were members of the T & GW union, but a number of them were former railwaymen and thus members of the NUR and drawing all sorts of allowances; a lump sum payment was eventually made to these men and they were persuaded to join the Transport & General Workers Union so that all staff could be paid on the same basis. Claude and his brother went round on Bank Holiday Sunday, 1 August 1933; they visited every Western Transport depot to get the assent of all the staff to this arrangement.

Telford's suspension bridge of 1826 across the Menai Straits had a weight limit on it of 4 tons 5 cwt which meant a single-deck bus of 20 seats on all Anglesey services if there were to be through running. The opportunity was taken to do some strengthening when the holding bolts on the Caernarvonshire side broke; Crosville arranged a luncheon on 26 March 1945 to organise a pressure group for sanctioning double-deckers over the bridge. The work of improving the bridge was completed in 1945 and the first double-decker across the Menai Straits came into use that same year.

Cumberland Motor Services Ltd started off on 8 August 1912 as Whitehaven Motor Service Co. Ltd and changed its name when more general territorial titles were popular with British Automobile Traction subsidiaries. Originally the Whitehaven company centred on the Meageen family and the original capital was the very modest sum of £1,500. The authorised capital was pushed up to £20,000 in 1920, to £35,000 in 1923 and to £60,000 in the following year. Manxland Bus Services Ltd, was formed as a subsidiary in the Isle of Man in 1927. Services by this company began in May of that year. A fleet of 30 Guy single-deckers was obtained, the issued capital being £30,000. Garages were located at Douglas, Peel, Port Erin and Ramsey. The seating capacity of the Manxland vehicle was 28, although the island traffic regulations specified 20 as the maximum permissible capacity. The Act granting permission for larger vehicles was passed after the order was placed. A limit of 20 seats continued on private hire vehicles. Manx Motors Ltd was formed in 1927 with an authorised capital of £16,000 (£7,066 issued) of which £6,000 was supplied by the Isle of Man Railway Company. It is interesting to note that £3,000 in debentures was issued and that capital expenditure by 1928 amounted to £16,721. The fleet consisted of 19 vehicles, mainly Thornycroft, but in June 1928, having disposed of its holding in Manx Motors it purchased 22 buses for operation in its own fleet. A decision to purchase all the rival concerns and end cut-throat competition was taken in February 1929 and a consolidated undertaking, Isle of Man Road Services Ltd, was formed on 17 June 1930. Embracing much of the island's transport facilities, the Isle of Man Road Services shares its management with the narrow-gauge steam railway which is now used as a tourist attraction. The present fleet of IoM Road Services is 33 double-deck and 22 single-deck. Douglas Corporation Transport operates 31 horse tramcars (as an archaic novelty), 27 double-deck and 14 single-deck buses (31 AEC, 8 Leyland, 2 Bedford); excursion and tour operators on the island include Castle Rushen Motors, A. A. Corkish, T. A. Corlett, Darnills Motors Ltd, Fargher's (Peel) Ltd which dates back to the 1920s but is now with the same directorate and livery as Tours (Isle of Man) Ltd which owns 46 coaches and 8 minibuses and is jointly owned by Corkill's Garage Ltd and the Isle of Man Railway Ltd. Other excursion operators are Mrs A. Roberts and W. H. Shimmin (Tours) Ltd, the last-mentioned being one of the more sizeable, with 10 vehicles.

Cumberland Motor Services Ltd became a British Automobile Traction Company at the beginning of the 1920s and when the Tilling & British Automobile Traction assets were split up in 1942 it was transferred to the Tilling group. Its growth was slow but steady, occupying a sparsely populated part of Cumbria. A typical consolidation took place in Aspatria in 1934 when the services of John William Stoddart were taken over. The new structure of routes was Aspatria–Gilcrux–Cockermouth; Aspatria–Plumbland–Mealsgate–Wigton; Ireby–Mealsgate; Uldale–Mealsgate–Wigton; Cockermouth–Blindcrake; Wigton–Patterfoot–Wigton; and Aspatria–Allonby.

I went to Whitehaven to see the undertaking in 1955; it was in a lively state, as diesel railcars had just been delivered to the West Cumberland area of the London Midland Region, so as a counterblast the Tilling management board had provided Lodekka low-height Bristol buses for the Carlisle–Whitehaven service. At the same time I was able to see something of what was being done at that time to relieve the depression that had cursed the West Cumberland industrial area before the Second World War. Judging by the flow of passengers on the buses this had already largely lifted.

When the London Midland & Scottish Railway took a shareholding in the company it paid 55s for each £1 share. There are one or two places of remarkable road formations on the Cumberland Motor Services network, the most remarkable being Ireby, where the space between houses is barely more than 8 ft and special skill is needed to negotiate the small slit. The other interesting stretch of Cumberland territory is between Keswick and Seatoller, a route that traverses the length of Derwentwater, although not on the shores of the lake. This demonstrates the ability of the Tilling & British companies when under British Automobile Traction influence to live in harmony with their neighbours, as a small one-man bus on this route was inherited from an independent operator.

12 Some Rapid Developers

The most romantic development of a small omnibus company into a big one, in the writer's view, was that of the sudden expansion of the National Steam Car Co. Ltd into the National Omnibus & Transport Co. Ltd. The steam fleet at its maximum was 173 in 1919; by the time of the Tilling purchase, at 43s per £1 ordinary share in February 1931, the fleet, by then divided between Eastern, Southern and Western National Omnibus Companies, totalled over 800 buses. At the time of the railway investment in 1929 Northern and Midland National Companies were registered, but the Northern was never activated, the title being used to prevent anyone else exploiting the name, and it was found impossible to separate the assets eventually transferred to Eastern national between the London & North Eastern and London Midland & Scottish Railways to form a Midland National bus concern as at first intended. In 1928 the National fleet totalled 861 petrol buses covering 4,496 miles of route. This expansion was not achieved without some traumatic difficulties; the National Omnibus & Transport Co.'s former routes can be distinguished to this day by irregular operation to cover times when passengers gathered in bulk; many of the services are market days only; all carry indications that they were begun with too few vehicles to cover the mileage and have a different atmosphere from other services in the south of England where the regular headways and ample coverage of the territory are witness to ample capital resources and adequate rolling stock and staff. Alas! it is too late now; if the population has not the bus habit today, they are never likely to acquire it in these days of the motor car. As Douglas Mackenzie once said to me, if a service was showing signs of being unsuccessful, he would try doubling the frequency to see if that would bring them off their bicycles! The result is that in similar territory, ex-National Omnibus & Transport routes take less revenue per car mile than more frequent services. In fact, stringent necessity compelled the fast-expanding NO & T and its officials to expect a minimum sum per car mile from the beginning even on a new route, so much so that the story goes that on one new route in Weymouth the decision for withdrawal was made before the notices announcing the times and where the service was intended to go were distributed.

Sidney Garcke was still suffering from pique over the besting of the BET by the Underground group when in 1914 young T. E. Thomas, the youthful commercial manager of the Underground, on behalf of the LGOC and Underground offered him the Bedford garage which the New Central company had brought into their assets. He refused to assist the LGOC to carry out the sale of the Bedford garage to implement the agreement the LGOC had signed in 1912–13 not to compete with the BET in the provinces. A T & BAT company based on Bedford might have resulted. With the end of the First World War the National Steam Car Company found that the Metropolitan Police were adopting a less amicable attitude towards high-pressure steam which some members of the force seemed to confuse with the atom-bomb. The price of naphtha had gone up by 2,700 per cent and the National men sought the conditions which had been accorded the General staff of an eight-hour day. The National Steam Car Company therefore decided to abandon its steam fleet, adopt petrol vehicles and to exchange its garages at Putney Bridge and Nunhead for that which the London General had obtained in 1914 from the New Central Omnibus Co. Ltd at Bedford. The LGOC in fact rebuilt the Bedford garage during its occupancy and for many years evidence was to be seen in the form of its initials on manhole covers. Eventually the Central transferred its interests to the Wellingborough Omnibus Co. Ltd (which later became the United Counties) during 1913 and the London Underground for a time took over the assets of the Central in the London area.

Two acquisitions which affected the National fleet should be mentioned. The Great Eastern Railway began bus operation from Chelmsford to Danbury, Writtle and Great Waltham on 9 September 1905. The National Steam Car Co. Ltd actually began provincial operations by purchasing the Chelmsford GER group of routes, which by July 1913 included a Tuesday and

Friday run to Leaden Roding and daily services to Boreham and Galleywood and Stock. During the First World War extensions by National steamers were made to Billericay, Braintree and Maldon.

There were 12 London Central Leyland 34-seaters at Bedford and the LGOC in 1914 purchased Burridge's Bedford Omnibus Company on the Kempston route with a 20-seat Argyll and a 20-seat Ryknield bus. The fleet at Bedford had grown to 30 vehicles by 23 November 1914 when the War Office commandeered the rolling stock. The depot was handed back on 9 August 1919. Operations were resumed with eight buses. The name of the company was changed to National Omnibus & Transport Co. Ltd on 13 February 1920. During 1919 depots were opened at Brentwood and Bishops Stortford. On 19 November of that year the last National steamer ran in Central London on route 12 from Dulwich to Shepherds Bush. The garages at Nunhead and Putney Bridge were occupied the following day by LGOC B-type buses. In the 1919 agreement with the LGOC the National company had freedom to operate anywhere in the country outside the London area. The eight vehicles with which the National management began operations at Bedford were deployed on routes to Biggleswade, Cranfield, Kempston, Newport Pagnell, St Neots and Woburn. By contrast some of the routes initiated by the London Central were more in the nature of town services, such as Clapham to Goldington via Tavistock Street, Bedford.

The London & North Western Railway operated a range of motor-bus services, mainly with Milnes-Daimler vehicles, from 11 July 1905 in North Wales and from 1906 onwards in the Harrow and Watford areas, which were suspended during the First World War. From September and October 1920 these services were revived by the London General Ominbus Co. Ltd. From 1 June 1921 they were transferred to the National Omnibus & Transport Co. Ltd, which worked them as operating agents on behalf of the LGOC. About six months previous to these events, in January 1921, Hertford & District Motor Omnibus Services Company, had been started by F. A. Harvey & F. Burrows who had a depot by Ware Town Hall. The LGOC purchased this concern in June 1924 and transferred it to National management. I remember taking a Harvey & Burrows Straker-Squire (they had 3, with 18 Daimlers) from Waltham Cross to Hertford and being interested in the light bulbs on the bus, all labelled 'LGOC', despite it being nominally 'National', and the driver, a real countryman, stopping in a patch of woodland near Wormley to rescue a hedgehog which was putting itself in peril by crossing the A10 main road.

Road Motors Ltd began on 6 May 1910 and was purchased by National in 1925 with 42 vehicles, mainly Dennis, but including a few Palladiums. Mr and Mrs Attree controlled the company and services ran from Luton to

Wheathampstead, to St Albans, to Dunstable, to Toddington, to Hitchin, to Letchworth and Norton, to Stotfold, to Markyate, to Upper Sundon and to Caddington and from Hitchin to Arlesey.

National services were begun from Grays in 1922 and a garage was built there two years later. Grays & District (Abercrombie and Collis, two ex-General drivers) was absorbed about this time and a service was started from Romford.

On 18 January 1932 it was announced that all the services in the environs of London which had been worked by agents for London General were being transferred and the East Surrey Traction Co. was being renamed London General Country Services Ltd. Some 627 route miles and 42 separate services were handed over to the London General Country Services at this time, only to be handed over to the Country Service and Green Line department of the London Passenger Transport Board on 1 July 1933.

By 1921 garages were opened by National at Bridgwater, Stroud, Taunton, Trowbridge and Yeovil. In 1921 I remember being in the Cotswolds with Noel Jackson and looking down from the escarpment near Cheltenham seeing a white National double-decker followed closely along the same narrow road by a blue single-deck 4-ton Bristol and thinking how stupid of two responsible bus operators to be competing for traffic in such thin territory.

The Hardy Central Garage Co. Ltd was absorbed by the National Omnibus and Transport Co. Ltd in 1927. The company began on 19 November 1919 and took in R. Dymond & Son of Bideford and Colwills (Ilfracombe) Ltd, and joined Hardy Central Garage on 12 July 1924 to become Hardy-Colwills. As well as operations round Ilfracombe some activities were included round Bideford, Bude and Bodmin.

S. Edwards & Co. of Bude, Rowlett of Stroud, Smith & Hoare of Portland and J. Kershaw of North Petherton were a representative bunch of National acquisitions about this time and in December 1927 Devon Motor Transport Co. Ltd was taken over. This company had pursued a similar career to National on a smaller scale but had accumulated 135 vehicles by 1927. These were mainly 31-seat Bristol 40 h.p. single-deckers, Albion 28-seat and Thornycroft 20-seat buses and coaches. This company was registered on 3 December 1919 and the founder, Lieut-Commander F. T. Hare, did his utmost to persuade my former chief, David Lamb, fresh from the Army, to join him during the Christmas holidays, in time for a start on 1 January 1920. As he had become a magnate in the bus business the careers of several people, myself included, might have been quite different. Hare gathered about him several other ex-Army and ex-Royal Navy officers who lived round Tavistock and Okehampton where the headquarters of DMT were placed, and he was attracted to Lamb because he had been one of Sir Sam Fay's bright young men on the Great Central Railway.

National acquired Cornwall Enterprise Motors in September 1923 and A. C. Turner of Plymouth in May 1924. Penzance & Jeames (Weymouth & Trelawney Tours) were acquired in 1929. The fleet consisted of 16 AEC, Dennis, Lancia and Leyland chassis and began operation on 11 March 1914. Hocking's Tours of Newquay, were also acquired in 1929, with 3 Albion, 1 Dennis and 13 Lancia chassis. From 1 January 1929 the Western and Southern National Companies were split off and from 1 January 1930 the Eastern National Omnibus Co. Ltd started its separate existence, although it was registered on 28 February 1929.

The Clacton & District Motor Services Ltd was registered on 4 December 1913 and during the war owned about three vehicles; after the change of name to Silver Queen Motor Omnibus Co. Ltd the fleet was returned as 45 Leyland buses and 25 Leyland coaches. Silver Queen, founded by W. P. Allen on 4 December 1913, was taken over with Blyth's business, Enterprise Bus Company (Clacton) Ltd with 14 AEC and Leyland and a small group of Lancia vehicles. These Clacton businesses were absorbed in 1926.

A controlling interest in Borough Services Ltd was obtained in 1933 and the takeover was delayed until 1947; services ran to Grays (begun 1927), to Colchester (begun by Rayleigh & District), and from Leigh Station to Eastwood and Leigh Station to Somerset Crescent – these two were transferred to the Westcliff-on-Sea Company at the outbreak of war. After 1 July 1933 a big acquisition of services in the Grays area took place; Tilbury Safety Coaches was acquired in 1934, the result being that east–west through services from Tilbury to Purfleet were interrupted to the public inconvenience. On the other side of the Thames, at Gravesend, the cocky young men who took a traffic census did it on an early-closing day with the results that in no time flat the London Passenger Transport Board had petitions from residents. Eastern National bought three Gilford coaches from Hillman with a view to operating them from Bow to Colchester, but the LPTB interpreted its powers rather rigidly in those days and the Eastern National found themselves unable to operate.

On 8 August 1934 Mrs E. S. Furber (East Bergholt & District) sold her business and was followed on 18 February 1937 by A. W. Berry & Sons Ltd of Port Lane and Artillery Street, Colchester, established as long ago as 1888, who handed over 13 buses including Dennis, LGOC and AEC vehicles to the EN, as well as garage premises at Brightlingsea, Colchester and West Mersea. Services in the neighbourhood of Tendring were abandoned.

Patten's Coaches sold the service from Pitsea Sation to Chignall Corner in November 1934. Bird Motor Services operated from Halstead to Braintree and also Braintree to Sudbury; there was also an express service; this was the first permanent Eastern National express service to London. On 24 August 1935 C. M. Taylor of the Horn Coach Company sold his express service from London to Braintree and Great Bardfield. In the transfer were included a service to Greenstead Green and Felsted Sugar Beet Factory. Harry Griffiths, who operated on the Halstead to Colchester route, became superintendent at the new Halstead garage. J. W. Gozzett (Quest) sold a Maldon–London express service and 11 stage carriage services and on 24 March 1940 Simpsons of Leaden Roding, operators of a number of services in the Chelmsford, Dunmow, Ongar and Bishops Stortford areas relinquished a group of routes to Eastern National; the purchase of Clavering & District (Wilson's) strengthened services local around Bishops Stortford.

Establishment of the London Passenger Transport Board involved the abandonment of Premier Line and its associate the Aylesbury Omnibus Company, which had set up in the premises just outside that town which had been occupied just after First World War by the Cubitt Car Company, one of the post-1914 hopefuls in the car industry. The fleet stationed there included 20 Leyland, mostly the Titan single-deckers which Premier favoured for its coach operations, 2 Daimler and 2 small Chevrolet. This undertaking was divided between London Passenger Transport Board, Eastern National, City of Oxford, United Counties and Thames Valley. Just before the formation of the LPTB I rode back from Oxford via Aylesbury to London beginning the journey on an Aylesbury Motor Company's Daimler when the company belonged to E. W. Young. The rolling stock was ripe for renewal and included 8 elderly Fords.

When 18 Leyland Tigers were introduced by Premier Line the fleet name 'Aylesbury Line' was adopted. The new Aylesbury Omnibus Co. Ltd was formed on 26 October 1931. Bowing to the inevitable the directors sold to Eastern National on 11 May 1933. Almost simultaneously an arrangement was made for most of the Eastern National Aylesbury area to be ceded to United Counties Omnibus Co. Ltd.

A. F. England's Union Jack (Luton) Omnibus Co. Ltd, dating from 20 November 1928, was purchased by Luton Corporation which made a provisional agreement to purchase in October 1932; 12 services and 14 vehicles were involved. A joint agreement was made between Eastern National and Luton Corporation, for pooling of services.

Beaumont & Priest of Leighton Buzzard, Slade of Offord and the 'Wonder' services of Bedford and St Neots, and C. Taylor (Reliance Safety Coaches) of Shillington, Seamarks of Westoning & District and Huntingdon Coaches Ltd, and Cambridge Blue Motor Services of Arrington Bridge were miscellaneous small purchases effected between 1934 and 1936.

Hicks Brothers Ltd, founded in 1913 with a market-day service from Felstead into Braintree, was purchased by Eastern National on 1 January 1950; the fleet totalled over 45, half being double-deck.

On 30 September 1951 the Grays area was transferred to London Transport Executive with 28 vehicles. On 1 May 1952 the logical step was taken of transferring the entire Midland area of Eastern National with 241 vehicles to United Counties Omnibus Co. Ltd.

The Westcliff-on-Sea Char-a-banc Company was registered on 23 April 1914 and carried on an enterprise begun by C. & C. Holmes and S. Smith, mainly in the provision of extended tours from Southend. Stage services around Southend were begun in 1921 and eight years later the coach fleet was known as 'Royal Red' and 23 stage services were operated. Edwards Hall Motors Ltd, the Blue Buses, which had been the subject of various agreements for some years, was absorbed in 1932. During 1933 Eastern National purchases included Thundersley, Hadleigh & District Motors and the services from Rochford to Southend, Creeksea to Southend and Stambridge to Southend of Rochford & District Motor Services. The first was founded in 1915 and operated from Hadleigh Church to Leigh Church with eight vehicles. The Tilling group took financial control of the Westcliff company in 1935. Although the Second World War caused some curtailment of facilities, the purchase of Multiways Ltd and a Southend to Hastings and south coast resorts service was carried out. The British Transport Commission also acquired Benfleet & District as well as a co-operative undertaking with 17 partners on a rota basis for driving, conducting, and other duties, Canvey & District Motor Transport, in 1934.

One of the best-known and most competent of the London independent proprietors was the City Omnibus Co. Ltd which did considerable rebuilds of its original 48-seat Leylands as a 55-seat open-top bus ('C1') and 62-seat six-wheeled covered-top vehicles ('CS' class); seeing the trend of the London business towards a compulsory merger, they took steps to ensure that they had a share in the coach business within easy access from the Metropolis. New Empress Saloons was in a somewhat run-down state and when the original proprietor, A. H. Young, was joined by Messrs Barnett and Collier, a new company was formed on 3 July 1928. The City board, W. F. and B. A. Mallender and Walter Crook, took possession of New Empress including two ex-London Public Maudslays and 7 Dennis E-type, on 20 November 1928. Between December 1933 and January 1934 the 18 Leyland Lions then operating the service (twelve 32-seat and six 29-seat) were all fitted with Dorman-Ricardo compression-ignition engines, using derv and saving £100 a week on the fuel bill; the fuel consumption on the service went down from 9·5 m.p.g. on petrol to 14 m.p.g. on diesel fuel and at that time diesel fuel had the great advantage of costing only $4\frac{1}{8}$ pence a gallon. City extended the service from Wood Green to Camden Town in October 1928 and a garage was shared with City buses at Leighton Road, Kentish Town. From 1 January 1929 the timetable was made joint with Westcliff-on-Sea Motor Services. In 1934 the Southend–Wood Green service was sold to the City Coach Co. Ltd. Local routes centring on Brentwood, including Nugus, were taken over and then the reverse process went on with the Kentish Town–Southend route being sold to Eastern National.

From 1921 onwards the National favoured Burford lightweight vehicles; after 1936 Bristol vehicles came into the fleet through Bristol becoming a marque associated with Thomas Tilling; from 1946 a number of vehicles based on lightweight chassisless Beadle parts were obtained; while petrol engines were used at first, compression-ignition engines were later adopted.

With high-speed rotating brushes hung from a frame in a garage, the Essex bus washer, designed by W. Morrison, chief engineer of Eastern National, was extensively adopted by Tilling companies after 1950.

During 1926 The National Omnibus & Transport Co. Ltd obtained the Isle of Portland Motor Bus Co. Ltd and in May 1927 Rex Charabanc Tours (R. H. Baker) of Plymouth. In 1931 the Southern General Omnibus Co. Ltd, with a name originally intended for a Southern Railway and London General Omnibus Co. Ltd subsidiary (which the LGOC, apparently lacking its usual acumen, omitted to register in advance of its need) was acquired by National Omnibus & Transport; it had been formed by incorporation of Hopper & Berryman of Plympton, Hendry Bus Service of Totnes and W. T. Coach of Plymouth; control was acquired by J. H. Watts of Red & White in 1930.

On 1 January 1933 Thomas Motors of Taunton (Lavender Blue) was purchased and on 30 March 1933 A. H. Broming of Totnes. Massatt Safety Cars (Eli Ford) was purchased on 3 March 1933 and Embankment Motor Company of Plymouth on 31 March 1933. In April 1933 Imperial Motor Service of Watchet (H. V. G. Williams) was acquired and in the same month Zenith Buses (E. V. Lowe & Co.) of Plymouth; E. Noyes & Co. came into the Western National fold on 30 March 1933 and Marazion Garage Ltd in August of that year. In May 1933 Dunn's Services of Taunton with 18 vehicles, was taken over.

J. R. Pollard of Kuggar was acquired in March 1934; in April Dartmouth & District Bus Co. Ltd was taken over; E. Smith of Taunton in June and in December 1934 Western & Southern National joined in acquiring Elliott Brothers Royal Blue Services. Elliott had long had an agreement which made them virtually the long-distance department of Hants & Dorset, an awkward arrangement which resulted in Bristol's Greyhound associate

173

being called on to provide road coach services from London to Bournemouth on behalf of the Southern Railway.

The Quay Garage Co. Ltd of Kingsbridge was another excursions and tours operator, taken over in April 1935. In May W. C. Glanville of Taunton and in the following November stage carriage services operated by Dartington Hall Ltd were absorbed. In July 1937 Mrs M. Hosking of Penryn and S. Pulsford of Lewilscombe and Mills & Lee were taken into the Western National structure.

Southern National acquired Wincanton & District Motor Services on 1 November 1932 and in 1933 the Braunton to Croyde Bay service of Mrs M. Bassett was acquired. Another 1933 purchase was Edwards & Hann Ltd of Bridport. The Great Western and Southern's joint bus service in Weymouth was taken over on 1 January 1934 and in February B. C. Toogood of Shaftesbury. In February 1935 A. F. Good's Silver Cars of Seaton were absorbed. In August of that year Reynolds Brothers were taken over and in March 1936 Scarlet Pimpernel Cars of Ilfracombe which kept up as a separate establishment for a year or two, providing holiday extras from London to North Devon with 20-seat vehicles. In the same month Hocking's Ensign Coaches was taken over at Appledore. In March 1937 the passenger business of Bird Brothers (Transport) Ltd of Yeovil was taken over and in May of 1937 the Swanage–Corfe Castle routes of G. Ford & Co. The bus services of Chard Motors, operating in Taunton, Chard, Axminster and Seaton area, since 1920 by Chaplin & Rogers of Victoria Garage, Chard, was purchased in February 1932. The service to Seaton ran via Colyton whereas the co-ordinated service of Southern National ran via Axmouth. The fleet was a little unusual in that as late as 1932 it included a chain-driven Hallford vehicle.

United Automobile Services acquired Norfolk Road Services in 1925 and in November 1926 acquired Robinson's Motors Ltd, Scarborough; on 1 January 1930 UAS took over LNER services in Northumberland and Durham and on the same day took over other LNER (or Thompson McKay, the LNER cartage subsidiary) associates such as Robert Emmerson (who gave UAS access to Carlisle) who had been painting their vehicles in Emmerson livery on one side and LNER on the other for a year. Reliance Express Motors, Eastern Express Motors, Amos Proud & Co. Ltd, Choppington, Red Line Motors, Crescent Omnibus Services, Blue Band Bus Services, Safeway Services Ltd, formed 1927 to amalgamate Frazer's Doreen Services, Redcar & Charltonian Services (Birkbeck), Carlisle & District Transport (jointly with Ribble, Caledonian, Cumberland and SMT) in December, 1930; in August 1931 J. S. Fraser (Saltburn–Warrenby), also in August R. Dunning (Middlesbrough to Kirby Moorside); on 1 September

1931 Scarborough Tramways Company; during 1932 National Coach-
ways Ltd (a Newcastle–London service) and in March Glenton Friars (Road
Coaches) Ltd and in November of that year Rutherford's Coaches and then
Jermy & Co. Ltd of Felton. In 1933 UAS purchases included Ennis & Reed
Ltd, Bridlington & District, Billingham & Haverton Hill Motors Ltd,
Scarborough & District Motors Ltd, with some AEC S-type buses finished
in London General style, and Carthope & District Motors. In 1934 additional
business included County Motor Services Ltd, acquired jointly with
Scottish Motor Traction; also purchased in 1934 was the United Auto-
mobile Association, a group of eight small operators around Langley Moor.
White & Timm of Bedlington was acquired in mid-1934 and Sleightholme
Brothers of Malton at the end and after November the Newcastle–London
service of Phillipson's Service was transferred from the London Control
Office to the Tilling-associated Orange Brothers. In June 1936 Bolton
Brothers was purchased; they were based at Embleton, Northumberland,
and operated seven buses.

Hants & Dorset Motor Services Ltd was formed on 17 March 1916 as
Bournemouth & District Motor Services Ltd to adopt an agreement with
J. B. M'Meekin. This was another company inspired by W. F. French. W. W.
Graham, the general manager, was on the board until all general managers
of THC operating companies were granted seats on boards of directors by
the Transport Holding Company. The name Hants & Dorset was adopted on
27 July 1920. In June 1927 Anna Valley Motors was absorbed. In 1929 the
Southern Railway paid 225 pence for each £1 share, acquiring a holding
equal to that of Tilling & British Automobile Traction Ltd (£213,556). In
January 1935 Elliott Brothers (Bournemouth) Ltd, operators of Royal Blue
Tours, was acquired. For many years this business had been the subject of
an agreement with Elliott under which Hants & Dorset was unable to
provide tours from Bournemouth or long-distance coach services, so that
when the Southern Railway desired a coach service from London Coastal
Coaches to Bournemouth, Greyhound of Bristol, a coaching subsidiary of
Bristol Tramways & Carriage, had to be employed. In May 1935 Tourist
Motor Coaches (Southampton) Ltd was purchased. This business was begun
in 1919 but the company was reincorporated in 1927 and took in Hiawatha
Motor Services. In July 1935 Hants & Dorset acquired W. A. Courtier,
Parma Violet Coaches, Bournemouth, Greyhound Coaches, Bournemouth,
Waterways & Docks Bus Company, Southampton; in the beginning of 1937
Gem Motor Coaches (J. A. Bright and R. W. Gardner) of Bournemouth was
acquired. The nominal capital rose from £75,000 to £125,000 in 1925; 6½ per
cent cumulative preference shares (£150,000) were issued in 1930; in 1934
£120,000 £1 fully paid ordinary shares were issued by capitalisation of

reserves. Throughout its early career Hants & Dorset had a dark green livery but after taking in Wilts & Dorset the livery, after some vacillation, was changed by the National Bus Company to red. In 1973 King Alfred of Winchester, Chisnell's fleet, was absorbed.

The Lincolnshire Road Car Company Limited has one of the more complicated histories, partly because it was started rather late on in the history of the bus business, on 8 August 1928. It was to take over W. P. Allen's Silver Queen services in Lincolnshire (he had another of the same name at Clacton in Essex) two years after Silver Queen took over Progressive Omnibus Service (Boston) Limited. Retford Motor Services was acquired jointly with East Midland in November of that year. During 1930 Bray & Company of Skegness was acquired; F. H. Brown's Bus Service was taken over in November 1931 and the Grove Motor Company of Newark in March 1932. On 10 March 1933 E. Drayton's Service was acquired and Godfrey Davis of Holbeach in May 1933. Two purchases in June 1933 were A. Arrund of Scunthorpe and Scunthorpe United Motor Services, incorporated 25 September 1931 to take over the undertakings of T. Cawkwell, L. Barnett, F. Mastin, R. Kemp, E. Stone and H. Parkes. In November 1933 the services of the Lincolnshire Omnibus Owners Association were taken over and in January 1934 Sykes Brothers of Normanby and the Mablethorpe & Sutton Motor Service, which had been incorporated on 9 March 1929 to take over a service operated by Tom Cory Ltd. G. and C. Rickett and M. A. Taylor & Sons, of Marsham-le-Fen, were taken over in June 1934. Also in that month Ada Services (Mrs Morley) of Grimsby sold her tours and excursions to Lincolnshire Road Car; her stage services had gone to Grimsby Corporation some time previously. In October 1934 Dobb's Ruby Bus Service passed to the large company.

In December 1934 the purchase of the Skegness Motor Service Co. Ltd was carried out; in January 1935 Blankley Brothers (Gem Bus Service) of Colsterworth was purchased and in February W. H. Dobbs & Son of Binbrook sold their excursions and tours to Lincolnshire. Hutson Brothers in February 1935, T. W. Yallup & Son in June 1935, and Atlas Motor & Bus Service Ltd in June made the decision to sell out; in June 1936 the tours of Provincial Tramways Co. Ltd formed the last part remaining to that once notable tramway empire. In March 1937 Lincolnshire took over the Spalding excursions and tours of Eastern Counties.

Enterprise & Silver Dawn Motors Ltd was registered on 8 July 1927 to acquire as from 1 June 1927 the branch of East Midland (formerly W. T. Underwood Ltd) at Scunthorpe and Frodingham, Lincs, and to enter into an agreement also with Progressive Motor Omnibus Services (Boston) Ltd which had an agreement with Lincolnshire Road Car Co. Ltd. Enterprise &

Silver Dawn acquired Humber Road Car Service in January 1934, Advance Motor Services Ltd in June 1936 (interest obtained June 1933), Blue Bus Services (Scunthorpe) Ltd also in 1936, and in March 1937 Immingham Queen Bus Service.

The Southern Vectis Omnibus Co. Ltd was formed on 29 August 1929 when the Southern Railway purchased a 50 per cent interest in Dodson Brothers Ltd, the London coachbuilder, who operated a bus business in the Isle of Wight. An early purchase was the Creeth business, then trading as Premier Bus Company, but which had earlier for a long time traded as the Isle of Wight Steam Omnibus Co. Ltd, the principal service being Ryde, Seaview and Nettlestone, begun in March 1909. A. H. Creeth & Sons had four Darracq-Serpollet steam double-deckers and another steam vehicle which was put down as 'own make'. In the 1920s the Ryde Seaview & District Motor Service had five Dennis single-deck, one Fiat and one Ford 14-seat petrol vehicles. The steam fleet had bodywork by Christopher Dodson. The Creeth business was absorbed by Southern Vectis in January 1930. Brown's Bus Company of Carisbrooke was taken in in 1934. In 1929 Isle of Wight Associated and Isle of Wight Tourist Co. Ltd (formed in 1922 and operating 12 vehicles from Ryde and Seaview) were taken over. Surprise Bus Company was a purchase of 1930 and H. G. Eames of Shanklin of 1937.

For some years the chairman of the company was unusual in being the assistant general manager of the Southern Railway, G. S. Szlumper, CBE, TD, but in June 1932 Tilling & British Automobile Traction Ltd purchased from Christopher and Frank Dodson the 50 per cent interest in the company; for a time S. E. Garcke was a BET representative on the board but then the company came under Tilling management, with Stanley Kennedy its chairman.

The United Counties Omnibus Co. Ltd had its real origin in Benjamin Richardson and his New Central company which established a branch at Bedford in May 1912. Richardson suspected that there were better pickings in the boot and shoe district of Northamptonshire and made a trial with a bus about March 1913. It did so well that he registered the Wellingborough Motor Omnibus Co. Ltd on 3 May 1913. Like the predecessors there was a strong bias in favour of Leyland vehicles although at one stage a number of Tilling-Stevens were obtained. Under Tilling influence a number of Bristol chassis were purchased. The United Counties Omnibus & Road Transport Co. Ltd was formed on 1 September 1921 to take over as from 24 September the assets and business of the Wellingborough Motor Omnibus Co. Ltd (agreement signed 7 September). An agreement was made 16 September 1921 to refrain from competition with Progressive Motor Omnibus Services (Wellingborough) Ltd. H. C. Merrett, who appeared in the administration of certain London independents and figured on the boards of National Omnibus & Transport and of H. M. S. Catherwood Ltd (in the latter case as chairman) was chairman under the Tilling regime which began in 1931. In April 1933 H. & F. O. M. Davis of Lavendon was purchased and Drage Brothers of Bozeat. In June Bagshaw & Sons (Kettering) Ltd was acquired. In December 1933 part of the Aylesbury Bus Co. Ltd was taken over from Eastern National and in the same month two important coach businesses were acquired – Allchin's Luxury Coachways (which had been applying to and refused by the Traffic Commissioners for the licences of Mayfair Transport Co. Ltd, operators of a London–Northampton–Leicester coach service) and W. A. Nightingale & Sons (Midland Motorways). The Mayfair company was formed on 16 April 1927 and Nightingale in October 1927. The Mayfair fleet consisted of five 27 h.p. 26-seat Brockway coaches.

Birmingham & Midland, which established services in the Buckingham area from its Banbury garage in 1921, reopened them in the end of 1933, having abandoned them for some years, by purchasing, jointly with United Counties Omnibus Co. Ltd (to which the name had been simplified in October 1933), A. G. Varney and Buckingham Orange Service (L. Tibbetts). The B & M Banbury–Brackley service was merged in this takeover with tours from Buckingham and Akeley. UCOC also took over the services of J. Dunkley of Buckingham. W. C. Nutt's Bluebell Motor Service was acquired in February 1934 with services from Harpole. R. Humphrey & Son of Old Stratford was acquired in August 1934 and the service thence to Woburn was cut back to Stony Stratford. When UCOC took over Frost's Motors Ltd on October 28 1934 with five Kettering local or works services, it made modifications to the timetables of others serving Corby, Burton Latimer and other long routes to incorporate Frost's times and on the Uppingham–Market Harborough route fares were agreed with Adams & Son of Middleton. In March 1936 the business of L. Timson & Son of Burton Latimer was taken over. H. Buckley & Sons of Rothwell was acquired in September 1936 and a year later R. L. Seamarks & Son of Higham Ferrers was acquired. In 1951 another transfer of Eastern National territory was made to United Counties.

The West Yorkshire Road Car Co. Ltd could trace its origins formally to the Harrogate Road Car Co. Ltd which was registered on 24 December 1906 and had as secretary Herbert Raworth. He developed several building estates and as a corollary a bus service to serve them. In 1926 Harrogate Road Car took over Dibbs & Warne of Tadcaster. When the West Yorkshire was incorporated it also took in Premier Transport Co. (Keighley) Ltd which had been registered on 11 September 1919 and included the Nelson & Colne Haulage & Chara Co. Ltd from 31 March 1926 and the Red Chara &

Motor Omnibus Co. Ltd from 1927 onwards. The 30 buses of this company were added to the West Yorkshire fleet and 40 buses (out of an 80-vehicle fleet including coaches and lorries) of Blythe & Berwick Ltd of Bradford, a firm dating from 24 March 1919, which were not taken over.

Burn's Motor Service, with headquarters at Boston Spa, was taken over in April 1927 and Warburton's Bus Service in July 1927. On 5 December 1927 the name was changed to West Yorkshire Road Car Co. Ltd. In 1928 the company had 190 single-deck buses and 36 coaches. In June 1928 Keighley Brothers Ltd of Keighley was acquired. In September 1928 John Cole & Sons of Leeds was taken over. In May 1929 Yeadon Transport Company was absorbed with its headquarters at Yeadon Transport Company was absorbed with its headquarters at Yeadon and Rodley. In January 1930 Hedna Bus Service was acquired with headquarters at Greengates, Bradford, and in May 1930 C. Chapman Ltd of Grassington. In the following month Wharfedale Motors was acquired. In May 1932 Cononley Motors Ltd was taken over.

The start of Keighley–West Yorkshire Services Ltd was by agreement dated 29 September 1932 on 2 October 1932 the assets being contributed equally by both parties. Previously Keighley Corporation had operated trams from 1889, buses from 1908 and trolleybuses from 1913. An excellent account of the history of Keighley Corporation Transport was published by J. S. King (Advertiser Press, Huddersfield) in 1964 to which those seeking further knowledge of this interesting system may be referred. The 4 ft gauge horse trams began in May 1889 and ended on 28 May 1904; the electric cars replaced them after a gap on 12 October 1904. The open-top cars seated 23 upstairs and 22 down. The eight cars came from Brush and had BTH electrical equipment. Later covered-up open-balcony cars were added to the fleet and the original batch were rebuilt with covers.

On 19 December 1908 an experimental service of motor buses was begun, a 36-seat double-deck Commer being lent by Commercial Cars Ltd; it worked from Utley, Ferncliffe Road, to Eastburn Bridge, reversing by going over the bridge to the Junction Hotel. The fare was 3d, with 1½d stage to Steeton. On 9 April 1909 Keighley Corporation took over the provision of its own buses and charabancs from Commercial Cars.

Although competition with the Midland Railway service was forbidden under a clause of the enabling Act of 1908 it was now possible to travel all the way into Bradford and Leeds by road transport by using the Keighley route to Nab Wood. Where Leeds and Bradford had demonstrated the reliability of the trolleybus of Schiemann type, Keighley adopted the Cedes system which had been demonstrated in Austria in 1902, and Keighley trolleybuses began on 24 April 1913. This complicated system had only one pair of wires, the over-running trolleys being exchanged from plugs on the cars when they met – to the dismay of other traffic! The Cedes had hub-mounted motors and it was difficult to get power enough, 28 h.p. being the maximum. A 20 h.p. unit burnt out its motors within a week or two of starting work.

With almost indecent haste Keighley, which had had an unsatisfactory experience with early motor buses, like so many operators, and had macadam roads which got churned up by solid tyres, led to the withdrawal of all motor buses about 28 February 1915. Enough Cedes to work the trackless service had arrived in early February, but an interesting addition to the fleet was the open-top dark-red Cedes demonstrator from Hove. A front-wheel-drive Cedes (adopted on the recommendation of a Leeds engineer) with a swivelling front axle (very hard to steer) was tried in 1921 but was disastrously unsatisfactory and was withdrawn after 2 December 1921, three Leyland buses being purchased almost in panic. This stemmed coach competition from the Premier company.

The Keighley tramcars, which had earned bad will owing to the state of the track, were given up in 1924, the last day of operation being 17 December, in the middle of the week. A public ceremony attended the lifting of the last rail, in South Street, on 4 February 1926. Keighley Corporation was thus the first to abandon a municipal tramway system and replace it by trackless vehicles, by this time converted mainly to under-running current collection. Captain C. Jackson, MC, the manager, gained some kudos from the work of conversion and an honorarium of £100 for his services and soon afterwards left for Oldham and eventually Plymouth.

The second trackless system at Keighley ended 31 August 1932. The last Keighley motor buses ran on 30 September 1932 (the last Keighley Corporation Guy buses were sold three years later in September 1935 to Lytham St Annes Corporation). From 2 October 1932 operation was carried out by Keighley–West Yorkshire Services Ltd, a company registered on 2 September 1932 to which assets were contributed in equal proportions by company and municipality, although one West Yorkshire Leyland Titan PD2 double-decker was temporarily in Corporation livery to effect the equalisation of assets. Three representatives of Keighley Corporation were on the board of the joint company and four of West Yorkshire. In 1937 55 buses and 3 lorries were numbered by the joint company, and in 1975 there were 52 buses.

The independent years of Keighley Corporation Transport were a long story of muddle, vacillation and incompetence; this was changed by association with West Yorkshire which produced some cash for the Corporation; in fact there were only two years from 1932 in which there was not a surplus. The joint arrangement came to an end on 31 December 1973;

like its beginning it could be attributed to *force majeure*; in 1932 it was the result of LMSR pressure that Keighley Corporation sought a scheme for co-ordinated working as an alternative to all-out competition with LMS road vehicles. Keighley bus station reverted to the Corporation and is now leased back to West Yorkshire. Keighley, owing to changes in local government boundaries, is now part of the Bradford Metropolitan District. It is curious that owing to legal complications it was autumn of 1974 before the Keighley-West Yorkshire fleet name began to be removed from the sides of the vehicles.

In October 1933 Overland Service (Tyne & Mersey) was taken over by West Yorkshire, jointly with Northern General, Yorkshire (WD), North Western and LUT. Also in 1933 the Fawdon Bus Co. Ltd was purchased jointly with Northern General, Yorkshire (WD) and Yorkshire Traction. In December 1933 Ideal Bus Co. (Corcoran Brothers) of Tadcaster was bought and in November 1934 London Midland & Yorkshire Services (formed 1933) was purchased jointly with East Yorkshire, Yorkshire (WD) and Yorkshire Traction.

On 1 April 1934 York-West Yorkshire Joint Committee was formed. The reasons were similar to the Keighley undertaking, but the York case was a joint committee and there were three representatives of each side, controlling 51 buses in the city. This total had risen to 68 by 1969.

Wilts & Dorset Motor Services Ltd was formed on 4 January 1915 as an independent venture by A. E. Cannon and A. D. Mackenzie who anticipated a need for bus services on Salisbury Plain with the development of the First World War and wanted something larger than the Worthing Motor Services, to which they had been brought in as consultants pending the formation in June 1915 of Southdown Motor Services, to occupy their energies. Thus, although Southdown had British Automobile Traction finance, Wilts & Dorset had an initial capital of £4,000 and Cannon and Mackenzie relied on finance from Lephards, the Brighton paper merchants. In 1932 Wilts & Dorset purchased N. Horny of Andover and in January 1934 Victory Services (Sparrow & Vincent) of Salisbury. In July 1936 L. T. Alexander's Queen of the Road parted with his stage service to Wilts & Dorset, his excursions being retained. Other acquisitions were Victor Service (W. A. Swadling) of Tisbury and Rawlings & Stevens of Shaftesbury. On 6 June 1963 an important purchase was carried out when White & Shergold (Silver Star) was put under the Wilts & Dorset banner; it had become the most notable of the Salisbury Plain camp undertakings and in 1957 had renamed itself Silver Star Motor Services Ltd when it had 16 express licences (mainly tailored to the needs of HM Services weekend leave traffic), 20 picking-up points at military camps, and no fewer than 90 setting-down points as far off as Glasgow. Those who looked at the sparsely populated Wilts & Dorset territory marvelled that they were able to sustain such close headways, but the secret was in the founder's belief in bus service. The W & D frequency of service protected the company from intense competition in the 1920s.

The first W & D rolling stock were two McCurd and one Scout, obtained under the stress of war, and the first service was Salisbury to Amesbury. Later a number of AEC 2-ton chassis – the smallest AEC model – were obtained. The administration of the company was unusual, the secretary, garage manager and traffic manager reporting direct to the board. Pooling on the joint route Salisbury–Bournemouth began in 1920 and on Salisbury–Southampton in 1921, and eventually 30-minute headways were provided. From 1920 the Salisbury city service was half-hourly. The Southern Railway investment in Wilts & Dorset took place in 1930 and in 1931 the company became a Tilling & British subsidiary. In 1942 it passed to the Tilling group.

The Bristol Omnibus Co. Ltd was a name-change adopted on 30 May 1957 by the Bristol Tramways & Carriage Co. Ltd, itself a merger of the Bristol Tramways Co. Ltd and the Bristol Cab Co. Ltd, which took place on 1 October 1887. The Bristol Tramways Co. Ltd was incorporated on 28 December 1874 and commenced operations on 9 August 1875; the Cab company was incorporated on 21 June, 1886 and began work on 1 August 1886.

In the 1930s the Bristol Tramways & Carriage Company had the reputation of having more staff at salaries of £1,000 a year or more than any other bus company in the country. Many of these were notabilities in their own right such as James Clifton Robinson, who joined George Francis Train's staff at Birkenhead at the age of 12 and at 27 was appointed general manager of the Bristol company, was later knighted and played a great part in persuading Sir George White and the Bristol board to electrify. Clifton Robinson, who had had some time away from Bristol to run the Cork City tramways, now reorganised a horse system, the West Metropolitan, as the London United Tramways, which became an electric network with over 300 cars. He was also on the board of the Imperial Tramways Company which owned the Corris Railway in Wales (opened in 1858) and invested in the Bristol company and the Middlesbrough, Stockton-on-Tees & Thornaby Tramways Co. Ltd. Imperial was also interested in the Reading and Darlington systems in horse days and the Dublin Southern tramways. Imperial established its headquarters at Clare House, Colston Street, Bristol. Charles Challenger on 9 August 1875 drove the first of a convoy of three cars to open the Bristol system with a service from Perry Road (at the Colston Street junction) to St John's Church, Redland. The mayor rode on

34 (*above*) One of the first six-wheel Guy buses, used for tramway replacement in Morecambe

35 (*below*) The first underfloor-engined chassis in London Transport service was this TF type for Green Line and private hire work, 1937–9

36 (*left*) The last journey of an NS-type bus, on 10 November 1937

37 (*below*) These six-wheeled AEC 64-seat buses were in 1939 the largest in the country. They were ordered by Ben England, then general manager, for the replacement of Leicester Corporation trams

38 Rear-engined Leyland Cub in the London Transport fleet; forty-nine were built in 1939

39 Llandudno Coaching and Carriage Company 20-seat Bristol on Bangor service

40 A gloomy afternoon of fog at the Bank underground station, with two LT-type buses on service No. 11 held up by traffic

this car. From this humble beginning (he had started with the Midland Railway) Charles Challenger became traffic manager of the company, a position he held for 37 years from 1882; when he retired he was in 1919 appointed to the board.

Horse buses were begun in Bristol in 1877 as a feeder service to the tram terminus at St George, but this was merely a preliminary to tramway extension. Permanent horse bus operation began in 1887 with a service from the Drawbridge to Clifton Suspension Bridge. Whereas two-horse buses were deemed sufficient, some of the trams on hilly routes were provided with four horses and even five over the steepest pitches.

Electric traction on the tramways was first applied under a provisional order of 1894 to the Old Market–Kingswood line and service began on 14 October 1895. Although the corporation wanted to supply the power for the tramways, eventually it was agreed that company power should be supplied and a power house was built at Counterslip. In the meantime, a generating plant at St George did duty. The second line of electric cars, to Eastville, came into service on 1 February 1897. The process of electrification was completed with the Hotwells line on 22 December 1900. A peculiarity of the Bristol system was the archaic appearance of its 232 cars, all to the open-top four-wheeled design of 1895; the Tramways Act of 1870 required Bristol Corporation to take possession of the tramways at what Emile Garcke of the British Electric Traction Company always called the scrap-iron value in 1915 or any seventh year thereafter, so although the BT & CC Ltd always kept track and vehicles in good condition, it was never worth while expending big capital sums on updating the system. The outstanding curiosity of the Bristol track layout was at the top of the Colston Street climb from Tramways Centre where an acute angle curve through 250 degrees was protected by railway-type semaphore signals controlled from a box; besides the circles at Centre and Colston Avenue there was a four-track layout in Old Market and an exceptional number of both facing and trailing crossovers in Cumberland Street; notable suburban stub-end termini existed at Durdham Downs and Zetland Road. Durdham Downs was reckoned by the pundits as having a loading capacity of 9,600 passengers an hour. The BT & C Company in 1912 purchased the Clifton Rocks Railway which had opened in 1893. It was closed in 1934. At Temple Meads station there was a covered tram station until 1925, now a BR staff canteen. The track gauge in Bristol was 4 ft 8½ in.

The Bristol company took delivery of a specimen Thornycroft bus on 27 October 1905 and the first of a batch of 12 Thornycroft chassis on 1 December of that year. They had 37-seat United Electric Car Company bodies. The seating was arranged so that 16 were accommodated on longitudinal benches downstairs, 19 on garden seats on the open top deck and 2 alongside the driver. The tradition of seating two or more passengers alongside the driver long continued on Bristol country buses and I remember a demonstration by a driver on some route deep in Gloucestershire to Noel Jackson and myself of how to change gear on a Bristol 4-ton chassis without touching the clutch pedal.

The first motor-bus service operated by the BT & C Co. Ltd began on 17 January 1906, between Victoria Rooms and Clifton Suspension Bridge, fare 1d, and in February, a number of tram route extension services were added. On 20 August the service from Brislington to Saltford was extended to Newton St Loe, making connection with trams from Bath. At this period contracts to supply traders with commercial vehicles were made, customers including Cerebos, Rogers Brewery and the Post Office and chassis including Hallford and Pierce Arrow.

Bristol purchased in 1906 three Berliet driver-over-engine double-deck buses which were in later years converted to overhead tower wagons for the tramways department. The first Bristol-built chain-driven C40 chassis were 16-seaters which appeared on the Clifton route in May 1908 (the first on 12 May) and were notable for their silence about two years before London's B-type made a name for itself for quietness. Manufacture was not organised on the large scale adopted in London, which gave rise to the Associated Equipment Company (AEC) in 1912.

In 1912 and 1913 the purchase of a Dennis fleet was carried out; this enabled the first timetable leaflet, issued in May 1914, to refer to tram services 1 to 15 (numbers were adopted in November 1913) and bus services 19 to 33. These were mainly local to Bristol but the penetration of the outer suburbs was shown by services to Frampton Cotterell, Wraxall and Nailsea, Tockington, Thornbury and Newton St Loe.

The first of a large group of Charron and Clement-Bayard taxicabs and landaulette private hire cars was delivered on 17 September 1908 and this part of the fleet grew to 300 vehicles before 1914. In the summer of 1909 tours by charabanc were instituted, the first being to Wells and Cheddar on 7 June 1909. In the autumn, five of the Thornycrofts were re-bodied with charabanc-type bodies. Motor taxicabs were put into service at Bath in 1909; the Bath Electric Tramways Ltd began a bus service with six Milnes-Daimler vehicles in September 1905 and Commer motor coaches were introduced in 1912. Bristol coaches began operation in Bath but, owing to sustained opposition by the Corporation watch committee, inspired by the tramways company, not until 1 February 1911.

On 1 June 1910 motor-coach tours were begun from Weston-super-Mare. Later in this same year the Bristol company was awarded substantial damages from the FIAT company in respect of defective motor buses supplied by them. 22 May 1912 saw the inauguration of the BT & C Co. Ltd's branch at Cheltenham with motor coaches, fifteen taxis and hire cars. On 20 March 1913 taxis began plying for hire from Gloucester railway station although the public carriage stands in the city were reserved 'for a local syndicate'; an endeavour was made to force the issue by putting ten taxis and some hire cars in Gloucester city on 10 May 1913. A Wye Valley tour was offered on 12 May 1913. The Royal Show was held in July 1913 right in Bristol, on Durdham Down, and a service of 225 trams, 52 motor coaches, 230 taxis and cars with 150 horses for horsed vehicles and 50 commercial vehicles, was provided. A service of 21 coaches was run from Temple Meads to the Show at 2½-minute intervals, the fare being one shilling. A coach tour of historic buildings required six vehicles. Additional commercial premises were acquired in 1912 and 1913 at Brislington and were christened 'The Motor Constructional Works'. In February 1910 Sir George White had given instructions for a clearance of buses from some sheds at Filton which were to be allocated to the Bristol Aeroplane Co. Ltd and three other companies. These were all registered on 19 February 1910 and supplied with capital by Sir George White, his brother and son, because on the Bristol Stock Exchange the making of aircraft was thought a sign that Sir George had taken leave of his senses. In view of the part played by Bristol aircraft in the First World War this madness on Sir George's part was a very fortunate thing for Britain, 4,938 planes being built during the war. The taxi service was given up in 1930.

The existence in the fleet of a number of Dennis worm-driven chassis, which were much quieter than chain-driven types, inspired the appearance of a Bristol-built shaft-driven vehicle in 1915. In 1914 the company's bus fleet numbered 44 buses and 29 motor coaches; in 1920 construction of the 4-ton type described as experimental in 1915 was begun in earnest and 100 chassis were delivered after 30 April; output in 1921 was 223, of which 100 were stored at Filton, there being no buyers. During 1922 the company closed its last horse stable and abandoned the funeral business. The design department devoted some time to devising a two-ton chassis for a 12 ft 6 in. wheelbase and a body for 20 to 25 passengers. This was a forward-control vehicle which achieved a measure of popularity. On 12 June 1936 the Gloucester City Council leased its bus services to the company for a 21-year term. This involved a change of operating management for 23 Thornycroft and 15 Vulcan single-deck buses.

The Bath Electric Tramways Ltd and the Bath Tramways Motor Co. Ltd (formed in 1920) were both taken over in December 1936, with the Lavington & Devizes Motor Co. Ltd (formed 17 November 1922 and controlled by the

Bath Tramways Motor Co. Ltd from 1932). The Lavington company was put into voluntary liquidation on 31 March 1937. On 17 April 1937 the Weston-super-Mare Tramways ceased to operate. This BET undertaking was replaced by six Dennis-Duple petrol-engined vehicles of the Bristol fleet.

Control was obtained of Greyhound Motors Ltd (which had operated local services in Bristol with NS London-type AEC buses and long-distance coaches and begun as a haulage firm, Toogood & Bennett) on 31 March 1928 although the companies remained separate until 1 January 1936.

In 1924 the premises of the Bristol Wagon & Carriage Works Co. Ltd with 12 acres of land on Lawrence Hill was acquired and used for a central garage and repair works.

In January 1930 acquisition of a shareholding in Bristol Tramways & Carriage Co. Ltd was made known by the Great Western Railway Company. During December 1931 the Western National Omnibus Co. Ltd purchased these GWR shares, its capital being increased to enable it to do so. For some time, the White and Smith families continued in control of the Bristol company, but in October 1935 J. F. Heaton of Thomas Tilling took over the chairmanship from W. G. Verdon Smith and the other director members of the White and Smith families resigned, including the general manager, Colonel S. E. Smith. He was succeeded as general manager by Major Frank Chapple of West Yorkshire Road Car Co. Ltd, another Tilling company and a much more positive policy was adopted. Chapple naturally toured the garages to size up his new appointment and in due course visited Brislington garage. On his first inspection he discovered a man sitting in a small room at a large executive type desk reading a newspaper in the early afternoon. When he had occasion to go to Brislington again later in the same week and saw the same man as idle as on the first visit, he made some inquiries. The reply was 'Oh, he's the manager of the aeroplane works.' Further inquiries elicited the information that he had been Sir George White's chauffeur who had been kept on when the manufacture of aircraft ceased. Frank Chapple went to Brislington the next day, asked if three months' salary after 13 or 14 years with nothing to do would serve instead of the usual notice, and handed over a cheque for the amount. Not long afterwards he sought a boy to do an odd job at the St Augustine's Place headquarters and was told he was sanding the stands at Durdham Downs. Enquiry produced the information that at regular intervals all the bus stands used by the company were strewn with fine sand, because in the early days buses dripped oil over them. 'But we always sand them' was the answer to which Chapple pointed out that since 1911 buses had not offended in this way and he knew of nowhere else where such an archaic practice was followed. Chapple's most amusing habit, demonstrated during several talks I had with him while he was building producer-gas trailers, was trying to light his pipe. Chapple was trying to meet Sir Frederick Heaton's foible that this rather inefficient power source (40 per cent of petrol efficiency) was the way to win the war. London Transport and the BET group did not believe very heartily in it and some Tilling engineers (including one that had been brought up with the National Steam Car organisation) openly said that Sir Frederick's money would have been better spent on two-wheeled trailers to carry steam boilers.

Sir Frederick's biggest contribution to Bristol affairs was to take a positive stand with the Corporation over tramways which they had time and again postponed purchasing, including in 1922 and 1929 when the option was available. Now Sir Frederick Heaton, after he had taken over the chairmanship of the company, put it to the Corporation's Tramways Option Committee in 1936: 'If you think there is any value in the option to purchase the tramways, why don't you exercise it?' This terminated any belief on the part of the Corporation that they could extract a payment from the company for waiving the option. Heaton persuaded them to purchase the tramways from the company at £1,125,000 and the company would contribute its 'City' bus services to a joint undertaking. In addition buses were to replace the trams, estimated to cost £480,125 including reinstatement of roads. The necessary Bill for the purpose, the Bristol Transport Act (1937), provided for a joint committee of the two bodies. Replacement of the trams began 7 May 1938 on the routes between Centre, Westbury, Durdham Downs, Eastville and Hotwells. It was intended to continue some routes throughout the war to economise on liquid fuel, but Hitler determined this on 11 April 1941 by cutting the main cable from the power station with a bomb at St Philips Bridge in one of the several air raids with which Bristol was afflicted.

In the early part of the Second World War I called on Frank Chapple (Major Chapple as he was universally known in the bus industry) to talk about producer-gas and how best to apply it to bus operation. Chapple, like all engineers and managers of the Tilling group, was full of ideas to make a success of this rather doubtful medium of propulsion which had been enthusiastically taken up by J. F. Heaton, soon to become Sir Frederick. Bristol experiments had begun with some fireproof containers incorporated in the chassis of various vehicles, including one under the stairs of a double-decker from 1937 onwards; eventually a separate two-wheeled trailer was decided upon. Frederick Heaton's patriotic work for the producer-gas method of saving fuel was acknowledged by a knighthood in 1941 which resulted in his dropping his first Christian name as there was already a Sir John Heaton. Nearly 2,500 gas-producer trailers were built, of which 100 were used on Bristol's own buses and 630 were supplied to London Transport among 92 other operators.

Chapple was fond of his pipe and a space on his office desk was given over to an outsize box of Swan Vestas. My talk with him was punctuated by the scrape of matches as he tried (unsuccessfully) to relight his pipe. In the end I was compelled to say, 'You seem to be smoking matches rather than tobacco.'

Two companies had been taken over by Bristol, but kept as subsidiaries. These were Bence Motor Services Ltd of Hanham, Bristol, with 10 motor coaches, and Burnell's Motors Ltd of Weston-super-Mare in 1933. Burnell's fleet totalled 38 vehicles when the subsidiaries were counted, and was absorbed in 1936.

Bristol designers were able to display their talents with the Festival of Britain in 1951 when they produced the Lodekka, a vehicle which achieved a low height without the awkward off-centre sunk gangway inherent to models such as the ingenious Leyland Titan, by dividing the drive at the gearbox amidships, and locating the transmission shafts under the longitudinal seats near the headroom on each deck. A Bristol service vehicle was produced in October 1949 and a trial trip was graced by the presence of Sir Cyril (afterwards Lord) Hurcomb, chairman of the British Transport Commission. After the vehicle for West Yorkshire in April 1950 some 2,200 were produced in 1953 and after, and with a flat-floor edition the total came to nearly 5,000. In 1956 arrangements were made with Dennis Brothers for a version by that Guildford manufacturer. From 1 January 1955 chassis building was hived off under Bristol Commercial Vehicles Ltd, thus fulfilling a long-held ambition of Sir Frederick Heaton's, the separate company having been registered as long previously as 1943. A very complete story of vehicle manufacturing by Bristol is included in *The People's Carriage 1874–1974*, published by the company, now Bristol Omnibus Co. Ltd, the name adopted in 1957. It is noteworthy that besides managerial staff and directors of the National Bus Company, contributors include afficianados of the Bristol scene such as Peter Hulin who have long been known for their excellent collection of Bristol photographs.

E. Jones & Sons Ltd, a Bristol company, registered on 19 March 1923, and began a regular service to London (Morning Star) on 26 March 1928 in competition with Greyhound Motors, which absorbed it early in January 1933.

When the Bristol company and Red & White and Western National were all expanding they all opened depots at Stroud and in the Forest of Dean; Thomas Tilling Ltd having sold its business to the British Transport Commission for £35 million. The Bristol depot at Coleford in the Forest of

Dean was exchanged in a scheme of rationalisation for the Red & White depot at Stroud and the routes concerned changed their operators.

In 1950 the last independent service running into central Bristol (Dundry Pioneer) was taken over; this firm was owned by S. A. and W. F. Ball and possessed four vehicles. Henry Russett & Sons Ltd of Bath Road, Bristol, with 55 vehicles (mainly lorries) and trading as Royal Blue Coaches and with nine Bedfords and a Foden was also absorbed at this time.

In 1948 the control by Thomas Tilling Ltd was exchanged for that by the British Transport Commission and George Cardwell succeeded Sir Frederick Heaton as chairman.

Investment in Black & White Motorways Ltd, which had been founded by G. Reading in 1928, was acquired in 1930; the proportions were 40 per cent by Bristol, 40 per cent by Birmingham & Midland and the remainder by City of Oxford, which had always been somewhat tepid towards coaches and whose general manager, R. F. Dixon, a somewhat austere character, was reputed to have made a decision that no City of Oxford vehicle should be allowed to go more than 50 miles from the Oxford garage. Even after the Tilling group had purchased coaches operating between London and Oxford, City of Oxford refused to have anything to do with coaches. Under the general manager of Black & White, H. R. Lapper, the co-ordination scheme of 1934 which produced Associated Motorways was entered upon.

Red & White Services Ltd originated in the Forest of Dean where Lydney & Forest of Dean Motor Services Ltd was operating as early as 1914. One of the directors of Watts Garage Ltd of Lydney was H. T. Letheren, a member of H. T. Letheren & Sons, proprietor of Lydney Posting and Garage Company, which worked bus services under the fleet name Lydney & Forest of Dean Motor Services. As Lydney & Dean Forest Services, this company operated half-a-dozen services round Lydney and Coleford into the mid-1920s. In September 1926 it was incorporated into Gloucestershire Transport with Walkley's Motor Transport Service of Cinderford and the trading name of Gloster (Red & White) Services. Watts Garage Ltd of Lydney had been formed on 22 December 1920 with W. Mutton as chairman, A. J. Watts, managing director, and H. W. Berthon, A. T. Perkins, J. H. Watts, H. T. Letheren and W. K. Coxon as directors. On 14 July 1922 the haulage business of Watts Garage was transferred to Gloucestershire Transport Ltd. Back in February 1920 James Fryer Ltd, motor engineers of Hereford, began market-day services from that town, consolidated as Hereford Transport Ltd on 29 April 1920.

In 1919 T. J. Jones and Guy Bown, who had been in business in Brynmawr, opened a garage in Old Griffin Yard and in 1920 purchased a new Dennis charabanc for tours; miners sought use of the same vehicle, but in the days before pit-head baths a second-hand bus was deemed good enough for the Griffin Motor Company; this began operation between Ebbw Vale and Bourneville (near Blaina) on 5 February 1921; there followed almost at once a National Coal Strike, throwing the economics of South Wales out of gear. Griffin were the first bus operators in the area to adopt the penny stage and to issue return tickets; Jones and Bown were presently counselling Watts and his friends on the board of Red & White. The Griffin Motor Co. Ltd was formed as a limited company on 6 March 1926. In the 1920s I had travelled with a railway-minded friend from Paddington to Chepstow, but the only convenient train had been non-stop from Paddington to Newport. As a result we had travelled back to Chepstow by bus by the road through the villages. The direct route had been operated on the fringe of its territory by South Wales Commercial Motors and was by now shed to Newport interests who took it over as South Mon Motor Co. Ltd in July 1927; in October of that year a controlling interest was acquired by Gloucestershire Transport Ltd and it became known as Red & White Services (South Mon Section). We spent the night in Chepstow at this interesting time and I took a photograph of a Red & White group vehicle alongside a Bristol 4-tonner on the Bristol service No. 100 (Plate 23).

On 7 August 1925 Western Services Ltd was formed by T. R. Jenkins to operate around Tredegar (to Blackwood in fact). This organisation was a joint concern with Valleys (Ebbw Vale) Ltd and really assisted in overcoming licensing difficulties in the days before the Road Traffic Act when operators were very much at the mercy of the local authorities who interested themselves in the dispensing of licences. The Crimson Rambler Bus and Charabanc Service was acquired from Wood & Company on 17 March 1926. In January 1921 the Aberdare Motor Service was founded and in 1927 it was taken over by J. H. Watts and five partners.

An event of 1928 was the purchase of Hereford Transport Ltd by Gloucestershire Transport Ltd; then Aberdare Motor Service bought control of Rhondda Motor Services Co. Ltd and Aberdare took over the management. Rhondda Motor Services Co. Ltd was incorporated on 23 April 1925, to acquire David Morgan & Co. of Tylorstown, Rhondda. Five limited stop trunk services were developed during the summer of 1928; they were Cardiff–Newport–Chepstow–Gloucester; Merthyr–Rhymney–Ebbw Vale–Abergavenny–Monmouth–Gloucester; Hereford–Ross–Gloucester; Abertillery–Pontypool–Usk–Chepstow–Gloucester; Blackwood–Newport–Gloucester. Rural England Motor Coaches Ltd was incorporated on 29 April 1927 and its principal service was between London and Gloucester. From August 1928 to April 1929 this company operated in association with Red & White; then Rural England began operating its own coaches from Cardiff via Gloucester to London on one route and from Merthyr via Abergavenny and Gloucester to London as an alternative. On 18 July 1929 the name of Gloucestershire Transport was changed to Red & White Services Ltd. A grand consolidation followed, Hereford Transport being wound up and most of the minor companies of the group being dismantled in the same way. Valleys Motor Bus Services took in Valleys (Ebbw Vale) Ltd in December 1929. The Griffin Motor Co. Ltd remained a separate company operating closely with Red & White. Among other companies wound up were South Mon Motor Co. Ltd, Rhondda Motor Services Co. Ltd, Aberdare Motor Service, Blue Star Coaches Ltd and Western Services Ltd.

Red & White was prominent in the consolidation of long-distance coaching service – what may be termed the Cheltenham scheme or what was sometimes called the 'Clapham Junction of the Coachways' in the popular newspapers. The coach station used was St Margaret's Coach Station at Cheltenham where at least twice-daily coaches met contributed by services of Greyhound Motors (then a Bristol subsidiary), Birmingham & Midland Motor Omnibus Co. Ltd, Black & White Motorways Ltd, Elliott Brothers (Royal Blue, Bournemouth) Ltd, later succeeded by Western National Omnibus Co. Ltd and Southern National Omnibus Co. Ltd, United Counties Omnibus Co. Ltd, and Red & White Services Ltd. The Black & White station in Cheltenham was particularly suitable for the in-auguration of the project because of its large covered accommodation, 168-hour-a-week service of meals, large parking accommodation, and an old mansion, typical of Cheltenham Spa, as headquarters. A certain amount of adjustment took place between various coach routes from 19 March 1934. Later licences were obtained for coach services in this scheme under the name of Associated Motorways, formed in July 1934, which had a com-plicated management structure of its own. The combined annual mileage totalled 4,949,908.

In the first four years the annual mileage was reduced from 4,674,024 to 3,966,665, whereas the number of passenger journeys by Associated Motorways rose from 673,320 in 1936 to 907,559 in 1941 when it was ruthlessly cut down in the interests of saving fuel and rubber.

Red Bus Services Ltd of Stroud was developed by an Australian, N. D. Reyne, and the buses carried a picture of a kangaroo on the side. The fleet totalled 37 about 1933 when it was taken over by Red & White Services. A daily service from Stroud to London was a feature of Red Bus Services. South Wales Express with a Llanelli to London express service was also taken over in 1933. Some other Red & White purchases included Nell Gwynne Coaches with a Cardiff–Blackpool service in 1930; Samuelsons Saloon Coaches (London, Birmingham and Liverpool) in 1932; and Great

Western Express (operated by the former London independent operator, Orange).

MacShanes Motors Ltd of London and Liverpool and All British Travel of London and Chester were also taken into the group in 1932. In 1936 Gough's Welsh Motorways, based on Cardiff and Aberdare, was acquired; and in the following year the acquisition was completed of Imperial Motor Services, based at Swansea, Aberdare, Cardiff, Merthyr and Ynysybwl. Between 1930 and 1946 eleven other concerns were purchased; additions to the Red & White group included Newbury & District Motor Services in December 1943, Venture Ltd of Basingstoke in March 1945 and South Midland Motor Services based on Oxford in October 1945. Red & White thus mopped up quite a number of undertakings left undeveloped between the large area agreement companies of which King Alfred Motor Service (run by the Chisnell family until 1973) of Winchester was a good example.

Red & White Transport Ltd was formed on 19 May 1937 to take over Red & White Services Ltd, Eclipse Saloon Services Ltd, Basset-Enterprise Ltd and Gower Vanguard Motors (1920) Ltd; later United Welsh Services was incorporated to provide a Red & White company comparable to the BET group's South Wales Transport Ltd. Some eleven businesses went into this merger which was put together in 1938 just in time for the combined strength of the undertakings to be available for the Second World War.

On 10 February 1950 the entire Red & White bus empire was purchased by the BTC. The group was then known as United Transport Ltd and a number of overseas transport investments which were formerly joint with Commander Hare were replaced by British Electric Traction shares. Red & White investments are very diverse and include haulage concerns, quarry companies, engineering firms and investments in 16 overseas countries.

13
Scotland

Aside from the curiosity that a great many medium-size Scottish bus companies had the word 'General' inserted in their title so that they were apt to be looked upon as distant, if not close, or at any rate financial relations, the growth of the motor-bus industry in that country was not as fast as in England and when it came it tended to be more concentrated on Scottish ownership and especially round the Scottish Motor Traction group. Other differences from the English scene are the natural ones based on population and its distribution. In Scotland the system was simplified by being based on the SMT and not suffering the quarrels that damaged the BET and Tilling relationships.

I once wrote that the road system of Scotland seemed to separate the towns rather than join them together. North of the Border the undertakings were in some ways among the pioneers and in others lagged behind.

There was comparatively little activity by the big English financial groups. As early as 1897 the British Electric Traction group appointed a district superintendent for Scotland for its widely separated undertakings at Rothesay, Greenock & Port Glasgow and Airdrie & Coatbridge. With one of these concerns, the Rothesay Tramways, it embarked on a purchase agreement and soon afterwards bought a share in an operator of horse buses, brakes and cabs.

Motor buses began under BET auspices by the Airdrie & Coatbridge Tramways operation in October 1911 and six bus chassis were ordered two years later for the Greenock & Port Glasgow undertaking. During that year, 1913, however, the BET decided that area companies could serve a number of tramways, and so on 24 September 1913 the Scottish General Transport Co. Ltd was formed to develop motor transport in Scotland and particularly to consolidate the interests of the Airdrie, Greenock and Rothesay companies, a move towards accomplishing which was made on 1 January 1914; on that day the bus businesses of the Airdrie and Greenock (this latter not yet in operation) and McKirdy & McMillan in Rothesay were taken over. On the mainland McKerrow's Largs & West Coast Motor Services was taken over. Further development was prevented by the outbreak of war.

Pioneering included the early efforts of Norman D. Macdonald with motor wagonettes in Edinburgh and the tough struggle put up by a young man from Caithness, William J. Thomson, to get the Scottish Motor Traction Co. Ltd on a satisfactory basis. Another pioneer road motor operator was the Great North of Scotland Railway Company which established a number of services from 1905 onwards on Deeside and in the territory north of Aberdeen.

Norman Dorien Macdonald provided Edinburgh with its first motor-bus service from 19 May 1898, the vehicles being 10-seaters of MMC and Daimler type which won some popularity soon after that time in London. But in three years of operation this pioneer service of any in the United Kingdom piled up a crippling load of debt, owing to the cost of repairs and the very high cost of tyres.

William J. Thomson began his operation with double-deckers after tyre merchants had reduced their contract price to two old pence (about $\frac{1}{2}$ p) a mile. The Scottish Motor Traction Co. Ltd was registered on 14 June 1905 and later the same month the initial capital of £12,000 had enabled a purchase of 34-seat double-deck Maudslay buses which were put on an outer suburban route in Edinburgh from Corstorphine to Bathgate, and then on a circular route from Edinburgh, Corstorphine, Newbridge, Broxburn, Uphall, Mid-Calder, Hermiston and Edinburgh. A big garage was built in Fountainbridge. Another chairman of the SMT, James Amos, joined SMT as traffic manager in 1925 from a small Border undertaking; when independent his bus had been known to stop on the road from St Boswells to Galashiels and tout for business. It had the picturesque name of *Flower of Yarrow*. Amos used to say that when he was engaged by Thomson that redoubtable busman gave him some advice: 'Always, when you can, make friends; always make friends with the police; and always make friends with the press. There's another piece of advice I'd like to give you: I'll do all the drinking in the SMT!' The present structure of the Scottish bus business was largely the creation of Sir William Thomson, although the first large undertakings centred round tramways.

The British Electric Traction Co. Ltd endeavoured to set up tramways at Airdrie & Coatbridge, Greenock, Rothesay and Stirling, but their negotiations were only occasionally successful. The tramway from Greenock to Gourock was built by Greenock Town Council under powers of 1871; it was worked by the Vale of Clyde Tramways Company which also worked the line from Glasgow to Govan. Electric traction began on 3 October 1901. The Rothesay Tramways Co. Ltd was incorporated in 1879 and it obtained its powers in 1880. In 1900 the BET horse-bus and brake company founded on Bute on 6 January 1898, McKirdy & McMillan, was taken over. This was the first BET investment in buses in Scotland. Electric trams began at Rothesay on 19 August 1902.

A leading figure in Balfour Beatty & Co. Ltd was George Balfour, among whose tramways was Paisley Tramways Company, and Hamilton, Motherwell & Wishaw Tramway Company (name simplified to Lanarkshire Tramways Company in 1903 – originally registered 3 November 1898). In 1912 Lanark County Council obtained further powers to extend the system. Other Balfour Beatty or British Thomson-Houston Co. Ltd promotions of tramways included Falkirk & District Tramways Company (opened 1905); Dunfermline & District Tramways Company (opened 1909 to 1918); Wemyss & District Tramways Co. Ltd (opened 1906, running powers to Kirkcaldy Corporation system); Dundee, Broughty Ferry & District Tramways Company (opened 1905); Dumbarton, Burgh & County Tramways Co. Ltd (opened 1908). The National Electric Construction Co. Ltd, rival to the British Electric Traction Co. Ltd in England, incorporated the Musselburgh & District Electric Light & Traction Co. Ltd; the tramways were inaugurated on 12 December 1904.

The Great North of Scotland Railway started a bus service on 2 May 1904 which virtually extended the Deeside branch railway nearly 17 miles from Ballater to Braemar and between then and 1912 six other services were begun. Buses were begun in association with the Airdrie & Coatbridge Tramways in October 1911. Two years later the Greenock & Port Glasgow Tramways decided to have six buses and with a change of mind an area company, Scottish General Transport Co. Ltd, was formed by the BET to take over the rather disparate businesses at Airdrie, Rothesay and Greenock. It began operation on 1 January 1914 and took over McKerrow's Largs & West Coast Motor Service.

In 1908 the Lanarkshire Tramways obtained powers to run motor buses five miles from any tramway route and a BTH petrol-electric vehicle was obtained and was used experimentally at Hamilton. Regular bus service was begun on 25 April 1913 between Newarthill and Gleekhimin with a 26-seat Daimler. At that time the Scottish General Transport was operating Belsize buses between Coatbridge and Hamilton; competition developed between the two companies on this route. It was resolved by division of the route at Bellshill Cross.

From 24 June 1913 the Balfour group got some buses in circulation by the Falkirk & District Tramways Company. These were taken over by the Scottish General Omnibus Co. Ltd as from 16 August 1919. On 19 November 1920 the Fife Tramway acquired the shareholdings of Falkirk & District Tramways and of the Scottish General Omnibus. The Wemyss & District Tramways began bus operations in 1922 and in 1926 acquired control of the General Motor Carrying and Scottish Utility Motors. This complicated structure was completed by the Scottish General Omnibus Co. Ltd becoming manager of the omnibus department of the Dunfermline & District Tramways. In all Scottish General Omnibus totalled 161 buses in 1927; the chairman was Kenneth Sanderson and the general manager Douglas Hays. The fleet at that time was largely of Albion and Leyland make although the original tramway bus fleets had had a large element of Tilling-Stevens vehicles.

There was a gap of three miles between the end of the Glasgow Corporation Tramways at Bailleston and the tram terminus at Coatbridge. As the dates of the rights of purchase fell on a series of different dates the Airdrie & Coatbridge Tramways Trust formed by Act of 1920 was used for the purpose of obtaining control by Glasgow Corporation. This enabled work to begin on the Coatbridge–Airdrie single-track and turnouts and its replacement by double track, a task which occupied 15 months. Glasgow Corporation bought the line for £82,250 and then had a temporary bus service maintained over the route by Scottish General Transport Co. Ltd. J. D. Hendry provided a bus between Clarkston, Airdrie, Bailleston and Cathedral Street, Glasgow, in competition with the trams. This tramway-sponsored bus service gave the public a taste for bus-riding just like the relayings of horse tramways and their interruption to service did in London.

Eventually on 23 May 1925 through trams from Glasgow (and Paisley, which had been taken in Glasgow Corporation's ambit) began from Anniesland and Paisley to Airdrie (both trips were over 20 miles). Buses soon regained public patronage after a brief period when the new tram service enjoyed popularity. I travelled by the tram service and judged that the reason for the decline in the tram traffic was the frightening performance of four-wheeled cars lurching round curves, and when bogie types superseded them, swaying round bends at still higher speeds. One or two disastrous accidents left a mark on public consciousness, although, to tell the truth, Glasgow buses had a bad record of wholesale accidents, such as turning over.

At the beginning of January 1925 the Lanarkshire Tramways took over the Coatbridge fleet of Scottish General Transport and also that of Donald Munn of Harthill and Bellshill. Laird of Bathgate and Joseph Tennant & Sons of Armadale were other operators in this part of Central Scotland to be acquired. The J. D. Hendry fleet was taken over by Henry Lawson Ltd and almost immediately John Sword's Midland Bus Services began working from Airdrie to Glasgow and right through to Paisley, profitably despite the new tram service.

R. B. Dick was another of the coming men who rose to Thomson's notice as a director of Stewart & McDonald Ltd, incorporated on 4 June 1925 and operating between Glasgow, Motherwell, Lanark and Biggar. On 3 April 1926 J. W. & R. Torrance Ltd was incorporated and operated mainly between Hamilton, Cambuslang and Glasgow.

The Glasgow General Omnibus & Motor Services Ltd was incorporated on 23 June 1926 and began bus services on 29 August. It had an agreement with the London General Omnibus Co. Ltd for advice about its fleet of AEC buses. The first chairman was Sir Thomas D. Pile, a former director of the LGOC. There were more adequate capital resources than new bus companies opening up new territory usually have available and they had put 30 buses into service by the end of 1926, 100 by September 1927 and 221 by November 1928.

William J. Thomson was the founder and master architect of the Scottish Motor Traction Co. Ltd and welded its components into the operating companies of the Scottish Bus Group as they are today. He made the LMSR and the LNER his partners in this process and took a different line from that of the English British Electric Traction Company. Whereas the BET required whichever railway company to acquire and retain a holding equal to that of the BET or Tilling & British, the SMT asked for the railways to part with a half share of the bus companies they acquired. The agreement to this effect was announced on 19 July 1929 and the two railway companies agreed not to compete by passenger road services with the SMT or any of its associates within an agreed area covering, it was understood, the greater part of the Scottish mainland south of a line between Inverness and the Kyle of Lochalsh. During this period the LMSR had substantial bus shareholdings.

On 8 April 1930, in territory outside the area agreed between the SMT and the railways, the Inverness & District Motor Services Ltd, formed in Edinburgh on 18 April 1925, was restructured as the Highland Transport Co. Ltd with a 50 per cent LMSR shareholding. Activities which at one time had been confined to Strathpeffer to the north-west and Nairn eastward were soon as far afield as Wick and Thurso and a branch was opened in Skye. This, however, did not prosper and on 30 March 1935 it was transferred to A. Nicholson of Portree who made it into the Skye Transport Company. A capital return was made of 3s a share and henceforward from 1935 Highland Transport shares were of a nominal value of 17s (85 pence). W. H. Fowke, the managing director of Highland, told me before the war he considered himself the luckiest Englishman in the Highlands, being received so favourably despite his failings.

In 1932 A. Robertson & Son of Wick was acquired; the local competitor, Grieg of Inverness, who ran the town services there, was bought much later.

The Scottish Motor Traction Company Ltd purchased the Dundee Mechanical Transport Company in 1920 with services to Arbroath, Forfar and Inchture and this remained an isolated projection into outlying territory for a number of years. In 1923 William Young & Son of Bathgate was bought and in 1925 the Peebles Motor Co. Ltd. In 1926 a controlling interest in Brook & Amos Ltd of Galashiels, and in 1927 the Border Motor Transport Co. Ltd of Hawick was obtained. Henry Lawson Ltd was obtained during 1926 with Glasgow–Bathgate and Coatbridge–Glasgow services.

Thomson chose some reliable lieutenants from the Scottish Motor Traction Company and its new associates to develop the subsidiaries on an area basis in conjunction with the railways. The Border territory in south-east Scotland where SMT had been established was kept for the holding company as an operator although in 1968 the fleet name was changed to Eastern Scottish.

In the turn of 1930–1 the business of the Carlisle & District Transport Co. Ltd replacing the abortive Carlisle municipal transport scheme, squashed by the Traffic Commissioners, was carved up between SMT, Ribble, United Automobile, Caledonian and Cumberland. The inauguration of the Road Traffic Act caused a distinct pause in acquisitions, the next big one being in June 1932 when W. Rendell & Co. of South Queensferry was taken over. In September SMT took in Liddell Brothers of Auchinleck and during that year Lamond Brothers was acquired. Two Dalkeith firms also came into the SMT ambit at this time – J. L. Dunn and William Sword and T. L. and H. L. Dunn. January 1933 saw the purchase of Azure Blue Services and April following the acquisition of W. Scott & Co. of Edinburgh. In February 1934 County Motor Services (formed by the Gordon family of Choppington on 12 January 1929 to run their bus and haulage interests and operating 22 buses and coaches and 10 freight vehicles) was jointly acquired with United Automobile Services Ltd of Darlington. A year later the whole of the issued share capital of the Fife Tramway, Light and Power Co. Ltd (controlling Dunfermline & District Traction Co. and Falkirk & District Traction Co.) was purchased (1,500,000 ordinary shares of 5s at 3s 9d a share). Prominent in acquisitions in 1935 was Westwood & Smith in July and James Browning & Sons of Whitburn in August. In 1936 W. & J. Lawson of Kirriemuir was a notable purchase. At the beginning of 1937 the Coast Line Bus Service was taken over. It had been started by Musselburgh & District Traction Company, BET (or National Electric) tramway operators, on 25 February 1928; a through electric service from Port Seton to Edinburgh began on 24 June 1923, when the Edinburgh system was electrified, it having previously been operated by cable haulage. On 7 May 1931 the rest of the system was sold to Edinburgh Corporation. In 1935, 22 Leyland, Albion and Bristol buses were operated by Coast Lines and 26 buses were transferred two years later.

In preparation for the railway-associated regime the Scottish Motor Traction Company had been re-formed on 15 August 1929; the purchase consideration was £800,000 in shares. The authorised capital was £1,000,000 in 6½ per cent cumulative preference shares of £1 each issued and paid up; of the ordinary £1 shares, of which 875,000 were authorised, 858,434 were issued by 1937 and these shares, many of which were issued at a premium, had been devoted to the purchase of other undertakings. The traffic manager was James Amos and after the acquisition of the SMT by the British Transport Commission in 1949 the general manager of Scottish Omnibuses Ltd (covering the area of the SMT operating company, now Eastern Scottish) was the genial Robert Beveridge who came in 1914 from the Great North of Scotland Railway bus operations. James Amos at that time became the chairman of Scottish Bus Group, Sir William Thomson having unfortunately died in 1949 after the arrangements for selling the Scottish Motor Traction group to the British Transport Commission had been made. In 1938 when I was in Scotland for a preview of the Scottish Exhibition, Beveridge was a most pleasant and informative guide to SMT activities.

Sir William evidently foresaw the Scottish Transport Group in the arrangements he made for the organisation of Scottish Motor Traction and its subsidiaries with the LMSR and LNER shareholdings. We have detailed the growth of the SMT itself, another fleet in blue livery until the war when green was chosen as being more lasting.

Between Inverness and the central Rift Valley the area was nearly all allocated to W. Alexander and Son Ltd. Walter Alexander Snr and his son operated that company and one of the assets of the azure blue fleet was the

41 (*above*) A Bedford 29-seat bus filling a narrow lane near Bishop's Castle in Shropshire

42 (*left*) Barton Leyland Lion taking town gas on board in the Second World War

reduction of layovers by means of the connecting up of long through routes. The Alexanders, *père* and *fils*, or Senior and Junior as they were usually known, had formed their company on 23 May 1924, having started in business the previous year at Kilsyth, about ten miles north-east of Glasgow, whence they moved to Falkirk. The SMT announced their purchase on 8 February 1929. In mentioning that they were of 'Falkirk, Glasgow, Stirling, Dundee and Aberdeen' their future area was briefly outlined. At the same time the acquisition of Midland Bus Services of Airdrie, Glasgow and Kilmarnock and J. C. Sword was announced and the entry to the group of R. B. Dick of Carluke.

Under the SMT early Alexander acquisitions were municipal businesses – the provision of local transport in Kirkcaldy was taken over in May 1931 and Perth City Transport (for a time kept separate in a red-liveried fleet) in May 1934.

The expansion of the Alexander business took place partly by extension facilities and partly by purchase. Elliott & Brigg, for example, was an acquisition of December 1927 and Lankin Brothers of April 1929. March 1930 saw White's Motor Hiring Company taken into the SMT fold. In that month the Scottish General Omnibus Co. Ltd was taken over; it had acquired a number of concerns, including Dunfermline & District Traction, Scottish General (Northern) Omnibus Co. Ltd, Wemyss & District Tramways, General Motor Carrying Co. Ltd, A. & R. Motor Services (Buckhaven) Ltd, and Scottish Utility Motors Ltd; SMT also purchased Northern General Motors Ltd. Having begun a through bus route from Braemar to Aberdeen in 1929, the LNER handed the services begun by the GNSR to yet another company of similar title – Scottish General (Northern) Omnibus Co. Ltd – during 1931.

The Pitlochry Motor Co. Ltd was registered on 4 September 1929; it took over an existing business but the separate undertaking was maintained as a subsidiary company of W. Alexander & Sons Ltd for many years. In 1935 it was operating 21 vehicles between Pitlochry, Struan, Kinloch Rannoch, Aberfeldy and Perth and an express service was operated to Ballater in summer months. The main Alexander company was operating some 960 vehicles at this time. The Alexanders – father and son – were hard-headed business men. There used to be a joke about the son that his conversation was mainly 'Aye' if he had to say something and if he was feeling loquacious he might go as far as 'Och Aye'. In speech or writing their pronouncements were simple and to the point.

In 1931 A. Baxter & Co. of Cowdenbeath was taken over and the following year the Bydand Motor Omnibus Company and Aberdeen Suburban Transport with its outer area tramway association, were acquired. Bydand remained separate for three years. An interesting acquisition was the Dundee–Manifieth service of Dundee Corporation in 1932. Also in that year the LMS local bus services round Oban were taken over. In 1935 Perth Corporation Transport and Lowland Motorways (Glasgow to Aberdeen express), begun by Scottish Clan Motorways on 7 April 1927 and transferred to Lowland in June 1930, were taken over. In February 1936 David Lawson Ltd of Kirkintilloch became a subsidiary which operated separately and had a freight business.

Under the Transport Holding Company regime it was thought that W. Alexander at 2,100 buses was too unwieldy a unit and it was divided into Fife, Midland and Northern portions with red, blue and yellow liveries respectively.

In May 1936 Elgin & District Motor Services were acquired; in July the bus services of Falkirk Tramways were bought and in May 1937 Dunfermline & District Tramways was abandoned, as eventually all the small tramways of Scotland, company or municipal, were replaced by buses. Alexander absorbed the General Motor Carrying Co. Ltd in 1937; they had replaced the Wemyss & District Tramways by buses in January 1932, having purchased them the previous year.

The south-west of Scotland was allotted to the Western SMT Co. Ltd run by John Sword, who had proved his mettle as a busman (he had previously been a baker and an air transport operator) with Midland Bus Services of Airdrie which was formed in March 1924. The company counted its original registration on the file in Edinburgh as 24 September 1913, that being long before the association of the railways and the SMT, and the date of the registration by the BET of the Scottish General Transport Company, which had been formed to provide a bus organisation for three separated tramway undertakings, as mentioned much earlier in this chronicle. A controlling interest in this concern was announced by SMT in November 1931 and the change of name to Western SMT was announced on 7 June 1932. Midland Bus Services of Airdrie was, of course, a prominent constituent from 1 April 1932 and I travelled a token journey to Scotland (half-way in fact) on a Midland vehicle on 10 March 1932, the day the new station of London Coastal Coaches was opened in Buckingham Palace Road. The trip to Glasgow was notable in that diesel coaches (AEC Regals) were used on the service for the first time, a typical piece of Sword enterprise. It was interesting that at that time the Traffic Commissioners were very keen on coaches keeping to 30 m.p.h. and on this trip, where the first gear-change was in the tortuous streets of Stamford, 92 miles from London, long stretches of the route were covered at 29 m.p.h.; one piece of 26 miles was covered at 26·5 m.p.h. and the whole trip took 16 hours 23 minutes.

Other concerns amalgamated in Western SMT were Southern Bus Services of Newton Mearns, Kings Bus Services of Glasgow, Currie & Thompson Ltd of Calderbank, A. V. Pyefinch of Greenock, Muirhead & Co. Ltd of Glasgow, R. & W. Ferguson of Inchinnan, Ayrshire Pullman Motor Service of Ayr, Ayrways Motor Service of Ayr, Fingland's Motor Service of Ayr, Carrick Pullman Bus Services of Crosshill, J. W. Graham of Johnstone, Liddle Brothers of Auchinleck, Ayr & District Motor Services Ltd (routes opened May 1923 by William Young & Son; company formed June 1927), and Kilmarnock Corporation Omnibus Services (purchased by SMT for Western SMT); Ayr Corporation Transport was also taken in by the SMT undertaking.

I first met John Sword in his office at Kilmarnock as a journalist and enjoyed his hospitality from the ever-open whisky bottle on top of his high desk, when he gave me a concise account of his company's activities. Later I got to know him quite well at post-war conferences of the Scottish Road Passenger Transport Association, first at Pitlochry and then at Turnberry. This body for many years had only nine member undertakings but was generous in its invitations (the only proviso being that you paid your own hotel bill). On these occasions Sword's sense of humour and his appreciation of fun came out as well as his sound busmen's common sense, especially when it was his turn to take the presidential chair and he would start off 'Boys and Girls'.

The dour Dicks (another father and son with the same initials) guided the fortunes of Central SMT Co. Ltd which was formed by change of name on 18 June 1932 from the Glasgow General company; from 1 January 1932 it had absorbed the undertakings of the 80-bus Stewart & McDonald Ltd (LMSR purchase February 1929) and J. W. & R. Torrance Ltd. Purchase by the LMSR of the Glasgow General took place in May 1930. The Lanarkshire Traction (name adopted by Act of December 1929) interests were obtained by SMT in July 1932, the tramways having been abandoned on 6 October 1930.

The Central SMT consolidated its position (territory mainly south of the Clyde between Peebles, Biggar, Muirkirk, Stonehouse, Airdrie, West Calder and Carnwath and on the north between Glasgow Dumbarton and Helensburgh) and on the purchase in October 1932 of MacPhail's Bus Service of Newarthill; in June 1934 of Thomas Orr, of Shotts, with a Shotts–Motherwell–Hamilton service, one that was found surplus to traffic requirements before the end of the same year, and in June 1936 of Clydebank Motors Ltd (dating from 1914) and Baillie Brothers Ltd.

The first railway investment in Scottish bus business had no relation to the Railway Road Transport Acts of 1928. David MacBrayne Ltd having got into difficulties, a new company was created, jointly by Coast Lines Ltd and London Midland & Scottish Railway, on 31 October 1928 to take over the existing business of that title. As extensions of its shipping services the company provided motor-bus services which began in 1907 and employed some 60 vehicles (many of them 14-seaters) by the outbreak of the last war. Before the Scottish Bus Group (how lucky the National Bus Group did not take the at one time proposed name with the fatal initials 'N.B.G.') took over MacBrayne management it had 140 vehicles.

We have completed the outline of the SMT group story; under the nationalisation legislation of the immediately post-war period. Sir William Thomson deemed sale to the British Transport Commission the best course in 1949. At that time, as Sir Cyril Hurccomb, chairman of BTC, once pointed out to me about area schemes, Scotland could have had an area scheme to itself. No doubt that threat influenced Sir William's action in offering the Scottish Bus Group to the Commission for £35 million. Area schemes which were at that time proposed as a means of nationalising all bus transport. Areas proposed were North East Coast, South Western (both stemming largely from Tilling companies) but owing to the opposition of the BET companies the legislation was not implemented. Under the 1962 Act the Transport Holding Company was created to control the diverse separate companies interested in bus operation and under the 1968 Act the bus shareholdings of the English and Welsh companies were transferred to the National Bus Company created for the purpose. Those of the Scottish companies were dealt with differently; they were merged with shipping interests (the railway subsidiary, Caledonian Steam Packet and the islands and highlands shipping undertaking, David MacBrayne Ltd) to form a Scottish Transport Group.

In the south-west of Scotland one of the less notable Tilling & British ventures was formed by registration in Edinburgh on 9 April 1927 of the Caledonian Omnibus Co. Ltd; it was the only British Automobile Traction enterprise in Scotland at a time when British Electric Traction interests were looked after by the Scottish General Transport Co. Ltd, formed to merge the bus interests of three BET tramways in Scotland. Not long was to pass before the Scottish General Transport was reorganised by the SMT group into the Western SMT Co. in June 1932.

On formation the Caledonian company incorporated H. Brook & Co. Ltd in and around Stranraer, J. & J. Scott around Dumfries, Brook Motor Company around Kirkcudbright, Annandale Motor Company based on Lockerbie, and G. P. Bell, based on Carlisle and district. During 1932 the company purchased the bus business of the South of Scotland Motor Co. Ltd, Dumfries; Farrer & Faulder, with a Carlisle and Dumfries service; Andrew Harper, Peebles, with a 28-vehicle fleet (half Thornycrofts) operating a total route mileage of 220, services having been begun in 1923; and Huntington Brothers, with a Gretna and Carlisle service. The accession of Harper to Caledonian was important as it gave the company entry to Edinburgh; as Central SMT already had a Glasgow–Peebles service the Harper Glasgow–Walkerburn was discontinued, but the Edinburgh facility was retained by Caledonian until after Tilling was sold to the British Transport Commission, when it was decided that a competitive service was no longer needed. In 1942, with the splitting up of Tilling & British shares, Caledonian had become a wholly Tilling subsidiary. At the end of 1931 the business of Richard Percival of Carlisle, with a garage for six buses, was purchased.

From its inauguration on 10 June 1929 the service between Glasgow and Stranraer was joint between Caledonian and Scottish General Transport, the interests of the two companies meeting at Girvan. With the passing of control to the SMT interavailability of tickets was instituted between Midland Bus, Ayrshire Pullman Services and Scottish General Transport on this road and after may 1932 and after a Traffic Commissioner's hearing the Caledonian was left with only its own journeys on the joint service, and short workings from Stranraer to Girvan. On 1 October 1933 the services acquired from Harper round Peebles were exchanged for SMT services from Langholm and Penton to Carlisle via Longtown. Protection for Caledonian on the Sanquhar–Dumfries section of the Glasgow–Dumfries route was removed by the Commissioners in October 1933.

There used to be a favourite rhyme in Scotland to the effect that the earth is the Lord's and David MacBrayne's; it typifies the universality of the west of Scotland shipping organisation that linked everywhere from Glasgow to Stornoway and provided also much road transport in the way of essential links in the transport chain. David MacBrayne as a shipping company started in 1851; forty years later it first received a Government subsidy (of £10,200) by virtue of its services in providing transport facilities to remote communities on an all-the-year-round basis. In 1928 MacBraynes refused to tender for the mail contract; there were no other offers, and the eventual solution was a new joint company formed between Burns, Laird & Co. and the LMSR; the Burns, Laird interest was rapidly handed to Coast Lines Ltd. The new company was formed 31 October 1928 and the road fleet which had begun in 1907 and now numbered 13 vehicles, rapidly grew in size. Before the Second World War there were 60 vehicles, including 11 large Maudslays and a number of 14-seaters suited to narrow roads; on most of the road routes mail could be posted on the buses and the territory served ran from Inverness along Loch Ness and extended into Glasgow from 1929. Drivers were smart at picking up letters at speed when they were held out.

It was often the practice to operate baggage vans along with coaches and to omit local service times from the general timetable. For many years MacBrayne timetables between Inverness and Fort William were co-ordinated with Macrae & Dick, the Inverness tour operators, but MacBrayne out of pique would not show Macrae & Dick's times in its publications as Macrae & Dick was the preferred nominee of the LNER. Actually MacBrayne would apparently have rather had MacIntyre to share the route with, although in 1933 MacBrayne had opposed A. MacIntyre & Sons (who had entered into a tentative agreement with the LNER) at the traffic courts. Eventually in 1935 A. MacIntyre & Sons was purchased by MacBraynes. Previously in March 1932 Link Lines Ltd was acquired and in September 1934 the Kinlochleven Road Transport Co. Ltd was taken over. In 1936 A. & J. McPherson of Fort William purchased the Fort William and Achnacarry service of R. Campbell. So in the remotest parts of the Highlands the process of consolidation went on.

In the north-east corner of Scotland there was an enclave served by James Sutherland (Peterhead) Ltd, which had a substantial fleet; Sutherland's Bus Services operated 34 buses on five routes in 1933 and some freight services calling for 24 lorries. At one time the fleet was as large as 86 vehicles (made up of 36 buses, including one double-decker, 10 other passenger vehicles and 40 lorries).

In the north-west some of the long bus services that have fulfilled the at one time hoped-for railway branches to such places as Ullapool (under 'rationalisation' the terminus of roll-on-roll-off steamer services from Harris and Lewis) are operated by Sutherland Transport & Trading Co. Ltd, which has only a small fleet of five or eight vehicles at various times, but provides passenger and mail transport over the 58 miles from Lairg to Durness; to Scourie (44 miles) and to Tongue (37 miles).

Young's Bus Service Ltd of Paisley was acquired on 1 March 1950 by the BTC at the same time as James Sutherland (Peterhead) Ltd and in 1951 the BTC obtained the 50 per cent interest in the Highland Transport Co. Ltd not taken up by the LMSR, under the name Highland Omnibuses Ltd.

A feature of recent years has been the participation of the Post Office in rural transport, testified by the Scottish Postal Board operating 40 minibuses, with 8 on order in 1975, worked from 27 different centres.

For English and Welsh companies the Tilling Group Management Board was used for administration until the Transport Act 1968 posed a threat, the British Electric Traction group yielded and sold out to the Commission and the National Bus Company was formed. At the last minute some intelligent civil servant warned the Ministry of Transport from adopting National Bus Group, a name parallel to the Scottish Transport Group, with the devastating initials 'N.B.G.'

14
Coaches

The medium-distance coach service established itself on a firm basis with routes between London and the coastal resorts in the period immediately after the First World War, when the war-torn railway system was unable to meet the renewed demand for pleasure traffic. Even during the war a pioneer effort had been made by Chapman's of Eastbourne, an old-established firm of horse-bus and -coach proprietors, which had adopted the motor for touring in 1913. A twice-weekly coach service was begun between Eastbourne and London (Grosvenor Hotel) in June 1917, and, as petrol was restricted, the Dennis open coach ran on coal gas taken from a balloon container fixed in a tray above the vehicle.

For the seed which grew into a nationwide industry, credit must be given to 'Len' Turnham, who was born in Sloane Street, near Victoria, and attended King's College. He qualified as a motor engineer and in 1912 set up in business in Eccleston Street East as a motor hirer and repairer. Leonard Mark Turnham, to give him his full name, decided to run a regular daily motor-coach service between London and Brighton, which he launched at Easter 1919. He said later that he was impressed by the long queues gathered to book for Brighton line trains and went along the queues selling coach tickets at 10s 6d single and £1 day return to waiting would-be train passengers. The pioneer vehicle of Turnham's was a 28-seat AEC with the seats arranged mainly in rows of five and the Brighton service ran from Grosvenor Gardens by Victoria Station to Cricketer's Hotel, Ship Street, Brighton. This type of vehicle, usually with a cape-cart hood which could be drawn over in inclement weather, was a motor coach to the proprietor, but to the majority of passengers it was a charabanc – a survival from horse days.

Chapman's resumed their thrice-weekly seasonal Eastbourne–London service on 17 March 1919, using petrol-driven vehicles; Alexander Timpson began working regularly between Plumstead and Hastings; and Elliott Brothers inaugurated weekend seasonal journeys between Bournemouth and London. Nevertheless, most of the coaching activity in 1919 was in the form of day excursions and not regular services. Although the Armistice had been signed on 11 November 1918, the war was not over until the Peace Treaty was signed on 28 June 1919. Meanwhile, there were shortages of vehicles, of men, and of petrol. Towards the end of the season, railway transport was paralysed for nine days by a strike from 26 September to 6 October, and this gave a great fillip to the motor coach. Many visitors were stranded in the East Kent coastal towns, and the East Kent Road Car Co. Ltd inaugurated emergency coach services from Folkestone, Deal, Thanet and Herne Bay to London. There was considerable excitement, and the coaches were given a parting cheer by a large number of spectators. Southdown Motor Services Ltd ran between Brighton and London as a temporary expedient, and indeed the railway strike produced a lot of ephemeral services such as W. P. Allen's distinctive greenish-yellow Straker-Squire with Allen's bodywork incorporating transverse seats on the lower deck) on the run from London to Mersea Island.

For the 1920 season, numerous coach proprietors introduced regular workings between London and the South Coast, of which one of the most important, in the light of subsequent events, was Pickfords Ltd. Initially it operated to Brighton, Eastbourne and Hastings. Turnham & Co. Ltd placed a Thornycroft coach on the Victoria–Eastbourne run at Whitsun and of course continued the successful Brighton service. Southdown also came on the Brighton road as a permanent feature. A name which became very well-known in the industry was Francis Arthur Flin who formed the MT Co. (a title clearly derived from the First World War) and launched a New Cross–Margate service on 29 May 1920. By the end of June the *Daily Mail* commented that 'motor charabancs were becoming very popular and that trains were losing passengers at an alarming rate'. The Westcliff-on-Sea Motor Char-a-Banc Co. Ltd began working between Woolwich, New Cross, East Ham and Southend daily from 10 July. During 1920 Shirley James of Pickfords Ltd suggested formation of a pool which was organised very quickly as London & Coastal Motor Coach Services. The various London firms who were the first members were soon joined by provincial bus companies working coaches to the Metropolis. Thus the associated proprietors were able to offer a twice- or thrice-daily schedule on many routes and were possessed of a sound traffic and mechanical service at each end of the journey. The London control was originally in the hands of Pickfords, but was taken over by Turnham & Co. in the autumn of 1921 and has since been located at Victoria, which has also been the main starting point. A central booking and control office was established at 7b Lower Belgrave Street, opposite Victoria Station, and for a few years Lower Belgrave Street was used as a terminal for the coaches, but it rapidly became congested, as did adjacent streets. Nevertheless, some years were to elapse before a private terminal could be established. Another development of 1920 which is worthy of record was the beginning of medium-distance coach services not touching London. The East Kent Road Car Co. was a pioneer in this field when it began a Margate–Hastings service on 12 July 1920, serving coastal resorts of Kent and Sussex.

This popularity of the motor coach with the travelling public, causing many to regard the journey as part of the holiday, resulted in what the industry regarded as an invasion of outsiders without operating know-ledge. The first of these was the Samuelson Transport Co. Ltd, a business established by George Berthold Samuelson, a film producer, which was incorporated on 14 April 1921 to work motor-coach services on a large scale. As a result of his experience in the entertainment world, Samuelson launched his enterprise with a volume of press and poster publicity which was exceptional in the road transport industry of the period. In the first three months more than £5,500 was spent on advertising, a very large figure for that period. He began trading on 7 May with six coaches, but, with the assistance of hired vehicles, inaugurated daily services from London to every coastal resort between Yarmouth and Bournemouth. Luggage vans were also run and 56 lb of baggage was conveyed free (including collection and delivery) in respect of all routes excepting Yarmouth and Bourne-mouth, thus covering the resorts between Clacton and Portsmouth. By the end of July this involved 99 coaches and 23 luggage vans, of which no fewer than 56 coaches were held under hire-purchase agreements. Of the coaches, 83 were 27-seat vehicles, mainly Dennis and Thornycroft, and by reason of their weight were subject to the 12 m.p.h. maximum speed that then applied to what were classified as 'Heavy Motor Cars'. Samuelson wished to go further afield than this permitted, and the remaining 16 coaches were 14-seat Talbot vehicles allowed a maximum of 20 m.p.h. With these he began some 'first class express' services to health resorts on 1 July

1921, namely Bath, Lynton and Ilfracombe, Dawlish and Teignmouth, Newton Abbot and Torquay, and Stratford-on-Avon, Rhyl, Colwyn Bay and Llandudno. Two others which were announced were Matlock and Buxton, and Harrogate, but these apparently were never worked.

Samuelson was followed closely by the Cambrian Coaching Company, founded by Athole Murray Kemp-Gee of the Cambrian Catering Company, and by Cornells, the meat transport carriers of Smithfield Market. The year 1921 also saw numerous provincial developments. The Birmingham & Midland Motor Omnibus Co. Ltd launched 'Midland Red' workings from Birmingham to Weston-super-Mare on 9 May, and from Birmingham to Llandudno on 16 June. A joint venture was that of the Hereford Motor Co. Ltd and Jones Brothers of Aberystwyth with their once-weekly service between Hereford and Aberystwyth beginning on 18 June. Another name which should here be mentioned is that of George Samuel Dicks, who has come into our story already as the originator of the route number with the Vanguard buses in London. He was also the pioneer of long-distance motor-bus operation with the Vanguard London–Brighton service of 1905–6, which, but for the Handcross accident which damaged public confidence, might have led to development a decade and a half earlier than was the case. At the great London merger of 1908 he became one of the joint traffic advisers of the LGOC and on his retirement in 1918 he settled at Brighton. After the war he took up excursion work under the name Vanguard Motor Conveyance Services, and in 1921 began some regular routes, of which the first was the London run. This was followed by a Brighton–Ashford–Canterbury–Margate route and in 1922 with numerous others, some with intermediate single fares as low as 1s. He joined forces with the Cambrian group in 1922 and these cross-country activities were not long-lived.

The increasing volume of traffic resulted in the London & Coastal partners forming a separate company capable of entering into contracts in its own name, and London Coastal Coaches Ltd was incorporated on 30 April 1925. The Company then sought a private site, lighting on a plot put on one side in the early days of London County Council Tramways when it was hoped that many West End thoroughfares such as Park Lane and Edgware Road would be traversed by trams. This idea persisted until 1920 when attempts at authorisation were abandoned and the Western generating station scheme was finally given up. From 1 April 1928 the Lupus Street Station of London Coastal Coaches provided space for a terminal and removed many of the police objections to the terminal work being carried out in Central London. In this year 200 departures daily were recorded and 12,000 passengers. In 1929 on 1 April control was moved to Bessborough House, Lupus Street. Later a number of concerns developed a small station at Kings Cross, but no other group of operators has had the success of what was known from 1925 as London Coastal Coaches. One of the factors in this success has been the refusal to allocate particular seats to particular travellers and to the high standards observed by all concerned.

In 1926 a number of London independent proprietors sold their businesses to the establishment, with the result that they were looking for some other remunerative occupation. Several of them hit upon the idea of operating limited-stop services from London to the country in emulation of the service begun by Greyhound Motors Ltd of Bristol on 11 February 1925 from London (Clarendon Hotel in Hammersmith Broadway) to Bristol. Regular year-round operation, a published timetable, and fares graded to stages were regarded as essential and in the Road Traffic Act of 1930 regard was paid to them as express carriage services with definitions as to the length of minimum fare stages. When Greyhound began such definition had not been given and over several sections of the London–Bristol route there were local stage carriage fares. Conductors were usually carried on Greyhound vehicles, but one conductor would sometimes be made responsible for several vehicles if the total seating capacity did not exceed 26. This, of course, was long before the general acceptance of the one-man bus on every sort of service. I was fortunate in being able to take a holiday from my job in the haulage business soon after the inauguration of the Greyhound Bristol service; I remember particularly the remark of an ancient man in the coach as we passed Silbury Hill that 'there is a volcano, surely'. This is perhaps an extreme example of how the motor coach brought a new aspect of the countryside before many citizens.

It is impracticable here to outline the history of the many businesses which have contributed to the evolution of the present nation-wide network, but one which is deserving of special mention is that of the Royal Blue Services of Elliott Brothers (Bournemouth) Ltd. Thomas Elliott of Bournemouth began operating horse coaches in 1880 and his sons bought their first motor vehicles in 1909. Almost immediately tours of up to 100 miles in length were operated – a great deal for the period. An agreement was made with Hants & Dorset in 1921 when the Elliott business was valued at over £14,000 that it would do all the long-distance work for the two undertakings. It was arranged that the London service should run to the Pall Mall office of Thomas Cook & Son, but from 1927 it worked to Lower Belgrave Street. From 1922, the daily summer seasonal service was inaugurated with Daimler 45-h.p. coaches, with sleeve-valve engines. On 31 March 1928 the Bournemouth–London service was altered to run via Basingstoke and Southampton twice daily; the fare was 12s 6d single and 20s return. The Torquay–Exeter–Bournemouth route was introduced twice

43 (*above*) The first journey by diesel-engined coach, an AEC Regal, from Glasgow to London seen at the Baldock refreshment stop. The operator is Midland Bus Services of Airdrie

44 (*left*) The Leyland Titan double-deck bus was low enough to pass through the medieval arch, the Stonebow, in the centre of the City of Lincoln

daily from 5 April 1928, and other services were London–Bournemouth daily and London–Reading–Bath–Weston-super-Mare (later diverted via Bristol). During the winter of 1928–9 additional services via Salisbury were inaugurated and were extended to Shaftesbury, but the route was later amended to serve the Salisbury Plain camps. From 25 March 1929 new services were begun: London – Guildford – Winchester – Romsey – Bournemouth; Bournemouth – Salisbury – Swindon – Gloucester – Cheltenham – Stratford-on-Avon – Coventry – Birmingham; Bournemouth – Southampton – Portsmouth – Arundel – Brighton – Eastbourne – Hastings – Folkestone – Dover – Margate, thus including every Kent and Sussex coast resort between Worthing and Margate; Bournemouth – Yeovil – Taunton – Weston-super-Mare; and Bournemouth–Dorchester–Taunton–Ilfracombe.

Early in 1930 route letters were adopted for timetable purposes. The frequency of Service A (London–Southampton–Bournemouth) was increased to ten journeys daily. From 9 May 1932 co-ordination was approved with Southdown and this involved the use of the Southdown station at Hyde Park Road, Portsmouth. From 19 July 1933 co-ordinated Royal Blue–South Midland timetables were in force. From October 1933 the Southern and Western National omnibus companies obtained the licences formerly held by Highways Ltd. The Tilling group secured control of the Royal Blue business in November 1934 and long-distance services were transferred to the Southern National and Western National companies.

Although honoured more in the breach than in the observance, the maximum speed which applied to most buses and coaches remained at 12 m.p.h. until 1 October 1928, when the Heavy Motor Car (Amendment) Order (1928) increased this to 20 m.p.h. for vehicles fitted with pneumatic tyres. It was further increased to 30 m.p.h. from 1 January 1931. Another major change was the new licensing procedure introduced by the Road Traffic Act (1930). The 1930 legislation brought many struggles before the Traffic Commissioners as to the level of coach fares – largely with the railways, despite their ownership of up to 50 per cent of the share capital of many bus and coach operating companies after 1929. This was a struggle the railways were happy to give up after a surprisingly short period. An unacceptable aspect of capitalism as it came to be termed concerned the unfair way some coach operators were treated in the traffic courts. The MT Company, which had been on the London and Thanet route since 1920, was passed over in favour of the East Kent Road Car Co. Ltd when it came to the issue of licences. This was felt to be gross favouritism of the large company, but the Traffic Commissioner, Rowland Harker, KC, took the view that the East Kent had to maintain a large mileage of unremunerative rural services. Some of these were once maintained by operators who kept the characteristics of country carriers, such as the Magnet, which plied from Gloucester Green, Oxford, to remote villages with mixed cargoes of passengers and goods on a Ford, or F. Bulmer of Charing, Kent, who continued to set out from Faversham from a phalanx of green Maidstone and Districts on his daily trips to the villages including Hockley, Stalisfield and Otterden, on the way to Ashford from 1922 into the 1930s. Nowadays they are replaced by services provided with minibuses operated by the Post Office.

Lupus Street coach station of London Coastal Coaches completely vindicated the policy of providing terminal arrangements on private ground, but it was an uncovered station and not so conveniently situated as was desired. As soon as a suitable site on freehold land could be obtained, plans for building a permanent station were put in hand on a corner site fronting Buckingham Palace Road and Elizabeth Street. On 10 March 1932 the present Victoria Coach Station in Buckingham Palace Road was opened by Percy J. Pybus, Minister of Transport at the time. It was said that never before had there been assembled such a representative gathering of important people – many of them pioneers – in the road passenger business. A prominent technical journalist who was present paid a deserved tribute when he wrote: 'When the history of the industry comes to be chronicled, there will be no more romantic chapter than that describing the growth of London Coastal Coaches Ltd.'

It provided the terminus for all the railway-associated bus companies (26) working to London and for some half-dozen independent companies. The opening day was marked by a collapse of seating in the restaurant and the use for the first time in long-distance service of diesel-engined vehicles. These were AEC Regents of Midland Bus Services, Airdrie, a member of the SMT group, soon afterwards to be merged in the Western SMT Company. I was invited to join the inaugural run from London to Glasgow as far as Boroughbridge, and was very impressed with the fact that the first gear change for other than acceleration purposes was at Stamford, 92 miles from Victoria, the tortuous streets of the town being well-known to coach drivers as a 'shoulder-breaker'.

At a time when traffic commissioners paid great attention to coach speeds it was interesting to note how closely the drivers adhered to 30 m.p.h. without exceeding it. On the London–Glasgow service the scheduled speed approved by the traffic commissioners was 30 m.p.h., except in the Northern area, where it was 25 m.p.h. The 7 miles from Biggleswade to Baldock were covered at 29 m.p.h. and 26 miles to Wetherby at 26·5 m.p.h. The entire 403½ miles was in 1932 scheduled in 16 hours 23 minutes. The time came down to just over 12 hours later and with road improvements reducing the mileage and the raising of the speed limit for coaches many services were covered at higher speeds. Today the time for over 400 miles to Edinburgh and Glasgow from London is 11 hours, or 9 hours from Glasgow by the M1 and M6 motorways, and years before the war, when the railways attacked coach services, I satisfied myself as editor of *Modern Transport* that the coaches were much more reliable timekeepers than the trains in bad weather.

With the opening of the M4 motorway the time on the London–Bristol pioneer coach route came down to 2½ hours. The London–Blackpool time has come down to 7 hours 1 minute via the M1 and M6 motorways and 10 hours 13 minutes by the A roads.

Northern long-distance coach services began for the most part in 1928 and 1929, but there had been some interesting efforts during the previous two years. The Leeds–London service of the South Yorkshire Motor Co. was inaugurated in September 1926. It was the Newcastle–London road, however, which first attracted widespread attention. At that period it competed not only with the railways but also with coastal shipping. The pioneer was Orange Brothers of Bedlington, which began a once-weekly service on 12 June 1927 that at once proved so popular that it became twice weekly on 23 June and daily from 10 October. An immediate competitor was the Majestic Saloon Motor Coach Service of Robert Armstrong & Sons, which began in July and became daily from 9 October; it was extended to Edinburgh and Glasgow on 23 March 1931. Also in 1927 the Leeds–Newcastle Omnibus Co. Ltd began to work between the points indicated by its title on 3 August.

Of particular interest in the north was the adoption by the large associated bus companies of the principle of coaching pools which enabled operators to avoid wasteful mileage; placed the services under supervision for the whole route; and enabled larger-scale publicity to be employed.

Of the companies operating the Yorkshire Services pool, West Yorkshire was the first, starting in July 1929 between Harrogate and London and, in the following month, between Harrogate and Birmingham. The pool with the title of Yorkshire Services was begun in July 1930 and the services inaugurated were Harrogate–London via Great North Road; Bradford–London, via the Midlands; Keighley–Birmingham via Sheffield; and Harrogate–Birmingham, via Doncaster and Nottingham. The East Yorkshire company began in July 1929 from Scarborough to Birmingham; it joined the pool in 1931 and further co-ordination was effected, the Scarborough–Leeds feeder service being withdrawn. The pool operators also obtained licences for the previous operations of East Yorkshire – Scarborough–York–Leeds–Barnsley–Birmingham; Scarborough–

Bridlington–Barnsley–London; Hull–Barnsley (feeder service). In 1933 the London–Leeds service via the Great North Road and Papworth of Hale Garage Coach Co. Ltd and Coachway Ltd was acquired by the pool. In October 1934 it was joined by the East Midland Motor Services Ltd, contributing its Sheffield–London service which had been previously operated by Underwood Express Services Ltd that had sold to the London Midland & Scottish Railway Company. Going back to 1933, the Fawdon Bus Co., with a service between Newcastle and Coventry, was purchased by Northern General Transport Co. Ltd on behalf of the Limited Stop Pool.

At the beginning of 1935 London Midland & Yorkshire Services operating between Bradford and London via the Midlands and Phillipson's Service Ltd between Doncaster and Scarborough were taken over. The independent operators who had previously been interested in London Midland & Yorkshire were South Yorkshire Motors, B & E Services, and Wilks Parlour Coaches. In summer four of the pool services met at Barnsley and three met at Doncaster giving a choice of routes between the Midlands, West, East Anglian resorts, and West Riding towns. A night service gave connections to the South Coast and the Continent.

The Northern General Transport Co. Ltd inaugurated what became known as the Limited Stop Pool on 1 May 1928. It was a service of charabancs between Newcastle, Manchester and Liverpool which at that time had to be licensed by the police authorities of the three towns. Experimentally it was operated during the following winter and the result being profitable an increased service was planned and begun on 15 May 1929 by Northern General, West Yorkshire, Woollen District and North Western companies. The timetable provided for a coach every two hours; subsequently certain journeys were extended via Altrincham to Liverpool. About the same time a Hull–Manchester service was begun by East Yorkshire and this was incorporated in the pool from February 1930. Two years later the Lancashire United joined the pool and the Manchester–Liverpool service was increased to hourly. On 18 October 1933 Tyne & Mersey Services (Newcastle–Bradford–Liverpool) was purchased and the Newcastle–Leeds section of the Fawdon Bus Co. was taken over. From 31 August 1932 joint operation on Leeds–Middlesbrough (originally operated by Redwing Safety Services Ltd) was begun by West Yorkshire and United Automobile Services (the Leeds–Middlesbrough service had a Redcar summer extension) but permission to add United Automobile Services to the pool was held up by the Traffic Commissioners who did not always see eye-to-eye with operators about economies in working. The Leeds–Hull section was withdrawn on 9 December 1934 and the East Yorkshire company ceased to be a member of the pool. It was not until 21 October 1934 that the

Commissioners gave their blessing to the UAS joining the pool. Just before the war the Limited Stop Pool comprised three services every two hours; (i) Liverpool and Newcastle via Altrincham, Dewsbury and Leeds; (ii) Liverpool and Middlesbrough (Redcar in summer) via Eccles, Liversedge and Leeds; (iii) Leeds and Newcastle (Saturdays only); the pool also included one return journey between Liverpool and Newcastle via Eccles, Bradford and Leeds; and one return journey between Coventry and Newcastle via Wetherby and Leeds. This gave an hourly frequency between Liverpool and Leeds and an hourly frequency on Saturdays from Leeds to Newcastle.

West Yorkshire began a service from Bradford to Blackpool on 16 July 1928; an extension to Leeds followed in 1929. This met a more favourable reception from the Commissioners, restoring order out of chaotic conditions, although several schemes were turned down by the Commissioners owing to the strenuous opposition of the railways. Each of the pools provided pamphlets for its drivers and conductors giving general and specific instructions for the service, with stopping places and plans of the main towns en route. Expenses chargeable to the pools included agent's commission, lodging expenses, bus station charges, and foreign vehicles hired for duplication.

The scheme of co-ordination, usually known as the Blackpool picture, brought some order out of chaos after 1932 when the Commissioners for Yorkshire and the North Western areas brought their combined talents to bear on the matter. In 1934 a comprehensive arrangement was put before them and the pool eventually combined West Yorkshire, Yorkshire Traction, Ribble, Woollen District, and Hebble companies. This was approved in the following year. This provided for the co-ordination on a rota basis of Hanson, Bullock and other competitive operators. General publicity for all the pools and timetables, etc. was done by the West Yorkshire company and one company acted as clearing house for the entire pool.

Because of its profound influence, a little special attention is worth while for Black & White Motorways. In the early 1920s G. Reading was in business with a garage and motor-coach business at Charlton Kings and Cheltenham under the name of Black & White Luxury Coaches and he formed a limited company to operate the property on 12 April 1928. Members of the Reading family originally managed the undertaking, with H. R. Lapper as secretary, but on the acquisition of the company by Birmingham & Midland Motor Omnibus Co. Ltd, Bristol Tramways & Carriage Co. Ltd and City of Oxford Motor Services Ltd, H. R. Lapper became general manager. His brother, L. B. Lapper, became well-known in the world of railway enthusiasts as a joint founder of the Railway Correspondence & Travel Society in 1928.

In 1933 Black & White and St Margarets Coach Station at Cheltenham were selected as the focal point of a co-ordination scheme which involved the meeting at Cheltenham of many services in the south-west area. The first stage on 19 March 1934 comprised Birmingham & Midland, Black & White, Greyhound and Red & White and two principal exchange times, one around 1300 and 1400, when lunch could be taken while exchanging vehicles, and the other around a tea interval. In May the second stage was achieved, bringing in Elliott Brothers (Bournemouth) (Royal Blue), United Counties, Ribble, and seeking the licences for the whole organisation under the name of Associated Motorways.

In the first flush of enthusiasm for the coach there were many thought that the sleeping car on the railways might be parallelled on the road. In 1928 Chergwin (the White Kaffir) operated coaches with sleeping accommodation, arranged in bunks parallel to the direction of travel, on the London and Manchester route; the reason for the failure of this venture was understood to be the cost of washing the bedlinen.

Similarly there have been several attempts at restaurant vehicles, mainly in the way of provision of facilities for special events, although double-deck coaches have attracted attention for the purpose, with the object of allocating one deck or the other to meal preparation, washing up, or whatever, but on the whole coach travellers appear to prefer to stretch their legs and patronise a motorway or other restaurant as well as what has come to be called a 'comfort stop'. For this reason built-in lavatory facilities are not deemed essential upon coaches as they have become even on short air trips, although the cross-Channel car air carriers were unprovided.

15 The Small Provincial Proprietor

Much of our story so far has been concerned with bus and coach operations in urban and interurban service, as might be expected. It would be lacking in balance, however, to conclude without paying tribute to the provincial independent operator, often a direct descendent of the country carrier, who had rendered valuable service in rural areas. As has been claimed on numerous occasions before the Traffic Commissioners, some of the 'area agreement' companies maintained a large mileage of unremunerative rural services, including those taken over from local operators of the country carrier type. This was often a desire to serve the whole area and to afford less reason for the small operator to 'intrude', but in practice the large company often found it impracticable to render the friendly personal service of the local man. It would take a sizeable book to chronicle even the more important of such activities throughout the country, and much of the contents would be of local rather than general interest. All that can be done here is to give a few representative examples.

Despite the apparent uniformity produced by the operating companies of the British Electric Traction and Tilling groups being united in the National Omnibus Company and many of the municipal undertakings being merged in passenger transport areas while the very vehicles are to a large extent standardised, differences still exist and it has been part of our task in this book to draw attention to these idiosyncrasies and the individuality of some of the small proprietors. It was the Eastern Counties that decided on its apparent traffic figures to buy a certain small business and after purchase found the receipts in no way tallied. Inquiry brought the explanation that the operator reckoned on doing all the shopping for his village even to buying 'little Johnny's boots and shirts'. A small commission on these transactions increased the fares taken to a worthwhile amount. There is no doubt that the relative closeness of the population to some rural proprietors has brought a loyalty of the users to the proprietors, much more noticeable than in the case of the subsidiaries of the National Bus Company.

On the Welsh Border during the war we boarded a bus in Shrewsbury for Llanymynech. The bus was an OWB Bedford with seats for 29 persons. By cajoling his customers – 'Breathe in Mrs Owen,' 'Turn your toes out, Mrs Jones' – the owner, Tony Vagg, managed to squeeze 54 people into the tiny body and all went happily the best part of 20 miles in this overcrowded state. On the return trip from Llanymynech the driver stopped at what was obviously his garage, and I took the opportunity of asking him for a timetable; he was gone about 20 minutes and I apologised for having sent him on such an errand. He then produced a time sheet and explained that he had had a cup of tea. The whole episode was very typical of the intimacy engendered by the small proprietor, the numbers of whom have, nevertheless, dwindled almost as much as the services of the subsidiaries of the National Bus Company.

The rural bus has been undermined by the private car almost as much as the town and interurban service. To a limited extent it has been superseded by the General Post Office which has been able to replace some facilities by services combining passenger transport with letter delivery. Where, as in Cornwall and Devon, the services of whole garages have been withdrawn, local entrepreneurs spring up and venture on the scene, sometimes with success.

In Norfolk the Eastern Counties Omnibus Co. Ltd has sponsored a scheme under which a certain number of volunteers arrange to man the local bus without charge. In other areas there have been official census figures taken with the object of ascertaining how many passengers would present themselves if a bus were to be run, but almost always the results have been disappointing. If 40 people say they would go shopping at a particular time, only 25 find it convenient to turn up; on one municipal endeavour to find passengers for an evening trip in the Midlands, 10 offered and none came.

A typical market-day operator who provided valuable service was Bob Carpenter of Bishops Castle, using the trading name of Hope Valley

Services. At the peak of bus prosperity Carpenter used a garage built out of the former Bishops Castle Railway station (the Bishops Castle Railway had been in the hands of the receiver from 1867 until it faded away in 1953). In its last years a railway-owned bus had operated from Craven Arms to the town as a supplement to the railway service but from about 1935 until the end of the Second World War Carpenter operated about 20 Bedfords on a succession of market-day services coupling Bishops Castle to Shrewsbury (daily); Craven Arms Station (daily); Shrewsbury via Lydbury and Plowden (Wednesday and Saturday); Welshpool (Smithfield) (Monday); Ludlow (Square) (Monday); Newtown (The Gravels) (Tuesday); Bridges (Horseshoe) (Friday); and Bishopsmoat (Friday). I remember going down with Bob Carpenter driving on the afternoon journey to Bishopsmoat, which was operated as a circular service, when an old lady suddenly piped up, 'Mr Carpenter, Mr Carpenter, you've passed my turning.' Quick as a flash, despite the impediment in speech from which he suffered, Bob replied, 'Oh we wouldn't want to do that, otherwise we'd have to keep you for a week!'

Carpenter used to work on Fridays to Asterton Prolley Moor and Wentnor Prolley Moor, remote hamlets at the foot of the Long Mynd and reached along some of the narrowest lanes traversed by full-size buses in the country. (When I knew Bob the maximum width of any vehicle was 7 ft 6 in. and some of his neighbouring Shropshire operators kept the width of body to 6 ft 6 in. to minimise damage in narrow lanes.) Bob took a number of precautions against snowfalls, which can be heavy and unexpected in these remote Shropshire uplands. All buses carried a large shovel in winter in case they had to be dug out and he had also four Tilling-Stevens Express because they were very sure-footed vehicles on icy roads. Carpenter began business at Church Stoke and disposed of it in 1957; Messrs W. E., M. E., G. G. and F. A. Lewis took it over and a new limited company, Valley Motor Services (Bishops Castle) Ltd, was formed in 1961. In the recent fleet Commer, Leyland, Ford and Seddon vehicles have figured.

Barton Transport Ltd had its origins in the oil-engine department of Hornsby & Sons when Thomas Henry Barton, after training at University College, Nottingham, rose to be manager of the department. He moved to the family quarry business in Derbyshire and moved on again, pursued by ill-health, to a smallholding near Mablethorpe. With this as headquarters plying for hire was done with a pony and trap. Sophistication brought a 9-h.p. Benz eight-seat wagonette with which he began a service along the Mablethorpe sea front on 19 September 1899 at the novelty fare of 6d for one mile. Ill-health drove Barton to Weston-super-Mare; on the way there the Benz gave so much mechanical trouble that shafts were fitted for horse-haulage.

The next venture into motor transport was achieved with a 12-seater Daimler wagonette which the Barton family used between the old pier and the new at Weston; ill-fortune still dogged the Bartons as the local horse-lobby, very strong in 1900, persuaded the Weston councillors to rescind the Barton licence. After trying a 20-seater which they were compelled to sell, even on their home ground back in Derbyshire, the permanent start of Barton was found in a 28-seat Durham-Churchill charabanc with which they cashed in on Goose Fair traffic between Long Eaton and Nottingham, after which they never looked back, despite an unfortunate experience in 1907 with a Clarkson steam vehicle which was unsuited to limestone water. The service from Sandiacre or Beeston ('old man' Barton's reminiscences varied with fading memory) to Nottingham was begun in 1911, although Barton buses were to be seen three years earlier, as regular operation (as distinct from trips and excursions) began in October 1908.

The Barton service attracted national interest when the *Daily Mirror* of 3 July 1913 had an illustrated article headed 'Girl as Chauffeur of Omnibus; sisters as conductors'. The girl was Miss Kate Barton, then aged 21, and the vehicle a single-deck Ryknield. Three years later, during the petrol shortage of the First World War, Bartons again became known as pioneers when they introduced a gas-driven bus in June 1916, taking its fuel of town gas from a collapsible bag or balloon on the roof. The firm also fitted other people's buses for coal-gas operation.

Barton innovations were numerous and included a road train that was intended for the Beeston and Nottingham route; it was an utter failure (it swallowed petrol and with its excessive consumption it was very slow). Competition demanded a light, speedy vehicle and the Barton six-wheeled 'glider' was evolved. He embraced the compression-ignition engine in 1930 and was among the earliest users. The first one had a four-cylinder Gardner engine and began work on 15 March 1930. By reason of his early association with the Hornsby-Ackroyd engine, Barton would not term these 'diesel engines', as the 1890 patent of Ackroyd-Stuart was prior to any of Dr Rudolf Diesel's for a compression-ignition engine.

In 1931 one could find a coach in the Barton fleet with a powerful Sunbeam eight-cylinder car engine; 'old man' Barton, who for many years distinguished himself by wearing a peak cap out of somebody's uniform, just could not resist buying the unusual and on one occasion he fitted a Blackstone oil engine to one of his 32-seat coaches and insisted on taking this entirely untried vehicle – in which he had great confidence – for a demonstration run with members of the Omnibus Society and four or five directors and officers of the Blackstone company. In 1932, makers' prices having been reduced, it was announced that Barton's had ceased to construct their own vehicles; this resolve was indeed forced on them by the increased standards required by the Traffic Commissioners and the economic requirements of greater efficiency and longer life that made it worthwhile to buy standard vehicles. Also in 1932 his sons and the company secretary (E. L. Taylor, who later became a BET group director) persuaded him that more conventional vehicles were desirable and the 500,000 deferred shares were halved in nominal value from 1s (5 p) to 6d (2½ p).

When motor-bus operations were begun on a permanent basis the name of the business was Andrew Barton Brothers. A limited company called Progress Motor Services Ltd was incorporated on 24 January 1913 but the title was changed to Barton Brothers Ltd in December 1920. Barton Transport Ltd was incorporated on 25 November 1927 to acquire its predecessor; it had as a subsidiary the South Notts Bus Co. Ltd (formed on 19 January 1928). The present fleet is 316 (of which 45 are double-deck); South Notts has 34 vehicles (24 double-deck and 8 coaches).

For 50 years, until its recent absorption by the South Yorkshire Passenger Transport Executive, Felix Motors of Hatfield, near Doncaster, has operated as an independent. Operations began in 1921 and the fleet name was taken from a well-known cartoon cat which achieved some fame at the time. The undertaking was notable for Miss Phyllis Thompson who was the first woman driver in the country to be licensed (in 1941) to drive a double-decker. Services extended from Doncaster to Hatfield and Moorends and towards Bawtry. There was a tendency in the early days to use small vehicles but latterly Felix obtained some large double-deckers.

To take an example from a different part of the country, a Dorset operator may be cited. The late R. W. Toop was typical of many small proprietors in the p.s.v. field; he began in October 1929 with one Model T Ford. It was a 14-seater with benches on either side for seven passengers. He operated from Bere Regis and business success came to him quite quickly, so that in 1930 he was able to buy additional vehicles and also the business of W. J. Ironside of Winfrith. Toop next formed an alliance with R. W. Davis of Bloxworth and joined him in March 1936. He brought in a Poole–Bere Regis–Dorchester route; also acquired over a period of years was W. J. Law (Briant's Puddle–Tolpuddle–Puddletown–Dorchester – June 1940), N. Russell (West Knighton–Broadmayne–Dorchester and a Dorchester–Weymouth licence – December 1941); C. E. Jeanes and H. Hawker (Puddle Valley – December 1941); F. Whitty (Dorchester and Frampton – 1942); F. Thorne (Dorchester–Cerne Abbas–Minterne Magna – 1942); E. Markey (Dorchester–Little Bredy – 1942); L. Sprackling's Ivory Coaches at Winterbourne Stickland with services centred on Dorchester and Blandford Forum – 1942; G. Lugg of Hazelbury Bryan with services running to

45 (*left*) An East Yorkshire double-decker with roof contoured for passing through Beverley Arch

46 (*below*) The first 8-ft wide bus, the Leyland RTW, came into service in 1949

Dorchester, Sherborne, and Sturminster Newton and Yeovil – 1944; C. Fripp of Okeford Fitzpaine with services to Blandford and Shaftesbury – 1945; G. Churchill and A. Pitcher, Dorchester–Bridport; E. J. Bale of Hurst 1946; Winborne Queen and Rambler of Longham – 1949 and 1951 respectively; A. E. Seager of Sherborne – 1954 and Antelope Tours, Sherborne – 1955; H. E. Butler, Milborne St Andrew, 1961. Today Bere Regis & District, the legal name of which is R. W. Toop deceased, is managed by his executor and operates 86 vehicles; in 1969 the total was 91. At the present time six of the vehicles are described as minibuses; the fleet comprises 6 AEC Reliance (Duple and Plaxton bodies), 1 Albion VT21L; 1 Austin J2, 56 Bedford with bodies built by Duple, Burlingham and Plaxton; 5 Ford (with Duple and Plaxton bodies); 4 Leyland with Panther and Leopard chassis and all with Plaxton bodywork. The headquarters of the concern is at Bridport Road, Dorchester, a site obtained from F. Whitty in 1942. Garages are maintained at Bere Regis, Blandford Forum, Dorchester, Hazelbury Bryan, Sherborne and Wimborne. We are indebted to articles by John Parke in *Modern Transport* in 1947 and more recently by Norman Aish in *Buses* for some of the details given of Bere Regis activities, because apart from the loss of its founder the Toop business has suffered to an unusual degree from a loss of regular customers and depends very much on private party work and on Monday to Friday the transport of schoolchildren to and from the centralised schools which remain open in the area of the Dorset County Council. With great enterprise value-for-money excursions are provided at seductive rates – Southampton £1; Chartwell £1.60; Cardiff £1.45; five days in Cornwall in October £36 inclusive.

In recent years a new facility has played a not unimportant part in serving rural communities. This is the Post Bus, which cannot be regarded as an 'independent' but is recorded here as its services cover what was formerly often an independent operator's sphere that had become uneconomic with the enormous increase in the use of the private car. Although post-office-operated buses are familiar in Germany, Austria and Switzerland, among other European countries, until 1967 they were unknown in this country. The General Post Office announced its intention of conducting experiments in 1965 when it became apparent that the Beeching cuts had left the railways incapable of conducting a lot of essential rural transport and that without subsidy many rural buses would disappear from the scene. The GPO is represented on the Ministry of Transport Working Party on Rural Transport and much research preceded the inauguration of experimental running, which took place with a Morris J2 minibus on 20 February 1967 between Llanidloes and Llangurig. It was started with a once-daily journey each way and three stops were arranged en route. This service was extended on 2 October 1967 on what is called the Wye Loop Extension. On 19 January 1976 the 100th post-bus service was inaugurated between Glenluce and Stranraer in Galloway.

Some of these services have quite obviously met what used to be called in old-fashioned sales literature 'a long-felt want'. The 45-mile Laide to Achnasheen route is one of those catered for and a 20-seat vehicle is needed. Besides bagged letters, parcels and miscellaneous goods, this trip makes the Kyle–Inverness rail connection at Achnasheen. A mail bus starting about the time of writing is between Henley-on-Thames and Frieth, taking over from Alder Valley section of the National Bus Company. The first Land Rover route was Killilan to Dornie, beginning 7 November 1973. The first operated by a Marina was Melrose to Maxton which was begun on 7 January 1975. South-east postal region vehicles are lettered 'Royal Mail Post Bus' and it is understood that vehicles allocated to Scotland will be lettered similarly. There are a number of larger vehicles beside the J2 minibuses. Among these are 9-seat Bedford Dormobiles, 11-seat Commers, 19-seat Leyland Terriers and 20-seat Leyland Boxers. The network of Post Bus services has added a new and much-needed facility to the national arrangements.

In the autumn of 1935, having achieved stable employment with a technical journal, which was to last 35 years in fact, I fulfilled the ambition of three years' standing and got married. In the words of the local paper, the honeymoon was to be spent touring Scotland. In the course of doing this we arrived at the little town of Callander, where we booked for a tour of the Trossachs organised by the London Midland & Scottish and London & North Eastern Railways. In those days the minimum price of the trip was 15s 6d, or 77½ pence. The first part of the journey was by what the timetable discreetly called 'Trossachs Motor' but which in 1935 was not operated by the Scottish Bus Group but by a freelance contractor engaged by the railways. This rather tatty vehicle took us away from the Pass of Leny under the slopes of Ben Ledi along the north shore of Loch Venacher near such places as Coilantogle Ford, written about by Sir Walter Scott in *The Lady of the Lake*. Then we skirted Loch Achray and passed through the Trossachs – 'where twines the path' in the poem, but a remarkably twisting road today. From Trossachs Pier we boarded the little Loch Katrine steamer and for the next 45 minutes glided over the lake entranced by the scenery and forgetful that it was the Glasgow Corporation waterworks.

We got off at Stronachlachar (a renowned tongue-twister which elderly Scottish ladies are fond of trying on unsuspecting Sassenachs) and then rode on the four-horse coach on the road to Inversnaid. This way of traversing the 4½-mile journey alongside Loch Arklet on the private road was unfortunately abolished when the owners purchased four AEC coaches in 1939, modernisation being thought essential, although less romantic. The rest of the tour went on by steamer along Loch Lomond to Balloch Pier and thence by train into Glasgow, with the driver breathing heresy against Sir Nigel Gresley by asserting that his 0-6-2 tank engine 'had nae boiler', and finishing up by a tram trip along Sauchiehall Street, just to obtain a halfpenny ticket which had disappeared in London with the coming of the London Passenger Transport Board.

Later in that same journey we went by train from Inverness to the Kyle of Lochalsh and were enheartened at Dingwall by the solicitude of a porter who asked, with faint belief, 'Are you for the Kyle?' In Achneshellach Forest a golden eagle spread his wings at the train and at Strome Ferry we were very tickled by the Highland engine crews taking advantage of exchanging engines to have a quarter-of-an-hour's cosy domestic chat. Eventually the train arrived at the Kyle and we arranged to spend the night at a modest hotel where the bed in our room was about eight feet wide and must have posed a problem in provision of sheets and blankets. The next morning we discovered that the local bus magnate was running an excursion to Dornie for a cattle fair. At that time the Kyle was isolated by ferries, there being no road bridge across the mouth of Loch Long. The coach excursion attracted us because we wanted to visit the Castle of Eilean Donan and there was a party of drovers, some of whom were anxious to buy cattle. There was also a pronouncedly Jewish gentleman, who attracted comments from the Highlanders such as, 'Vant to buy a vatch?' At the Dornie Hotel the yard was fixed up with cattle pens but we went on to the junction of Loch Alsh and Loch Duich, where a bus was waiting to go on to the little ferry boat to cross Loch Long. We went over and walked to Eilean Donan where we were shown round by the Macrae who was glad to expound on the good work he had done in rebuilding the ancient edifice. We arrived back at Dornie in good time for the coach, not all of whose passengers were ready to return. When we did start the driver demonstrated that he too had been occupying most of the turn-round time in drinking whisky; in fact he elected to drive half-a-dozen recalcitrant beasts with the bus and so made the journey back to the Kyle pretty exciting. He drove with great skill and aplomb but we were quite glad to debus safely.

On Skye next day we took the Ford bus from Kyleakin to Broadford and on the return took the timetable for gospel as southerners are apt to do. The bus came along about the time that seemed right, but about a mile from Kyleakin the driver met a mate with whom he found it necessary to conduct serious business. 'You've got my coat,' said one. Coat and trousers had been exchanged between drivers at a 'jag' that had accompanied a ceilidh and the following morning brought a lot of Gaelic to the surface. Conscious that the MacBrayne steamer for Mallaig was due to go and would not wait for us while we were in the purlieus of Kyleakin, we got anxious about the time of arrival there; and then in those days before a roll-on-roll-off ferry we had to charter a private MacBrayne motor boat to get across to the Kyle; the boatman deposited us nominally at the railway pier, but actually we were a long way off across several lighters. While we were still running down the railway tracks of the pier the MacBrayne steamer sounded its siren for departure and the gangplank had just been withdrawn when we arrived at the pier head; fortunately second thoughts brought about its replacement in time to prevent a plunge into deep water, but my impetus brought me down on to the deck of *Loch Hourn* precipitately and with a resounding bang. Such are the perils of casual timekeeping by buses in the islands and highlands – at least in 1935.

We spent our summer holiday in 1938 walking in Wales and I see that I evidently wrote to W. S. Jones, of Gwynfa Garage, Beddgelert, for a timetable. His reply mentions his 24-seat Daimler bus which he had bought in 1923 from J. M. Roberts of Shepherds Bush, the London dealer who negotiated a number of Daimler double-deck buses, approved by the Metropolitan Police, into London independent fleets. The chassis were overhauled War Department stock. A body by Strachan & Brown was mounted and by 1938 the vehicle had covered 386,000 miles, nearly all over the 13 hilly miles between Caernarvon and Beddgelert. The certifying officer had that day (17 October) renewed his approval for another three years.

The timetable showed 15 journeys each way on the main route, taking 55 minutes for the 13 miles. There was an extension on Saturdays to Nant Gwynant which had a widely varying journey time and twice a day (not on Saturdays) Jones ran down to Portmadoc, a half-hour journey. One can easily see how the bus provided much more inviting facilities than the Welsh Highland Railway which, although it provided a refreshment car of sorts, ran three trips a day in 80 minutes. With these wide intervals I remember a railway enthusiast (none other than Charles E. Lee, in fact, at that time on the *Railway Gazette* staff) being very wrath when he arrived at Dinas Junction on the LMS crack 'Welshman' only to find that, with hours to wait for the next narrow-gauge train, the Welsh Highland crew had wrong-headedly gone off because the LMS train was two minutes late. 'Jones the bus' provided a much better service than the Welsh Highland line, and moreover the users of the bus were deposited right in Caernarvon and not 10 minutes away by LMS connection from Dinas Junction into the shopping town. With such a handicap the Welsh Highland not surprisingly faded out after the summer of 1936 and altogether after the following tourist season.

In 1939 we had walked the length of the Roman Wall from Brough-upon-Solway to Newcastle and then called at Durham on the way to some friends at Darlington. That night we stayed in Middleton-in-Teesdale and enjoyed the solid comfort of the Cleveland Arms, and walked from Low Force up the Tees to High Force. When we had absorbed the majesty of the falls, which are as impressive as any in England, we went up to the road again and in due course boarded the Teesdale Queen. The conductor issued a ticket, cancelled not with a Bell Punch but with railway-type nippers, and resumed his stance amid a pile of labelled newspapers. These were being delivered literally door-to-door; as the Bedford bus proceeded at fairly high speed, the conductor shot his labelled newspapers either to the left out of the door or much more dextrously right over the bus to the right. It made no difference which side was aimed at; all arrived well and truly at the front door of the premises. Although we were progressing steadily along the B6277 road, with the 1,100-ft contour giving way to 1,300 and the heights of Langdon Common, rising in successive folds to 2,000 ft on the right and Widdybank Fell running across to the Tees on our left, it was a surprise when the driver terminated the journey by reversing in the narrow road at a point 1,744 ft above sea level.

No settlement of houses, no steeper hill, determined this boundary of bus operations which walkers, wanting a daily service between Middleton and Alston, have long endeavoured to break down. A few miles of flower-decked walking, on which we admired gentian and mountain parsley (claimed by botanists to be relics of the last ice-age) beyond Ashgill Force, an attractive, although not spectacular waterfall, we turned aside into the village of Garrigill where we were nicely in time for a public-house tea and the bus into Alston, the highest market town in England. The remainder of the holiday was spent in ascertaining the answers to a number of problems concerning the ancient railways at Brampton and the 15-inch gauge Ravenglass & Eskdale Railway.

The youngest character in the bus business was probably the 12-year-old who in the days before the Road Traffic Act (1930) began as a conductor helping his father run an Albion bus in the suburbs of Inverness, from the centre of the burgh to Kessock Ferry, which plied from the south side of the estuary where a 'wee boat' would take a small bus load of passengers across the Beauly Firth to the B9162 road at North Kessock.

London Transport was delighted to find at the time of the tramway conversion that several near-70-year-old tram drivers were able to pass the driving test and carry on, for a short while at any rate, driving buses from Wandsworth depot. The East Kent Road Car Co. Ltd also produced a septuagenarian who was able to fulfil his ambition of driving on every route worked from Dover garage in the last week or two before his retirement. Needless to say that required the co-operation of the garage superintendent, to roster him specially on each of the routes in turn. The oldest active busman of whom we have a note was Jimmy Culshaw, a former Peterborough Traction employee and who was employed as an inspector in his last years by the Delaine, owned by Delaine Coaches Ltd of Bourne, Lincs. Culshaw, who was 89 when he died in 1971, had completed over 70 years in public transport and was working full-time until a week before his death.

Although Lanarkshire and the County of Middlesex, among a select few, operated tramways, ownership of bus undertakings has not fallen to the lot of county councils although had the Monmouthshire County Council followed the recommendations of N. J. Young, sometime general manager of Newport (Mon.) urban authority, who operated trams and buses in the town, that authority (or perhaps Monmouthshire County Council) would have operated services all over East Wales, occupying territory rather similar to that taken up by Red & White Motor Services.

The decline of the bus against the inroads of private car transport has made necessary some alterations in organisation to ensure maintenance of services. In Devonshire, for example, the Western National in 1972 closed its garages at Tavistock and Kingsbridge at short notice (in addition to garages in Cornwall, at Bude, Delabole and Liskeard). As a result, the people of the South Hams area rely on the work of independent proprietors for bus transport. Tally Ho! Coaches was asked by Devon County Council to maintain a service on a temporary basis after representations by the Kingsbridge Rural District Council, which, under reorganisation of local government has been succeeded by the South Hams District Council. Co-ordination of the local operators is managed by the Devon County Council which issues its own series of service numbers, Tally Ho! in fact being allocated Nos 600–607, of which 606 and 607 are schools services. Other operators have been taken over by Tally Ho! in the past year or two, these including South Milton Coaches, J. Hoare & Sons of Ivybridge; the mainstay of the business is 22 school contracts and a county council subsidy for the service buses, which is much smaller than the local organisation finds necessary.

The Tally Ho! company began in 1960 in its present form when an undertaking was taken over in an almost derelict state; hopefully, however, the bargain included some tours and excursions from East Allington and in 1964 it was possible to add the Salcombe Motor Company and further tours and excursions were taken over. By strict attention to the possibilities of traffic 40 vehicles are now required, and frequent journeys are made to Continental destinations; the strong local Manchester United supporters club made a return journey of 550 miles in the winter of 1976–7 to see every home game in addition to many other club bookings.

A curious result of the area agreement system, adopted eventually by all the large companies, but initiated largely by Flexman French and, to protect the companies of the British Automobile Traction group before the licensing system of the 1930 Road Traffic Act, by Sidney Garcke, were the gaps left at boundary towns of 'no man's lands' that nobody tried to develop. For example Aldershot & District Traction Co. Ltd had territory in much of Surrey west of a line through Staines, Guildford and Horsham. Westward, Aldershot territory lay north of a line from Horsham, through Petersfield and Winchester; it also lay east of Andover. Basingstoke was on this northern boundary between the Aldershot and Thames Valley areas. Hence, how expedient was the merger of these two companies with relatively small fleets, under the National Bus Company, as Alder Valley, an imaginative name which cloaked the fact that British Electric Traction and Thomas Tilling ideologies had once again met under *force majeure*.

The territory allotted to Aldershot & District led to the development of a service (No. 14) from Aldershot down the A325 road to Farnham and then by A31 to Alresford and Winchester. An interesting feature of the A & D territory was that it included a road right across Southdown country from Midhurst via Chichester to Bognor Regis. To some extent the Hants & Dorset did not exploit the south of Hampshire to the extent that it might have done and the through services to Winchester, joint with Southdown, were cut short at the Fareham boundary point in 1926, although the National Bus Company resumed through services quite recently. The outcome of this was that neither Aldershot nor Hants & Dorset were anxious to provide local services in Winchester; similarly Basingstoke, Andover and Newbury were likewise neglected. In each case a local organisation developed.

At Winchester I saw the whole process, as I was there in the summers of 1923 and 1924. While Winchester & District and an Alresford undertaking, covering somewhat similar ground, did not survive, the Chisnell family business, King Alfred Coaches, lasted from 1921 until 29 April 1973, when the senior partner passed it to Hants & Dorset, which promptly replaced the immaculate King Alfred vehicles with some rather tatty Hants & Dorset and Wilts & Dorset vehicles. The King Alfred livery was latterly green and cream with a representation of King Alfred on the side, or more literally of his statue in the Broadway, round the plinth of which most services terminated. Across the way was the ancient monastic building adapted as a waiting room and café, where few waiting customers could resist taking a cup of tea and some refreshment after shopping in the city, in Alfred's day the capital of England.

The first vehicles of the King Alfred fleet that I recall were coaches based on RAF military chassis of which type Leyland made several thousand during the First World War. Photos were passed to me by Chisnell Senior as a sort of peace-offering after he had been rather recalcitrant the first time I encountered him. I had spent the morning in Southampton on the business of *Modern Transport* and when I discovered from my friend Percy Baker that he was not going to be available in the afternoon it occurred to me that I might be able to make a good short article on the activities of the Chisnells. I arrived early in the afternoon and found Robert Chisnell wrath with me on two counts. One was that he did not like my arrival without an appointment and the other was the he feared repetition of a trick played on him in his early days where a representative of a local journal had gathered particulars for an article, along with some photos for reproduction, and published a very wordy article about King Alfred and some illustrations and accompanied a copy of the paper with a quite outrageous bill for the blocks that accompanied the article. I explained that *Modern Transport* was not that sort of paper and eventually we parted firm friends; my wife and I were glad in later years to have the younger generation of Chisnells as friends at busmen's meetings of the Public Service Vehicle Association.

Very quickly King Alfred seemed to graduate from its RAF Leylands to Lion single-deck service buses, hailed as a high-water mark of Leyland refinement and sophistication. In the early days Albion, Dennis and Thornycroft chassis appeared in the fleet; a Tiger coach or two then was numbered in the green and cream King Alfred vehicles (a London express service was maintained at that time) and when it was available advantage was taken of the low-height Titan double-decker for passing under low trees. Later Leyland Atlantean and AEC Bridgemaster vehicles were adopted without finding the objection once expressed to me by Theodore Thomas, general manager of London Transport, when the AEC Q-type double-deckers were being tried in London, that passengers in the queue at stops would not know whether the next bus was going to present its entrance at front or rear.

On the single-deck side Commer and Metro-Scania were added to the Chisnell repertoire, but there does not seem to have been the need for specially low single-deckers to go through the culvert-like bridges under the Southern Railway embankments on the south of the city such as are traversed by buses on the Stanmore route. The near suburbs traversed by

King Alfred lead to St Cross (by two routes), Oliver's Battery, Stanmore, Flower Down, Weeke and Colden Common. The town services started at two-hour intervals, between 10.30 and 20.30, but before very long 15-minute intervals were being advertised. Journeys four times a day gave place to six trips a day to such places as King's Somborne, Stockbridge, Whitchurch and Basingstoke. On my first visit to Winchester the yellow bus of Mobility Ltd was still running three times a day across country from Sutton Scotney and Andover; on the demise of Mobility Ltd this was one of the services that King Alfred filled a most useful function in replacing and developing. Not all developments are genuine progress and the replacement of these buses by a National subsidiary is a case in point.

Malicious fate has brought about several garage fires of a disastrous character. The division of London bus garages into small compartments seemed a typically cautious police way of safeguarding costly vehicles, but to my mind it is preferable to the sad holocausts at Bournemouth, Trent Motor Traction at Derby and then at neighbouring Blue Bus of Willington. Blue Bus was notable for its rather rich blue livery. Blue Bus was being maintained as a separate entity, although it was taken over by Derby Corporation (District Council) from 1 December 1973. The owning firm was previously Tailby & George and two additional Bedfords were delivered only on 1 September. Before the Second World War the rolling stock comprised 5 Leyland, 4 Maudslay and 1 GMC single-deckers, seating from 20 to 38. By 1969 the fleet was 13 Daimler double-deckers, and 6 single-deck (mainly Dennis, but including some Daimler Fleetline). The Blue Bus fleet retained its blue and grey colour scheme. Two routes were provided between Burton-on-Trent and Derby, one via Newton Solney, Repton, Willington, Findern and Littleover, the other by way of Streetton, Egginton, Etwall, Mickleover and Littleover. Neither route relied for far on the Roman road, or Ryknild Street, or the A38 as it has been classified by the Ministry of Transport, although services were sometimes hampered by floods where it crosses the Dove Valley, notably at Clay Mills near the confluence of Dove and Trent. On the night of 5–6 January 1976 fire destroyed almost the entire fleet; left outside the garage was the ex-WD Humber works truck (it was known as 'Monty' by the numerous enthusiasts that have gathered round Blue Bus), a bus that was scheduled to spend the night in the East Staffordshire (formerly known as Burton Corporation) garage at Burton, and a Loline that was under repair at Derby Corporation works together with a single-deck Daimler Fleetline. Included among the losses was the original Daimler Fleetline, the Daimler Roadliner in the fleet and two new Leyland Leopard coaches. Also saved were the prototype low-height Ailsa and three low-height Duple-bodied Daimler Fleetlines, but this was a chance of late delivery. Some of the vehicles lost are mourned by the cognoscenti who admired this friendly local concern, and the garage fire has brought to an end the use of Willington as a garage site.

Regular headway bus services are almost universal among the English companies except perhaps the descendants of the National Omnibus & Transport Co. Ltd, but in Wales and the Welsh border country it is not so much to be taken for granted. The Yeomans family, who were old-established cider pressers in Herefordshire, with headquarters at Canon Pyon near Hereford, in 1934 purchased a number of services from Birmingham & Midland Motor Omnibus Co. Ltd, including Kington–Leominster; Leominster–Staunton-on-Arrow; Kington–Staunton Park and various BMMO services that were modified. From August 1948 Radnorshire Motor Services, of which H. J. Yeomans was proprietor, operated round about every two hours, but with some gaps of as much as three hours, on such routes as Ludlow–Llandrindod Wells (with many short journeys to Leintwardine and Knighton; Hereford–Newtown; Leominster–Eltons Marsh; Leominster–Leintwardine; Knighton–Leintwardine–Leominster; Bishops Castle–Craven Arms; many of the services had facilities on certain days, or such things as 'Ludlow auction Mondays only' or 'Craven Arms auction Mondays only'. The August 1949 timetable shows more perfection in adhering to the two-hour intervals.

Leintwardine, a relatively small village between Ludlow and Knighton, was made a nodal point; previously there was a connecting point on some services between the Ludlow–Knighton–Llandrindod Wells service (the latter part usually by connections at Knighton) and the Leominster–Hereford service. The new scheme truncated the Ludlow service at Leintwardine and the Hereford service ran through to Llandrindod Wells.

Eventually, Radnorshire Motor Services was defeated by finance, as well as such unfortunate things to which a regular headway service is vulnerable as missing a shift at a factory by five minutes; the routes have been changed in nature as well as ownership and it is all too easy to say that it was too late to introduce such regular headway services, although it might have been better if there had been closer control of finances, because new vehicles sometimes arrived when money was not available and in any case a chain of cafés (mainly at bus stations) required support. Some students of the Welsh border area consider they can see the reflection of Radnorshire routes in some of the express routes set up later by the National Bus Company. It was at any rate a brave try. The full story of the bus ramifications of the Yeomans family and Radnorshire Motor Services is told by J. E. Dunabin in a supplement to the *Omnibus Magazine* (75 pence) (103a Streatham Hill, SW2 4UD).

Another bus undertaking with an unusual start is Premier Travel of Cambridge. A discussion on ways of improving Sundays in Cambridge resulted in a suggestion from H. L. D Beauchamp, of Jesus College, that a coach service should be run to some seaside resort, such as Skegness. Although the LNER and Eastern Counties objected, the inaugural trip was made on 15 April 1933. The energetic Arthur Lainson began running vehicles on hire slips, but soon expanded to a number of rural Cambridgeshire routes as Premier Travel Ltd, some of the money in which was derived from the London independent of the same name. Arthur Lainson, who proved to be a natural busman, with many excellent ideas in the way of publicity, recently celebrated his 65th birthday as chairman of the company which was an occasion for general rejoicing.

Index